IOWA
CONFEDERATES
IN THE CIVIL WAR

IOWA
CONFEDERATES
IN THE CIVIL WAR

DAVID CONNON

AMERICA
THROUGH TIME®
ADDING COLOR TO AMERICAN HISTORY

To Melinda, who has long awaited this book.

America Through Time is an imprint of Fonthill Media LLC
www.through-time.com
office@through-time.com

Published by Arcadia Publishing by arrangement with Fonthill Media LLC
For all general information, please contact Arcadia Publishing:
Telephone: 843-853-2070
Fax: 843-853-0044
E-mail: sales@arcadiapublishing.com
For customer service and orders:
Toll-Free 1-888-313-2665

www.arcadiapublishing.com

First published 2019

Copyright © David Connon 2019

ISBN 978-1-63499-155-1

Typeset in 10pt on 13pt Sabon
Printed and bound in England

Foreword

Although the reaction to the September 2017 airing of Ken Burns's and Lynn Novick's *The Vietnam War*—a T.V. Mini-Series—was not entirely unexpected, it was a stark reminder of how deep and emotional are the "scars" of war. Almost forty-five years after the official end of the war, Burns and Novick were either vilified for opening old wounds or praised for going where few have dared to go—a view of the war from the North Vietnamese perspective, both soldiers and civilians.

David Connon's *Iowa Confederates in the Civil War* is a thorough and superbly researched book into the minds and motives of Iowans who chose to fight for the Confederacy. In spite of General William Tecumseh Sherman's famous reminder that "War is Hell," young men by the thousands—both North and South—either volunteered or, later in the war, were conscripted. The seventy-six Iowans whom Connon identifies through letters, diaries, newspaper accounts, official documents, etc., had reasons or motives, some similar to and some very different from their fellow Iowans who fought for the Union. For some, the reasons were pretty straightforward: economic opportunism; love of adventure, compounded by peer pressure; or an almost "romantic" notion of "patriotic fervor," complete with a nice uniform. For others, the reasons were more complex: "State's rights" (or sovereignty) defending slavery as constitutional; maintaining white supremacy and defending their "country" and way of life; mixed loyalties and "divided families;" or familial concerns such as loyalty to a birthplace or parent's birthplace.

Although minuscule in number, compared to the approximately 75,000 Iowans who fought for the Union, the Confederates have an important story to tell, and Connon's exhaustive research fills in an important gap in Iowa Civil War history.

John Liepa
Emeritus Professor of History and Political Science,
Des Moines Area Community College

Acknowledgments

This book grew out of extensive research into primary sources dealing with the Grinnell branch of the Underground Railroad and then Iowa Confederates. I field-tested portions of stories before Civil War Round Tables of Des Moines, Cedar Falls, Milwaukee, and Chicago, and wonderful audiences throughout Iowa.

Many people have helped me. I'm grateful for advice and encouragement from David Hargrove, Tom Taggart, Amy Rosenquist, Bethany Connon, and Aaron Savage. They closely read the manuscript and made it better. Historians Bruce S. Allardice and Dr. David Broadnax (Trinity Christian College) offered useful suggestions. I appreciate Dr. David Salvaterra, John Liepa, and Marvin Bergman of *The Annals of Iowa* who challenged my thinking. If there are mistakes, they are all mine.

Many descendants of Iowa Confederates graciously shared family stories, letters, and photographs, especially Mary Lovell Swetnam, Phil and George Williams, Samuel Ross Penny, Barbara Wells, Dr. Wendell Lawther, Shirley Happs Martsching and Judy Gardner Phelps, Jim Chamberlin, Bob Ramay, Susan Cobb Beck and Darleen Cordova, Evalee Hunerdosse, Linda M. Kelley, Beth Shields, Christine Brugman, and Randel Bailey, Nelda Palmer, Jim Williams, and Rachelle Cooley.

I am thankful for research assistance from Walt Libby, Colleen Peterson, Sherman Lundy, Al Ourth, Anne O'Brien, historian John A. Moretta, Kent Folmar, Elspeth Olson, Dr. Terrence Lindell, Wartburg College, and Dr. Kim Porter, University of North Dakota.

Indispensable help came from librarians and archivists Sherry Stelling, Bruce Kreuger, and Becki Plunkett, State Historical Archives, Des Moines; Mike Gibson, Center for Dubuque History; Marykay Clarke, Irene Powell, and Jessica Whitmore, Mt. St. Mary's University; Grinnell Historical Museum; Grinnell College Special Collections; Curtis Small, University of Delaware Special Collections; Tim Noakes, Stanford University Libraries; John Coski, American Civil War Museum; Lynn Ellsworth and Joy Conwell, Iowa Wesleyan University; Jared Smith, Tempe History Museum; Tonya Boltz, Keokuk Public Library; Meghan Townes, Library of Virginia; and University of Memphis Libraries.

Much-needed encouragement came from Ken Allers, Galin Berrier, Tom Taggart, Bryan Crites, Pastor Dave Brooks, Bruce Peterson, Tom Krueger, Ken Wallace, Jean Koch, Tom Hoover, Kent Schlawin, Steve Dudley, Dr. Richard Guzman, Dr. Jim Guthrie, Martin Wissenberg, Kyle White, David and DeAnne Negley, Kelli and Adrian Anderson, Caroline and Gerald Lehman; historian Father Ed Gleeson, Bob and Marilyn Barnes, Charles K. Connon, and Jim Connon.

Artist Kathryn Neese was very helpful. Alan Sutton, Kena Longabaugh, Joshua Greenland, and the rest of the team at Fonthill Media provided editorial and publishing direction and support.

My wife, Melinda, has sacrificed to make this book a reality. My daughter, Bethany, knows perhaps too much about the Civil War.

Contents

Contents

Timeline

1846:	Iowa becomes a state, and Democrat George Wallace Jones becomes a U.S. Senator.
1857:	Financial Panic of 1857 begins.
1858–1859:	George Wallace Jones loses his Senate seat and is appointed minister to New Grenada.
1860:	Abraham Lincoln elected President, and South Carolina secedes, followed by six other states.
April 12–13, 1861:	Confederate troops fire upon Fort Sumter.
April 15, 1861:	President Lincoln calls for 75,000 militiamen; four Upper South states begin to secede.
May 17, 1861:	George Wallace Jones writes his lifelong friend, Confederate President Jefferson Davis.
Late May 1861:	Iowa General Assembly votes to send troops into the Union Army.
December 19–20, 1861:	Secretary of State William Seward orders the arrest and imprisonment of George Wallace Jones.
August 8 and 13, 1862:	Secretary of War Edwin Stanton orders arrest of civilians for wide range of disloyal conduct (i.e., discouraging enlistment).
July 3–4, 1863:	Union wins victories at Gettysburg and Vicksburg.
April 9, 1865:	Confederate General Robert E. Lee surrenders Army of Northern Virginia.
July 11, 1865:	The last Iowa Confederate surrenders.
1865–1867:	President Andrew Johnson extends pardon to all Iowa Confederates, but not the right to vote or hold political office.

Introduction

After I moved to Iowa with my wife and newborn daughter, I read an eyewitness account of Grinnell, Iowa's riot in 1860 over the presence of fugitive slaves in the public school. The shock and horror of the riot contrasted with today's leafy, quiet streets, a stone's throw from Grinnell College. Questions sprang to mind: Who instigated the riot? How did others show courage in the face of intimidation? How exactly did it play out? The more I learned, the more I wanted to know.

The aftermath of the story includes a historical footnote: Bushwhackers in southwest Poweshiek County (not far from Grinnell) murdered two federal marshals during Iowa's first draft on October 1, 1864. This gave me pause. Did any Iowans leave the state and serve the Confederacy? Historian Hubert H. Wubben answered yes; two Iowa state legislators "went South" and wore gray. But did any others? Who were they and what choices did they make? This book grew out of these questions.

It is common knowledge that Iowans flocked to enlist in the Union army and navy after Fort Sumter. Fifty-seven Iowans showed distinguished gallantry in battle and received the Medal of Honor. However, it may be surprising that these soldiers and sailors had counterparts in every branch of the Confederate service, and one Iowa resident is listed on the Honor Roll—the Confederacy's highest recognition of valor in battle.

I have documented seventy-six Iowa Confederates. These men included doctors, druggists, lawyers, law students, merchants, farmers, and a newspaper editor. The men included eleven sets of brothers who were scattered across the Confederacy in the Western and Eastern Theaters. Most of them served in the infantry, with the cavalry a close second, and artillery a distant third. One served in the Confederate Navy, and at least two worked in the Confederate Treasury Department.

Iowa Confederates could be called shadow images or "doppelgängers" of their 76,500 Union counterparts. Men on both sides had similar experiences, including time in POW camps. Like Iowa Union soldiers, some Iowa Confederates withheld financial support from wives and children.

This book features new research on loyal friends of Jefferson Davis (who contributed six Iowa sons to the Confederate service); routes that men took to go South during the war; and a tantalizing witness statement, suggesting that a Confederate recruiter was active in Iowa. Readers will gain new understanding of wartime Iowa, including violations of civil liberties and the Republican propaganda campaign that successfully demonized Peace Democrats. Readers will also be introduced to pressures facing Confederates who returned to Iowa after Appomattox.

This book draws upon unpublished or little-known correspondence and diaries, as well as newspaper editorials and histories. You will find an extensive bibliography.

I write a blog—Confederates from Iowa: Not to Defend, but to Understand. The title is meant to set readers at ease. In that spirit, I share quotes from two skillful authors. Biographer William J. Cooper Jr. author of *Jefferson Davis, American*, writes:

[Davis] believed in the superiority of the white race. He also owned slaves, defended slavery as a moral and as a social good, and fought a great war to maintain it. After 1865, he opposed new rights for blacks.... No reader of this book can condone any of these attitudes. My goal is to understand Jefferson Davis as a man of his time, not condemn him for not being a man of my time.... I will not keep pointing out that his outlook is different than mine and from that of our own era.[1]

I do not harbor romantic notions about the Confederacy, and I am not interested in entering a modern political discussion about the Confederate flag or Confederate monuments. Instead, I echo the words of biographer Clare Mulley, author of *The Women who Flew for Hitler*. She describes:

The sense you sometimes have of shaking hands—or joining a conversation—across history. Reading diaries and letters, or even less intimate material, can bring moments of profound empathy and a frequent sense of meeting of minds, but also the sudden shock of finding inexplicable prejudice, or worse....

Decisions and actions were rarely as clear-cut at the time as seventy years' distance might sometimes suggest, and reaching the many truths of any life, whether factual, moral, or emotional, requires empathy as well as inquiry, criticism as well as care.[2]

This book rests upon the definition of "Iowa resident." I define resident as one who lived in Iowa before the Civil War for at least two years, no earlier than 1850, and was thirteen or older during residency. These parameters exclude U.S. Army soldiers who served in the Iowa Territory, including Robert E. Lee and Jefferson Davis. I occasionally tell stories of Iowans who do not qualify as residents (that is, who I have not documented as having two years of pre-war residence). Their stories help convey the experience of documented Iowa Confederates.

Perhaps you, like me, wonder why someone left a nice young state like Iowa and served the other side. Consider a little data. Almost half of the seventy-six Iowa Confederates moved South during the lingering financial Panic of 1857. While seeking jobs, they were exposed to Southern influences.

A total 36 percent of Iowa Confederates left the state in early 1861 or afterwards, as the secession winter led to Fort Sumter.

One of every four Iowa Confederates had a divided family. In other words, they had at least one immediate family member (brother or son) who served the Union.

Why would an Iowa Confederate fight to defend someone else's fireside? Three main motives appear in the data; of course, some soldiers had interconnected motives. Fifty-one Iowa Confederates (67 percent) enlisted out of opportunism, often related to earning a living, with little regard for principles or consequences. Thirty-four Iowa Confederates (45 percent) enlisted out of familial concerns, often related to loyalty to their birthplace or the birthplace of their father or mother. Twenty-two Iowa Confederates (29 percent) had a philosophical motive, involving state's rights related to slavery and/or an interpretation of the Declaration of Independence and the Constitution. A love of adventure underlay these motives, especially for many young soldiers. A fourth minor motive appears in the data: feeling trapped. Three soldiers in this category (4 percent) felt peer pressure to enlist, or they were conscripted.

Slave ownership merits a few comments. Ten Iowa Confederates had some connection to slavery as children or as adults. Eight of them had grown up in households that held one or more slaves in bondage (for at least a short time). One of those households (containing two brothers who became Confederates) was in Dubuque. During the 1850s, one future Iowa Confederate moved south, married a belle, and bought two slaves. During the war, one Iowa Confederate received a slave as a gift, and another Iowa Confederate bought numerous slaves who were "refugeed" to Texas, away from Union troops.

Stories are the driving force in this book. The pages contain tales of capture and imprisonment, loyalty, desertion, strained marriages, tenuous romances, and adventure. Read them individually, as you like.

1

Context: Iowa and the Lead-up to Fort Sumter

Picture a burly blacksmith hammering on the anvil of slavery. Heated to a cherry red, the churches were the first to split: Presbyterians, Baptists, and Methodists. The Whig Party hissed and dissolved, and the Democratic Party blistered and cracked. The Whigs and the Democratic Party had formerly promoted national agendas that unified the country. However, historian David M. Potter states that as abolitionists grew in number and vigor, "the slavery issue ... transformed political action from a process of accommodation to a mode of combat."[1]

Slavery intersected with the free state of Iowa beyond receiving riverboats that paddled up the Mississippi River. Early settlers from the slave states elected many Southerners to political office. Southern influence began to diminish amid waves of settlers from the Ohio River Valley, New England, Ireland, and Germany.

The largest city, Dubuque, was rightly called "The Gibraltar of the Iowa Democracy."[2] Perhaps surprisingly, eleven Dubuque residents owned seventeen slaves in 1840.[3] Two of the slave-owners later became mayors of Dubuque, and a third mayor had grown up with slaves in his household.[4] The largest slave-owner was future U.S. Senator George Wallace Jones who held three humans in bondage. (The owners freed their slaves within a few years.)[5] Historian Robert Dykstra suggests that Dubuque County residents were the only Iowans bold enough to admit that they owned a slave in 1840.[6] Early Dubuque had a rather pro-slavery business environment.

George Wallace Jones was a Southerner at heart. Born in Indiana, Jones grew up with slaves, and he became a close friend of Jefferson Davis when they attended Transylvania University in Kentucky.[7] Jones was originally a miner and storekeeper who started his political career in Congress, representing the Wisconsin Territory (a forerunner of Iowa). He lost that seat, but he rebounded as surveyor of public lands and then U.S. Senator. His tight supporters, "Jones Men," professed personal and political loyalty.[8] Jones rewarded them with political appointments, and many went on to successful public careers. Jones also befriended many Southern congressmen and senators. Two of his closest Dubuque allies, Warner Lewis and Patrick Quigley, were also friends of Jefferson Davis.[9] Jones, Lewis, and Quigley each later sent two sons into the Confederate service, representing half of the Dubuquers who eventually wore gray during the Civil War.

Senator Jones and his fellow Iowa Democrat, Augustus Caesar Dodge, voted for the Compromise of 1850, designed to hold the Union together.[10] The bill also included the Fugitive Slave Act, designed to force bystanders to help deliver slaves to their masters. Abolition-minded citizens easily imagined being coerced into violating their consciences or paying a huge penalty. Grinnell resident Jesse Macy called the Fugitive Slave Act "one of the most barbarous pieces of legislation ever enacted by a civilized country."[11]

Four years later, Jones's senatorial colleague, Democrat Stephen A. Douglas from Illinois, inadvertently reignited the smoldering slavery debate. Hoping to build a transcontinental railroad, Douglas championed the Kansas–Nebraska Act.[12] This bill would bring both territories into the Union. Bickering over slavery began immediately, as Douglas promoted "Popular Sovereignty," where the majority of settlers would decide whether the future state would be slave or free. Predictably, pro-slavery men from Missouri and anti-slavery men (many from the Northeast) poured into Kansas. "Bleeding Kansas" attracted John Brown and his sons, who murdered five pro-slavery men at Osawatomie.

At the same time, the Underground Railroad passed through Iowa, and Democrats castigated "Negro stealers" who helped as many as 300 fugitive slaves find their way to freedom. In Grinnell (a stop on the Underground Railroad), Leonard F. Parker stated, "Slavery and anti-slavery filled the air, and John Brown was arousing every man to thought and action."[13] The State Congregational Association, meeting in Grinnell in summer 1856, expressed indignation over "the outrages that have been inflicted upon our fellow citizens of Kansas, by hordes of armed men from Missouri, for the purpose of crushing out liberty."[14]

Across the nation, the Whig Party fizzled, and out of the ashes arose the Republican Party coalition, combining former Whigs, Free-Soilers, and Democrats. Potter states that Republicans saw recent history as "one long shameful record of concession after concession to the insatiable Slaveocracy. The annexation of Texas, the Mexican War, the Fugitive Slave Act of 1850, the Kansas-Nebraska Act, all were designed to buy off the South."[15]

Iowa politicians in both camps tended to conceal their true beliefs. For example, Republicans claimed they weren't abolitionists while they railed against slavery. Democrats, on the other hand, could point out the constitutionality of slavery but say they personally opposed it. Democrat Henry Clay Dean, a former Methodist minister, was an exception. He boldly stated, "Since the crucifixion of Jesus Christ, there has not been so benevolent an institution known among men as African slavery."[16]

Iowa U.S. Senator George Wallace Jones cast pro-Southern and pro-slavery votes, but most Iowans in the mid-1850s, including Democrats, had grown tired of the wrangling. Iowa Republicans grew in strength, and so did anti-Jones Democrats. Jones's days in the Senate were numbered.

On the national scene, the Republican star was ascending, and the Democratic Party began to war against itself. The Democratic brouhaha pitted President James Buchanan and his fire-eating pro-slavery Southern allies against Senator Stephen A. Douglas and Southern Unionists. Buchanan and Douglas were virulent enemies. They first jousted over the Lecompton Constitution. Territorial Kansas residents had voted for the Lecompton Constitution under fraudulent circumstances. If Congress approved the constitution, Kansas would have entered the Union as a slave state. Fire-eaters joined Buchanan in demanding that all Democrats support the Lecompton Constitution.[17] Douglas defied Buchanan and opposed Lecompton, noting that it violated the principle of popular sovereignty. An ever-widening chasm reached from Washington to Des Moines. Senator Jones, up for re-election, voted for the Lecompton Constitution against the wishes of most Iowans.[18]

This was Jones's last hurrah as senator. In 1858, the pro-Douglas, anti-Jones Democrats in the Iowa General Assembly chose a different senatorial candidate. Jones railed against Douglas as "the most corrupt of all politicians," and his supporters shrank to a splinter movement within the party.[19] As Democrats fought against themselves, Republicans took control of both houses of the General Assembly.[20]

Across the border in Illinois, Republicans nominated Abraham Lincoln as candidate for the U.S. Senate to run against Stephen A. Douglas. Lincoln gave his famous "House Divided" speech on June 16, 1858, stating, "I believe this government cannot endure, half slave and half free.... It will become all one thing or all the other." Douglas analyzed the end result of Lincoln's words. He predicted that Lincoln would oversee "a war of sections, a war of North against the South, of the Free States against the Slave States—a war of extermination to be continued relentlessly until the one or the other shall be subdued and all States shall either become free or become slave."[21]

Congress did not approve the Lecompton Constitution, and Jones's term expired in the Senate. Fortunately for Jones, his political friend Buchanan appointed him minister (ambassador) to New Grenada, South America.[22] As Jones sailed to his new post, John Brown and his party of armed men and fugitive slaves crossed Iowa, heading eastward. Eight months later, Brown and company attacked the federal armory at Harpers Ferry, Virginia, hoping to start a slave rebellion. John Brown was hanged on December 2, 1859. Some Northerners called him a martyr and a hero. Bestselling author Ralph Waldo Emerson said that John Brown "made the gallows glorious like the cross."[23] Such adulation frightened and enraged Southerners who feared being murdered in their sleep.

Historian Bertram Wyatt-Brown writes that Northerners claimed the right to define and preserve the Union.[24] The day after John Brown was hanged, Lincoln spoke in Leavenworth, Kansas. He applauded Brown's execution, but he also addressed Southerners who warned of seceding if a Republican were elected chief executive. Lincoln vowed: "So, if constitutionally we elect a president, and therefore you undertake to destroy the Union, it will be our duty to deal with you as old John Brown was dealt with. We can only do our duty."[25] Lincoln hastened to add that he hoped "extreme measures" would not be necessary.

The antagonism between President Buchanan and Douglas continued during the presidential campaign of 1860. Buchanan supported the fire-eating secessionists by trying to undercut Douglas in every way, including dangling political plums in front of pro-Douglas Southern Unionists. The great showdown occurred in Charleston, South Carolina, where neither camp had enough votes for a presidential nomination. Fire-eaters bolted from the convention hall. Ultimately, two rival conventions chose different nominees: Douglas (representing Unionists across the land) and John C. Breckinridge (representing Buchanan and the fire-eaters). Lincoln, in contrast, fairly sailed to the Republican nomination. Complicating the mix was a fourth candidate, John Bell of the Constitutional Union Party.

A martial spirit had been building in Iowa in the late 1850s, with paramilitary guards forming in the larger cities, complete with weapons, officers, and drills. The Republican *Dubuque Times* stated, "We are pleased to see the military spirit on the rise in this city."[26] During the 1860 campaign season, young Douglas Democrats formed a "military company called the Dallas County Invincibles," built a 70-foot-high flagpole, and dared any Republican to approach it. Republicans formed cadres of "Wide-Awakes."[27] A rally in Glasgow, Iowa, featured 2,200 torch-carrying Wide-Awakes. A Democratic critic said the marching Wide-Awakes made the "night hideous with their sulphurous lamp smoke and their screams for Lincoln."[28]

Lincoln won solidly, but it was a regional, Northern vote. Potter explains, "All parties at the South were agreed in either threatening to leave or reserving the right to leave a government administered by Republicans." For their part, Republicans were able to tune out the growing cacophony of threats.[29]

Republican Henry Wilson once told Congress, "You cannot kick out of the Union the men who utter these impotent threats."[30] He ate his words when South Carolina seceded on December 20, 1860, and other Southern states followed suit. Iowa's Republican Governor Samuel J. Kirkwood called their actions "treason."[31]

The Iowa Democracy divided over the topic of secession, foreshadowing the later rift between Peace and War Democrats. Historian Hubert H. Wubben writes, "those disgruntled Democrats who appeared to condone secession too readily and too outspokenly found themselves belabored by other embarrassed Democrats."[32]

Some Iowa Republicans agreed with *New-York Tribune* publisher Horace Greeley, who did not want to live in "a Republic whereof one section is pinned to the residue by bayonets."[33] Greeley declared, "If the Cotton States shall become satisfied that they can do better out of the Union than in it, we insist on letting them go in peace."[34] Greeley and his supporters later accepted war instead of the prospect of having a separate Confederacy.

President-elect Lincoln kept a very low profile during the great "Secession Winter" prior to his inauguration. Panicky congressmen floated proposals to pacify and unify the country, and they inevitably touched on slavery. Lincoln gave marching orders to a Republican congressional ally in December 1860, "Let there be no compromise on the question of extending slavery.... The tug has to come, & better now, than any time hereafter."[35] Lincoln did not want to say anything that could weaken the Republican coalition before he took office.

Potter explains that Republicans thought most Southerners were loyal Unionists, and they would rise up against any attempt to secede. In effect, Republicans believed Southerners would quash any rebellion.[36]

The reality was different in the Upper South where Unionists fought a losing battle against ultra-secessionist fire-eaters. The Unionists cried for the president-elect to give tangible signs that he would protect slavery. Instead, Lincoln kept public silence, although he wrote a few Unionists of his kindly intentions.[37] Lincoln may not have properly reckoned with inflamed Southern honor.

Historian Bertram Wyatt-Brown states that outrage drove the Lower South to leave the Union. He explains: "To be sure, slavery was the root cause of sectional conflict.... The threat to slavery's legitimacy in the Union prompted the sectional crisis, but it was Southern honor that pulled the trigger."[38]

Wyatt-Brown continues:

Racism, white freedom and equality, and honor were not discrete concerns in the Southern mind. They were an inseparable part of personal and regional self-definition.... White liberty was sustainable, it was thought, only on the basis of black slavery.[39]

Southerners perceived a long-term threat to the peculiar institution because of the Republican Platform of 1856, and because President-elect Lincoln never retracted his "House Divided" speech or his remarks at Leavenworth.

The fire-eaters rushed to judgment. Potter explains, "If Southern public men had retained enough detachment of mind to weigh the factors involved, they might well have chosen not to inaugurate the program of secession."[40]

It seems that Lincoln did not anticipate secession, in part because he misunderstood the importance of Southern-defined honor. Potter writes that "when Lincoln moved to defeat compromise," he did so "as a partisan leader."[41]

Wyatt-Brown claims that both sides contributed to secession. Admitting that this summarizes the matter, he cites the interplay of "Northern conscience, guilt, and righteousness," and "Southern honor, dread of shame, and demand for vindication."[42]

Many residents may not have joined the C.S.A. if they had remained in Iowa. A seismic financial event moved them into a different culture.

The New York branch of the Ohio Life Insurance and Trust Company announced in August 1857 that it would suspend payments, touching off a financial implosion across the North.[43] Like an explosion deep in the bowels of a coal mine, shaking the ground above, the Panic of 1857 grew worse over time. Historian Morton M. Rosenberg writes that real-estate values collapsed, grain prices fell, currency was devalued, and many businesses failed.[44]

The South rebounded rather quickly.[45] The sunny business climate attracted many Iowans who found jobs and were exposed to Southern influences. Irish immigrant John Dooley describes a Northern-born-and-bred Confederate officer at Johnson's Island POW camp. The Maine native had married a Southern belle, and they lived in Tennessee. Dooley comments that he "became more Southern than many of the Southern people themselves."[46]

Homefront Pressures

The Propaganda Campaign in Iowa

While Union troops fought to crush the rebellion, Republicans back home waged a propaganda campaign against the Iowa Democratic Party. Starting very modestly, the strategy eventually targeted Ambassador George Wallace Jones (formerly a U.S. Senator from Iowa).

In the beginning, the firing upon Fort Sumter was a political game-changer. Iowa residents flocked to enlist in the Union Army and Navy, and Democrats divided over how to restore the Union. Some favored war; others favored negotiations and compromise.

Historian Hubert H. Wubben explains that Iowa politicians tried to define loyal and disloyal (traitorous) behavior. The editor of the *State Democratic Press* wrote:

> For God's sake, let not every vagabond in this community be permitted to make a definition of treason to suit himself, and then constitute himself accuser jury, judge and hangman, and proceed to wreak his vengeance and indulge his spite upon any personal enemies.[1]

Something else changed after Fort Sumter. President Lincoln began suspending the writ of *habeas corpus* in the North. This meant that federal authorities could arrest and imprison civilians, without any charges. The civilians would not get a trial, and their civil liberties would be violated.

Many Democratic editors in Iowa complained about this, stating that only Congress could suspend habeas corpus. Lincoln disagreed. He later argued that the Constitution allows the suspension "when, in cases of rebellion or invasion, the public safety may require it."

In summer 1861, a few months after Fort Sumter, there was a governor's race. The Democratic candidate, Charles Mason, had been the first Chief Justice of Iowa's

Supreme Court. Mason said the Union must be preserved, but he thought the war, at that time, was unwise and possibly illegal.

President Lincoln said in his first inaugural address, "In view of the Constitution and the laws, the Union is unbroken."[2] According to this view, the Confederacy was made up of insurgents who lived in states that remained loyal to the Union. Mason disagreed with this legal fiction.

Mason suggested that secession may represent "the uprising of a whole people against what they deem injustice and oppression."[3] He also suggested it may be "the voice of one-third of the Sovereign parties to our present Constitution claiming the rights of securing the happiness of their citizens by changing the form of their Government in accordance, as they contend," with the Declaration of Independence.

Mason agreed with Republicans that the Union must be restored. But, he said, the federal government must first exhaust every possible means of compromise and conciliation. Otherwise, the federal government was engaged in "naked, arbitrary, down-right coercion." Mason then predicted that "a republican government held together by the sword becomes a military Despotism."

Republican newspapers and politicians called Mason a "dis-unionist."[4] He felt great pressure and dropped out of the race. A Republican became governor.

During this period, the Lincoln administration began military arrests of civilians. Historian Mark E. Neely Jr. notes that "Secretary of State William H. Seward was given control of military arrests of civilians" after Fort Sumter until the War Department assumed control of them in early 1862.[5] Seward organized a secret service for this purpose.

There is a story, possibly apocryphal, that tells of Seward's power. He allegedly told Lord Lyon, the British minister in Washington:

> My Lord, I can touch a bell on my right hand, and order the arrest of a citizen in Ohio. I can touch the bell again, and order the arrest of a citizen in New York. Can the Queen of England, in her dominions, do as much?[6]

Not long after Fort Sumter, Secretary of State William H. Seward began intercepting Ambassador George Wallace Jones's correspondence.[7] Seward knew that Ambassador Jones was friends with Confederate President (and former U.S. Senator) Jefferson Davis. In addition, Seward probably had heard of Jones's stump speeches, predicting that Jones and his sons "would be found in the ranks of the Southern Army" in case of war.[8] Seward collected letters to and from Ambassador Jones, waiting to find incriminating evidence of disloyalty.

In the fall of 1861, the Lincoln administration recalled Ambassador Jones to replace him with a Republican. When Ambassador Jones returned to Washington in December 1861, his boss, Seward, honored him with a diplomatic dinner. Seward also introduced Jones to Abraham Lincoln as "my old friend." Lincoln invited Jones to his home. It was a memorable visit.[9]

The next night, Jones came to the White House and saw Lincoln with his leg thrown over the side of a chair. Lincoln said he had met Jones years earlier, when Lincoln was a state representative. Jones had asked the Illinois State Legislature for permission to operate a ferry from Dubuque to the shore of Illinois.

Lincoln said to Jones, "You were brought to my house one night by our old friend, Judge Pope, of the United States District Court for Illinois, the father of this 'lying Gen. John Pope' now of our army."

Jones said, "Yes, Mr. President, I got that John Pope into West Point Military Academy in 1838."

Lincoln said, "Judge Pope said to me, 'Lincoln, I want you to pass George's bill granting him a ferry privilege at Dubuque. I'll be damned, if you don't pass his bill tomorrow morning, you shall never come to the Legislature again.'"

Lincoln then told some funny stories and suggested that Jones get reacquainted with Mary Lincoln, whom he knew from his college days.

On Jones's last day in Washington, Seward pulled a bottle out from under his desk and said, "Let's take a farewell drink."

The next morning, Ambassador Jones rode a train to New York. When he arrived, a detective arrested Jones, without formal charges, at the order of his "old friend," William H. Seward.

Later that day, Seward told the press that Jones was in prison. Seward publicized one of the ambassador's letters to Jefferson Davis, highlighting passages that made him appear disloyal. For example, Jones had written Davis on May 17, 1861:

> My prayers are regularly offered up for the reunion of the States, and for the peace, concord and happiness of my country. But let what may come to pass, you may rely upon it, as you say, that neither I nor mine, "will ever be found in the ranks of our (your) enemies."
>
> May God Almighty avert civil war, but if unhappily it shall come, you may, I think without doubt, count on me and mine and hosts of other friends standing shoulder to shoulder in the ranks with you and our other Southern friends and relatives whose rights, like my own, have been disregarded by the abolitionists.[10]

However, Jones had clarified his thoughts in a different letter, written the same day, which had slipped by the State Department. The ambassador told a fellow Iowa Democrat:

> I tell [Jefferson Davis] he judges me & my friends rightly in supposing that we will not make war against ... our own beloved people who are driven from the Union for no other reason than because they were unwilling to submit to insult, injury & a palpable violation of our Constitution.
>
> No, I will not do battle against them & rather than do so I will leave my own beloved home & go South to join Davis ... & the true hearted & chivalrous Southerners.

Great God, has it come to this that I am to be impressed into a Northern Army, at the bidding of Kirkwood ... or other Abolition coward[s], to go down South with a rifle on my shoulder, do battle against the only brother whom I have living ... or turn my back upon the State which has honored me so highly?[11]

Ambassador Jones's arrest was a gift to the Iowa Republican party. Here was a Democratic former U.S. Senator who was a friend of Jefferson Davis, with one son in the Confederate Army and one about to join.

Republican editors jumped into the fray. The *Muscatine Journal* called Ambassador Jones "a traitor of the deepest dye."[12] The *Burlington Hawk-eye* editor equated "traitor" Ambassador Jones with "men in their arms, making war upon the Government."[13]

While Ambassador Jones was still in prison, one of his Confederate sons was captured. The *Chicago Post* said, "He was not only disloyal himself, but he encouraged his sons to be disloyal, too."[14]

Ambassador Jones spent about two months in prison. After he was released, the *New York Times* called Jones a minister to "Bogota [Colombia] and Fort Lafayette [Prison]."[15]

The *Burlington Hawk-eye* ran Jones's letter, defending himself, on July 12, 1862. He said he had intended to fight only abolitionists, through the political process, but not to "break up the Union."[16] But he was never allowed to defend himself in court.

The *Hawk-eye* tried Jones in the court of public opinion, stating:

The ex-Senator and Ex-Minister not only proves himself a traitor but an ass.... He is steeped to the very lips in treason and secession, and that his whole family, male and female are, all and singular, blind poison, vile secessionists.[17]

For the rest of the war, Republican editors used "George Wallace Jones" as shorthand for a sneaky, traitorous Confederate sympathizer, who had Confederate sons.

One of the ambassador's Dubuque Democratic friends, Warner Lewis, wrote:

All constitutional liberty ... [is] lost in this country. If Wm. H. Seward or any other dignitary is allowed to select his victim and incarcerate him in a cell or Fort without a trial or even examination, then this great Republic as founded by our Fathers ... has failed. Who would have thought five years ago that the American people would have submitted to such outrageous despotism?[18]

The following year, 1862, the state of Iowa and the Federal Government used force to silence Democrats who disagreed with them. Lincoln was keenly interested in having ample troops, and he opposed anyone or anything that would interfere with enlistment.

Early in 1862, Secretary of War Edwin Stanton took over the military arrests of civilians.[19] By that summer, the Union Army needed more troops. In July 1862, Lincoln signed a Militia Act (a first step toward a draft).[20]

In August 1862, Stanton authorized law enforcement officials throughout the country to arrest disloyal civilians and try them before a military commission.[21] A military commission was a court-martial for civilians. What crimes were subject to arrest? Anyone who "discouraged" enlistment "by act, speech, or writing," or who gave "aid and comfort to the enemy" or did anything else disloyal.

In effect, if a person discouraged enlistment, he or she was disloyal and could be arrested and imprisoned, without a civil trial.[22] No one defined the word "disloyal." Iowa Democrats were easy targets, especially if they favored an armistice.[23]

Lincoln explained his position to Erastus Corning the following year. He stated, "He who dissuades one man from volunteering, or induces one soldier to desert, weakens the Union cause as much as he who kills a Union soldier in battle."[24]

The life of the nation, Lincoln said, depends on "the existence and vigor" of the army. He stated that when prominent Peace Democrats waged "war" upon the military, that "gave the military constitutional jurisdiction" to lay hands upon those Peace Democrats.

Lincoln asked Corning:

> Must I shoot a simple-minded boy who deserts, while I must not touch a hair of a wily agitator who induces him to desert?
>
> This is nonetheless injurious when affected by getting a father or a brother or friend into a public meeting, and there working upon his feelings till he is persuaded to write the soldier boy that he is fighting in a bad cause, for a wicked administration, or a contemptible government....
>
> I think that in such a case, to silence the agitator and save the boy is not only constitutional but withal a great mercy.[25]

After Secretary Stanton gave his orders, the federal Marshal for Iowa, Hubert M. Hoxie, acted. Hoxie had been Chairman of the Republican State Committee.

This was election season in Iowa. Marshal Hoxie arrested two outspoken Democratic editors, Dennis A. Mahony and David Sheward.[26] Both editors had sometimes criticized the Lincoln administration and the war effort. Mahony had been the acting chairman of the State Democratic Committee. Hoxie threw Mahony and Sheward in to Old Capitol Prison in Washington, D.C. Neither editor was formally charged. Democrats nominated Mahony to run for Congress from his prison cell.[27] Unsurprisingly, he lost the election.

Historian Hubert H. Wubben estimated that thirty-six Iowans were arrested in August 1862. This was the high-water mark for arrests of Iowa civilians during the Civil War.[28]

President Lincoln wrote Corning:

Arrests [in cases of rebellion] are made, not so much for what has been done, as for what probably would be done....

The man who stands by and says nothing when the peril of his country is discussed cannot be misunderstood. If not hindered, he is sure to help the enemy; much more, if he talks ambiguously—talks for his country with "buts" and "ifs" and "ands."[29]

The following year, Democrats in Albany, New York, wrote Lincoln:

Your claim is, that when the writ of habeas corpus is suspended, you may lawfully imprison and punish for the crimes of silence, of speech, and opinion...

Your doctrine denies the freedom of speech and of the press. It invades the sacred domain of opinion and discussion ... even the refuge of silence is insecure.[30]

Meanwhile, in Des Moines, the governor was worried about Iowa's southern neighbor. He had reason to be worried: Missouri was descending into horror, and armed guerrillas were on the loose. Even worse, towns and sometimes even neighbors were pitted against each other, causing bloodshed, murder, and destruction. It was prudent to have an Iowa Border Guard—a militia—to prevent armed Confederates from slipping across the border into Iowa.

Wubben explains that the governor had another worry. Wubben states:

[Gov. Kirkwood feared] that secret societies of Southern sympathizers had gained a foothold in Iowa. Foremost among these was presumed to be the Knights of the Golden Circle. Worried Iowans believed the Knights were well organized, disciplined, and prepared to aid the rebels.[31]

This was not a legitimate fear, but it is understandable. Passions were running high, and rumors filled the state. Republican editor Jesse Clement of the *Dubuque Times* said that Dubuque harbored a Knights of the Golden Circle lodge.[32] He gave no evidence. Nonetheless, national Republican newspapers spread Clement's rumor, and so did other Iowa papers.

Soon, the *Dubuque Times* linked George Wallace Jones to the KGC lodges. The article was titled, "Secret Movements of Northern Traitors." It stated:

The emissaries of Jeff. Davis are busy at their night work in this State. Their leader is Brigadier George Wallace Jones.... Since he was released from Fort Lafayette, he has been as busy as the satanic spirit of treason can make him to be, and wherever he has been, secret lodges and "Democratic" papers have sprung up, with the rallying cry of "Down with the Abolitionists!" Wherever he cannot be, he has his tools, who take the lead of the "Democratic" element in their community, organize lodges, work hard o' nights, and damn the "abolitionists" during the daytime.[33]

The next year, 1863, Democrats and Republicans enthusiastically criticized each other. But Republicans raised name-calling to the next level. They called many Democrats "Copperheads."

Republicans used "Copperhead" to smear any Democrat who, supposedly, sympathized with the South and was too sensitive about violations of civil liberties. Copperhead came to mean someone who did not fully support Lincoln's war policy.

Historian Frank L. Klement calls this "the most vicious, most extensive, and most successful smear campaign in American history."[34] According to Klement, Republican wartime propaganda, which charged Democratic critics with being pro-Southern in sympathy and proclivities, "polluted the stream of history for more than a hundred years."

Historian Leland Sage writes that many Democrats supported the war "as loyally as the Republicans, earned the title, "War Democrats" and hated the Peace Democrats as fiercely as did the Republicans."[35] However, Sage notes, "when election time came around, the Republicans forgot this and smeared all Democrats as Southern sympathizers."

In late May 1863, someone in Burlington prematurely announced the fall of Vicksburg. Burlington residents formed an exuberant nighttime procession with bells ringing, firecrackers exploding, and cannons firing.[36] Afterwards, the *Muscatine Journal* said that "rebel sympathizers ... should be compelled to leave," "take the oath of allegiance," or be hanged.[37]

Six months later, in the third year of the war, Republican Governor William M. Stone stated:

> There is no longer any middle ground where loyal men can stand.... Those who hesitate now to yield an unreserved support to the Federal Government ... unmistakably array themselves on the side of its enemies.... If treason is a crime, to sympathize with traitors is also clearly criminal.[38]

In other words, Gov. Stone suggested that loyal citizens had to support everything the Federal Government did. Democrats never figured out how to disagree with Republican policies without being seen by the public as disloyal.

Midway through 1864, Ambassador Jones's son, Charles, was captured. The *Burlington Hawk-eye* wrote:

> Charles S.D. Jones, son of ex-Senator G.W. Jones, of Dubuque, was captured by Butler at Drury's [*sic*.] Bluff.... That is the sort of patriots the leaders of the Iowa Copperheads make of their sons. They have been honored beyond their deserts by the Democracy of Iowa. The return they make is to teach their sons to become traitors, to join the rebels in their efforts to destroy the Union, and to murder the sons of Iowa who are defending their country![39]

There is another aspect to the propaganda campaign in Iowa. Sometimes, soldiers or civilians reacted violently toward Democratic newspapers. Consider what happened in Keokuk.

There were seven hospitals for soldiers in that city. In February 1863, Thomas W. Clagett of the *Daily Constitution*, a Democratic newspaper, wrote an editorial, "Politics in the Army." According to historian Hubert H. Wubben, Clagett "reacted angrily to reports that … [officers from Indiana who were Republicans] subjected their regiments to political pressure."[40]

Clagett wrote, "Partisan officers in the army are pliant tools of … partisan bigots at home." Later that day, four soldiers, carrying sledgehammers, led a mob of their comrades in smashing Clagett's presses and tossing "much of the equipment into the Mississippi."[41]

It happened too fast for local and federal officials to intervene. The mob of convalescent soldiers destroyed $10,000 worth of property, and it took seven months to restart the paper. Wubben explains that Democrats across the state were incensed, but the soldiers said they had done their duty to get rid of the *Daily Constitution*'s "treasonable influence."[42]

Governor Kirkwood said he regretted the mob action, but he asked this question: "Is it strange that men enduring what soldiers are enduring should give such expression of their feelings towards the men in the North they believe are aiding the enemy?"[43] All told, mobs, mostly made up of civilians, destroyed four Iowa Democratic presses and wrecked a couple of newspaper offices in 1863 and 1864.[44]

The war finally ended in 1865. By this time, the Iowa Democratic Party was badly beaten.

Son of Former Iowa Governor Goes Bad: "Rebel Son" Becomes Campaign Issue

Junius L. Hempstead set down the chisel and ran his fingers over the marble contours of the bust. He was reminded that God, on the seventh day, looked at his creation and said it was good, very good.

A Dubuque arts patron was so impressed that he offered to send eighteen-year-old Junius to Europe to study art.[45] But Junius's father—a realist who had been Iowa's second governor—nixed the idea. Insisting that Junius receive a "good civil and military education," he tried unsuccessfully to enroll his son at West Point.[46] Another option appeared. Former Governor Stephen Hempstead and his wife, Lavinia (a native of Maryland), would long remember the day that Junius enrolled at the Virginia Military Institute—nine months before Fort Sumter.

VMI had a good reputation, and Junius did well in class. Governor Hempstead might not have known that being a cadet meant taking an oath to "support Va. against all of her enemies." Junius later explained that he "believed in State['s]

Rights, to the fullest extent," and thought every "state is a sovereign power ... privileged to withdraw at will."[47] He quickly identified with Virginia and the Southern cadets. After Virginia seceded, Junius wrote, "Her enemies became mine."

Junius and other cadets entered the 5th Virginia Infantry.[48] His service became a campaign issue for his father, who was running for Dubuque County Judge. A newspaper article criticized former Governor Hempstead. The article stated:

> [Gov. Hempstead] does not believe in the war to put down rebellion. On the contrary ... he believes in the war begun by the South to destroy the Government, for he has a son in the rebel army, fighting against his country. Who knows but that some of our own citizens may have a relative shot by the hand of this rebel son of a disloyal father?[49]

A letter to an editor accused, "THAT SON JOINED THE REBEL ARMY, AND DID SO WITH HIS FATHER'S APPROVAL!"[50] In spite of the uproar, Governor Hempstead was elected county judge.[51]

Meanwhile, Junius the artist was becoming a warrior. His superior officers asked Jefferson Davis to give Junius an officer's commission. They described him as "a worthy young gentleman" and a proficient drill-master who acted with bravery and coolness in two battles. The officers explained why Junius needed a commission:

> Mr. Hempstead's father & friends are residents of the State of Iowa, and though Southern in their feelings are unable to give him any pecuniary assistance, and as it would be unsafe for him to visit them, he is entirely dependent upon himself for a support.[52]

Governor Hempstead likely had fond memories of years spent in Missouri as an older teen and young adult, but he did not side with the Confederacy; he was a Douglas Democrat, and even Junius admitted that his father was a strong Union man.[53]

A month after the officers wrote Jefferson Davis, two of Junius's Dubuque friends visited him in camp. Junius made them feel welcome, and they "talked over Iowa matters."[54] Both friends later entered the Confederate service.

Junius became a lieutenant in the 5th Virginia Infantry. He was badly wounded in the shoulder at the Second Battle of Manassas, and after he recovered, he rejoined his unit. At the Battle of the Wilderness, amid a flurry of bullets, he was wounded and captured. Union authorities moved Junius and hundreds of other Confederate officers to Fort Delaware. All too soon, Junius was tested to the edge of his endurance.

Junius and 600 other Confederate officers crowded into the dark hold of a Federal steamer. Seasickness and lack of sanitation bedeviled them for two weeks.[55]

They arrived at Morris Island (outside of Charleston, South Carolina), and entered Fort Gregg. Its cannons were pointed at Charleston and two Confederate forts, Sumter and Moultrie. The prisoners were held behind the cannons, inside a wooden stockade, four men per tent.

The POWs were there because of vengeance. A year earlier, in 1863, Union troops had captured Fort Wagner, further west on Morris Island. They began firing cannons at a civilian neighborhood of Charleston; some of the shells were incendiary. Months later, seeking relief, Confederates placed forty-five Union officers and five generals in the besieged neighborhood. In retaliation, the Union Army placed Junius and the 600 other officers in the line of fire of Confederate guns aimed at Fort Wagner.[56]

The bombardments began on Junius's second night. He could not escape the screaming shells and convulsive, shaking ground. Some nights, he was so hungry, he drifted off to sleep. By day, Junius could see Charleston and hear the church bells.[57]

Junius poured out his feelings in a journal. He prayed, "O! God, how long will the misery continue?"[58] Hunger pushed him "to eat bean soup full of sand and gravel."[59] The guards stole parcels of food and clothing, but they gave the POWs tobacco. Junius started smoking, grateful for a distraction from his stomach.[60]

On September 18, 1864, Junius wrote: "Heard the bells in Charleston. Made my heart ache, to think of it, within sight of liberty and still not there. Like Moses running to the Promised land.... How long! will this misery continue?"[61]

Feelings poured out of Junius. He wrote on September 29: "[I] am getting so tired [of] retaliation. It is a mean thing, dishonorable in both governments to treat prisoners of war ... in the way they do ... I am home sick and want to get home so bad."[62]

After forty-two days, the Federal Government moved the POWs to Fort Pulaski, off the coast of Savannah, Georgia. Chilly Atlantic winds blew in. Junius couldn't get warm since he had neither blanket nor fire for warmth. Hunger continue to gnaw.

His parents were frantic. Judge Hempstead started pulling strings to free their son. He may have asked newly elected Iowa Governor William M. Stone to visit Junius in prison. Fellow POW Captain Henry C. Dickinson wrote in his diary:

29 December 1864. Still very cold, men coughing terribly. Yanks signaling from the fort. Governor Stone, of Iowa, arrives. Sent for Lt Hempstead, Twenty-fifth Virginia, son of ex-governor of Iowa, and begged him to take the oath. Brown [Union commandant] added his persuasions and told him we were to be fed on corn meal and pickles. Hempstead nobly refused.[63]

A month later, on January 27, 1865, Judge Hempstead contacted Charles Mason (a Democrat and former chief justice of the Iowa Supreme Court). Judge Hempstead wrote: "Prisoners cannot live long if they are treated in this manner.... I will take it as a kindness never to be forgotten if you will use your influence with Gen'l

Grant and others at Washington to affect his parole, and if that cannot be done, his exchange."[64]

Judge Hempstead explained that Junius felt he had to keep his promise to defend Virginia.[65] Junius thought he would perjure himself (that is, violate his earlier oath) "before God and man" if he swore allegiance to the U.S.[66]

Battling hunger and cold in mid-February 1865, Junius wrote President Lincoln. Junius explained his moral predicament and asked Lincoln to be "indulgent to the Prodigal."[67]

Judge Hempstead wrote Charles Mason that Junius "believes that he has done nothing wrong and is proud of what he has been able to do in defense of a brave people."[68] Junius's father decided not to push his son to do anything that he felt was dishonorable. "He is now of age to act for himself." The next month, prisoner Junius wrote:

Dear Father, Fort Delaware, 12 March 1865
After many disappointments and hopes, I have landed once more at this place. I am in a hard scrape have but one shirt to my name, and that is worn out. I am wearing a friend's underclothing; my suit is getting ragged and is very thin for such weather.[69]

Junius asked for clothes and family photographs: "Send the box at once for I have been naked and cold all winter. This place is Paradise compared with where we came from.... You all think I am a trouble I know."

He wrote his mother: "I am almost naked, my clothing is quite ragged, and I need some badly.... Come and see me, please. You have a splendid chance.... You can get me out of this hard scrape by using your influence."[70]

After President Lincoln's assassination, Judge Hempstead kept trying to free his son. He wrote newly installed President Andrew Johnson: "President Lincoln, through his private secretary, wrote to him [Junius], promising him a Parole for the War, and had he lived would have granted it.... My son is very young, was nothing but a boy when the War first commenced.... [He] is tired of the War and is anxious to come home."[71]

More than a month after Appomattox, Junius remained in Fort Delaware. By this time, Junius was ready to sign the oath of allegiance. His father kept trying to get him released. Judge Hempstead described Junius to Charles Mason as "a boy who went into the war without mature consideration, and as he supposed, to defend the state of Virginia."[72]

On June 16, 1865, Junius finally signed the oath of allegiance. He returned to his parents in Dubuque. While there, he wrote Paul Cantwell, a fellow former POW, "I am going to write a book and am going to publish to the world the cruelty of the Federals to Confederate Prisoners."[73] Junius later explained to Cantwell, "The book will show two sides to the question and open the eyes of a number of sensible men in the North."[74]

By Christmas 1865, Junius had written "some 350 pages."[75] His manuscript has been lost, but *Confederate Veteran* magazine eventually published his article, "How the Six Hundred Officers Fared."[76]

Junius thereafter lived in Memphis and then Louisiana, mainly writing poems and novels, often related to VMI and his wartime experiences.[77] Late in life, he became president of the Immortal Six Hundred association. Junius died on September 16, 1920, in Jennings, Louisiana.

A Family Friend in the Confederate White House

Sitting next to a general with gold braid on his sleeve, Charles noticed his own emaciated arm. His old priest back in Dubuque had preached, "Man is born to trouble." How true. He could think of his own health problems and a strained marriage. Maybe, just maybe, this meeting with Jefferson Davis would be a turning point.

Charles's life of struggle began in the Wisconsin Territory, even before he was born. His father, George Wallace Jones, had brought slaves up from St. Genevieve, Missouri, to Sinsinawa Mound, Wisconsin Territory, to help him mine and smelt lead.[78] George Wallace Jones went back to Missouri to court and marry Josephine Gregoire. They returned to Sinsinawa Mound to begin married life and start a family. Joy increased when Josephine conceived. Tension increased as Sauk Chief Black Hawk recrossed the Mississippi River and gathered hundreds of warriors, heading eastward.

The situation became so menacing that George Wallace Jones sent Josephine back to St. Genevieve.[79] Even *in utero*, Charles absorbed the message that the world is a dangerous place.[80] While Genevieve was in Missouri, warriors massacred her brother-in-law, Felix St. Vrain, the Indian agent at Rock Island, Illinois.[81] When the Black Hawk War ended, Josephine came back to Sinsinawa Mound and delivered Charles S. D. Jones.

Lt. Jefferson Davis visited Sinsinawa to renew his friendship with George Wallace Jones, his classmate from Transylvania University in Kentucky. Davis visited several times.[82] At least once, he reportedly bounced young Charlie on his knee.

When Charles was a boy, George Wallace Jones entered politics, becoming a delegate to Congress from Michigan Territory.[83] He lost that post and moved his growing family (and three slaves) across the Mississippi River to Dubuque, Iowa Territory.[84] He was the largest slaveholder in Dubuque in the 1840 Federal Census, a town that had seventeen slaves held by eleven owners.[85]

Culturally speaking, George Wallace Jones was a Southerner.[86] He modeled a Southern-defined sense of honor and built a political machine based on what he called "friendship," namely, personal and political loyalty.[87]

George Wallace Jones made friends of Southern congressmen and senators, and he often voted with the Southern bloc. For the first half of his life, Charles walked through many doors opened by his father and his father's friends.

In 1848, when Charles was sixteen years old, George Wallace Jones became one of Iowa's first U.S. senators.[88] Perhaps Charles first became aware of his new status as a senator's son when, at age eighteen, he enrolled in Western Military Institute (WMI) in Drennon, Kentucky, at the suggestion of Senator Henry Clay, the "Great Compromiser."

Charles received a Southern military school education, one that emphasized math and practical science applications, including the ability to survey land.[89] Senator Jones's influence was such that seven Dubuque notables followed his example by sending their sons to WMI.[90]

Charles made Southern friends at WMI. His social life included helping to manage a military ball on June 17, 1852. He graduated the following year, on July 14, 1853, at age twenty-one. Later that year, Charles visited the University of Virginia Law School as a prospective student. Late enrollment was the only option for him, so instead, he enrolled in Harvard Law School on December 16, 1853.[91] He graduated from Harvard in 1857, at age twenty-five, with an LL.B. ("*Legum Baccalaureus*"), the equivalent of Bachelor of Laws.

Charles returned to Dubuque and, probably due to his father's influence, quickly passed the Dubuque bar and served as secretary of one of its meetings. But Senator Jones's power and finances began to slowly melt away.

While Charles and his two brothers had been away at school, Senator Jones made stump speeches around Iowa. For example, he said, if civil war broke out, he and his sons would "be found in the ranks of the Southern Army, and that, altho' we might be few in number, we would be victorious as our cause would be just."[92] Perhaps this was a politician's bravado, but it was out of step with many constituents in the 1850s.

Iowa Democrats had increasingly opposed Senator Jones due to the Fugitive Slave Act, the Kansas–Nebraska Act, the birth of the Iowa Republican Party, and the failure to build a railroad in Dubuque.[93] The growing strength of Jones's opponents caused the Democratic Party to splinter in Dubuque (the "Gibraltar of the Iowa Democracy") and throughout Iowa.

The financial Panic of 1857 occurred just as Charles graduated from Harvard.[94] The panic slowly and inexorably caused the Dubuque economy to deteriorate, leaving Senator Jones and his Dubuque friends in precarious financial positions[95] In Washington, Senator Jones voted to accept the Lecompton Constitution. This unpopular move further fractured the Iowa Democratic Party, causing Jones to lose his senate seat, and his supporters to become a minority faction.

Senator Jones—land rich, but cash poor—mortgaged his house to pay debts.[96] President Buchanan gave a temporary reprieve when he appointed Jones in 1859 as minister to New Grenada (present-day Colombia), South America.[97]

The ambassador took Charles with him to South America as his personal secretary. Soon after they arrived, Charles contracted Chagres fever, a debilitating, virulent form of malaria.[98] Victims of Chagres fever suffered from high fever and delirium lasting from six to twenty hours.[99] They also had "intensely excruciating" headaches. Barely able to sit upright, some victims experienced these symptoms every day or two. Perhaps worst of all, the fever could come back every few years. One doctor wrote, "Chagres fever is the most obstinate ... form of intermittent fever."[100]

Chagres fever was likely a type of cerebral malaria, similar to that contracted by some 250,000 American G.I.s in Vietnam. Cerebral malaria eventually results in personality change and depression, similar to the neuropsychiatric symptoms experienced by many Vietnam veterans.[101]

Charles returned to Washington, carrying his father's dispatches.[102] He recuperated in Dubuque. On February 6, 1860, Charles was appointed first lieutenant of the Washington Guards, the second-largest military company in pre-war Dubuque.[103]

That summer, as the national Democratic Party was splitting, Dubuquers who opposed Stephen A. Douglas for president held a meeting. Charles joined John C. Breckinridge's presidential campaign committee along with some of his father's friends.

Ambassador Jones returned home on furlough, and Charles had a flare-up of Chagres fever. The Dubuque doctors could do nothing. Ambassador Jones took Charles to New York, prior to heading back to New Grenada.[104] They found a Venezuelan doctor who diagnosed and treated Charles.

Unlike the ambassador, Charles did not seek political office, but he agreed with his father that war loomed because northern abolitionists interfered with slavery in violation of the Constitution, and because of Democratic Senator Stephen A. Douglas's scheming. Charles knew that his father's circle of friends, including Jefferson Davis and other Southern senators and congressmen, did favors for each other. Jefferson Davis taught Charles a powerful lesson about the bonds of friendship.[105] On the eve of resigning from the Senate (to serve the Confederacy), Jefferson Davis tried to restore the military commission of Charles's younger brother, William A.B. Jones, in the U.S. Cavalry.[106] Davis was unsuccessful. In a short time, Davis's life changed greatly when he became president of the Confederacy. William A. B. Jones left for Colorado Territory, making him the only Jones son who did not serve the C.S.A.[107]

When Abraham Lincoln was elected president, the Jones family quickly entered dire financial straits. In late March 1861, Charles took time to visit Washington, D.C., where he met a captivating Kentucky belle, Annie Miller. He gushed, "It was love at first sight with both of us."[108] Charles explained to his father:

> She is none of your ordinary girls.... She refused a millionaire and a lawyer in
> Phila. last winter.... These secrets came out when she thought I had accused her
> of being influenced to love me by your honorable position and supposed wealth.

She said she never would have mentioned these things, but to convince me that she loved me for myself alone and that she was not aware that you were an Ex U.S. Senator.[109]

He returned to Dubuque and corresponded with Annie. Shortly before Fort Sumter, Charles cheered the young Confederacy.[110] He looked at his father's disintegrated political base, his family's financial hardship, the new Lincoln administration, and the growing prospect of war. Charles, whose blood ran hotter than his middle-aged father's, began to see the Confederate service as a viable option. Charles wrote his father (still stationed in South America):

I loved the Union dearly—but I hate abolitionism and love the Southern people. Come home and let's move South and help them fight for their Independence. The last news is that old Abe will commence a war on the South. God protect us if he does. I feel a conviction that I will fight for the South.... I [will] send you a pair of ... French pistols.... You must keep them for our Revolution—if we are to have one precipitated by these damnable abolitionists.[111]

At some point, Charles made the surely unhappy discovery that Annie's father was a Republican and a political friend of Abraham Lincoln.[112] Charles's mother, Josephine Gregoire Jones, fretted about the family finances. She wrote her husband: "If it were not for my faith I could not get along & would be in despair, for Charley and I have been worried with business matters until we are almost discouraged. I could not begin to tell you the bitter tears I have shed."[113]

At a time when an average man earned a dollar a day, the Jones family owed $10,000.[114] Their creditors threatened a sheriff's sale of some of their property, and Josephine Gregoire Jones considered selling their house.[115] Grasping for income, Charles hired two men and started digging a lead mine shaft. His mother wrote, "Charles ... has not come to mineral yet & I live in dread of the expense & no profit, but he thinks he must try something."[116]

Not unexpectedly, Ambassador Jones was recalled by the new Republican administration, taking away another source of income. Charles wrote his father:

I regard this act as the greatest favor to you that he could have done.... Thus you will not suffer the disgrace of having served Lincoln's abolition Govt. for pay when your sense of honor and lifelong principles condemned it as disgraceful....

I'd rather this minute accept with joy the most abject misery and poverty than ... support the war ... in any way.[117]

Amid the turmoil, Charles became engaged to Annie.

Charles's friend, Daniel O'Connell Quigley (son of Patrick Quigley), first considered joining a Louisiana unit. Shortly after Fort Sumter, Charles wrote a letter, introducing Quigley to his friend (and fellow *alumnus* of WMI), the commander of Hunter's Louisiana Rifles.[118]

Writing another letter to his father, Charles lauded Jefferson Davis and General Beauregard's victory at Bull Run. Charles stated: "God bless them all and their people is my heartfelt prayer. How much I wish that we could have been there to share in the glory of that day."[119]

By late September 1861, six months after the war began, Union Army enlistments had dropped. Iowa Governor Samuel J. Kirkwood hinted about having a draft. Charles wrote his father, "I [do] not wish to aid in this war even by getting a substitute if I were drafted."[120]

Charles's dream of leaving Dubuque for a career in the Confederacy was almost stillborn. He explained to his father:

> Like a dunce I promised Annie Miller that I would not go to war or do anything unless she gave her consent, and all because she had cried over the expectation that there might be Civil war at the North and that I would not be neutral. There's no telling what a silly man will not do on account of a woman's tears. If there is no other way to gain a livelihood but war, I've got myself into a miserable scrape.[121]

By late August 1861, Chagres fever began to have an effect on Charles's personality. His mother, Josephine Gregoire Jones, wrote to Ambassador Jones: "I think he has changed in his disposition since his first attack of illness, and I expect it [marrying Annie] will be the best thing for his health & happiness."[122]

Charles and Annie planned a Kentucky wedding—in spite of their economic uncertainty. On October 17, 1861, Charles, who was Catholic and a Democrat, married his bride—a Presbyterian with a Republican father—and they returned to Dubuque.

Unbeknownst to the Joneses, Secretary of State William H. Seward had been intercepting the ambassador's correspondence with his family.[123] Just a few years earlier, George Wallace Jones and William H. Seward were "brother Senators," and both were friends of Senator Jefferson Davis.[124] Seward demonstrated his friendship in early 1857 when Davis's "left eye became intensely inflamed," and he was confined to a darkened room.[125] Senator Seward visited Davis an hour every day, telling him congressional news and trying to lift his spirits.[126] Davis's wife, Varina, appreciated Seward's "earnest, tender interest" in her husband.

During that time, Seward had apparently heard of George Wallace Jones's stump speeches, predicting that Jones and his sons "would be found in the ranks of the Southern Army" in case of war.[127] After Lincoln's inauguration, Seward was given control of military arrests of civilians. Seward now wielded a powerful, concealed weapon. Because Lincoln suspended the writ of *habeas corpus*, Seward had the ability to arrest George Wallace Jones and jail him without a trial by jury.

When Ambassador Jones returned to Washington, Seward threw him a diplomatic dinner and took him to see Abraham Lincoln in his office, introducing the ambassador as "my old friend." Lincoln was busy but told Ambassador Jones to come by his house the next night, and he did. Ambassador Jones heard Lincoln tell funny stories, and he chatted with Mary Lincoln, who he knew from his college days.

Ambassador Jones proceeded to New York on December 20, 1861, where he was promptly arrested and thrown into Fort Lafayette prison without formal charges, all at the order of his "old friend," William H. Seward.[128]

Seward immediately told the press that Ambassador Jones was in prison.[129] Seward soon publicized one of the Ambassador's letters to Jefferson Davis, highlighting passages that made him appear disloyal. For example, Ambassador Jones had written:

> My prayers are regularly offered up for the reunion of the States, and for the peace, concord and happiness of my country. But let what may come to pass, you may rely upon it, as you say, that neither I nor mine, "will ever be found in the ranks of our (your) enemies."
>
> May God Almighty avert civil war, but if unhappily it shall come, you may, I think without doubt, count on me and mine and hosts of other friends standing shoulder to shoulder in the ranks with you and our other Southern friends and relatives whose rights, like my own, have been disregarded by the abolitionists.[130]

Dubuque attorney (and Democrat) Ben M. Samuels tried to intervene. Samuels asked the State Department for a copy of George Wallace Jones's letter to Jefferson Davis. Samuels wrote on Christmas Eve:

> The General's family is in the very depths of distress. The suspense in regard to the charges against him increases their anguish of spirit. Certainty will bring to them some measure of relief....
>
> Mrs. Jones informs me that she is acquainted with Sec. Seward and has always regarded him as entirely friendly with the General and the family.[131]

Ambassador Jones was freed from prison after two months on February 22, 1862.[132] He returned to Dubuque to his wife, Charles, and Annie. The pro-Union press excoriated him. Ambassador Jones later claimed that he had intended to merely speak up for the Southerners, but he never was allowed to defend himself in court.

Charles had seen the federal government trample on his father's rights. At the same time, rumors swirled around Dubuque about imminent conscription, and several of Charles's like-minded peers had already left Dubuque to serve the Confederacy. Charles, who was recovering from another bout of Chagres fever, took Annie and fled South.[133] She might have been carrying their first child. They first went to Frankfort, Kentucky (where Annie's father lived), and then to Richmond to "escape the abolition draft" and "despotism."[134, 135]

Upon reaching the Confederate capitol in the spring of 1862, Charles headed to President Jefferson Davis's office, probably seeking a civilian job. In that way, he kept his word to Annie. President Davis received Charles "promptly and cheerfully."[136] The meeting was a success. Some months later, Jefferson Davis helped him get a job in the Ordnance Department as part of the civil service.[137]

Now that Charles had a job in Virginia, he and Annie could settle down. Annie delivered their first child, Nannie Stribling Jones, but the baby died the same year. Charles changed to a job in the Confederate Treasury Department, with the help of Jefferson Davis.[138]

During this time, Charles's letter of introduction for his friend Daniel O. C. Quigley surfaced in the wreckage of Shiloh. *New York Times* reporter (and former Dubuque resident) Franc Wilkie found the letter and printed it. This gave a fresh opportunity to heap abuse on Ambassador Jones as well as Charles and his brother, George R. G. Jones, who had recently been captured at Fort Henry.

The following year, 1863, Charles threw a monkey wrench into his marriage. He passionately wanted to enter the Confederate Army. The record doesn't show what Annie thought about this.

Jefferson Davis helped Charles be appointed to the temporary staff of General Bushrod R. Johnson, his old principal at Western Military Institute. Charles wrote Davis: "I assure Your Excellency of my sincere and deep-felt gratitude for your favor in the past to my father, my brother & myself, and that I am anxious to serve the country which affords me such a happy asylum."[139]

Charles kept working in the Treasury Department until his appointment was finalized. On July 8, 1863, Charles had a relapse of Chagres fever, with "great physical debility and nervousness following it."[140] The following month, he confided to Jefferson Davis, "I am now almost unable to perform the severe manual labor required in our office, of numbering 4,800 notes from 8 to 3 o'clock." Charles implied that serving as a Confederate officer in the field would aid his health. Charles stated:

> A word of recommendation from Your Excellency ... will secure for me a position and livelihood till blessed Peace comes and the hateful foe shall have retired and abandoned his bloody purposes.... I approach Your Excellency with something like the confidence I would my own father.

Davis forwarded the letter to the Secretary of War, noting: "Mr. Jones is the worthy son of our friend Geo. W. Jones of Iowa. He has a Brother in our army." After Charles recovered less than a month later, he was appointed captain and assistant adjutant general on Bushrod R. Johnson's staff.

During this time, Charles caused the Jones family to receive rare praise in the pro-Union press. On November 29, 1863, the *Dubuque Daily Times* credited Charles with helping secure the release of Private Samuel Smith of the 21st Iowa from a Richmond prison.[141] But this positive recognition proved to be short-lived.

Nine months later, on May 16, 1864, Capt. Charles S. D. Jones was stationed outside of Drewry's Bluff, Virginia. Rising early, disoriented in the dense, dark fog, he rode his horse straight into Union lines.[142]

He languished in Fort Delaware prison, racked with Chagres fever, while Annie gave birth to their daughter, Josephine, near Richmond. Charles experienced the now-familiar "great physical debility and nervousness." Ambassador Jones tapped into his vast network to help relieve Charles's suffering. A former senatorial colleague from Delaware sent his son to Delaware Prison, bringing Charles much-needed fruits and vegetables.[143, 144]

When pro-Union Iowa newspapers caught wind of Charles's capture, they heaped fresh abuse on Ambassador Jones and his disloyal son.[145]

Annie's Republican father entered the picture, telling Charles to "take the oath of allegiance to the U.S. Govt."[146] But Charles said "he would rather rot in prison than give up his principles or allegiance to the South." Annie's father intervened again, traveling to Washington.[147] Due to his efforts, Charles was paroled just before New Year's Day 1865. But Charles was forbidden from fighting until he had been exchanged for a Union officer of same rank. While he waited, Charles's mother clandestinely sent him letters through people coming to the Shenandoah Valley.[148]

About a month before Appomattox, Charles was exchanged and eager to rejoin the Confederate Army. However, he needed a horse, so he asked Jefferson Davis to help him get one. Charles noted, "My good father (Geo. W. Jones of Iowa) is still on his parole and subjected to the taunts and espionage of the abolitionists."[149] Jefferson Davis scrawled a note: "Sec'y of War, with a request for special attention. Capt. Jones is the worthy son of a gallant father."

Charles was in Danville, Virginia, when he heard that Lee had surrendered to Grant. After the war ended, Charles sought amnesty, so his father-in-law, James. J. Miller, interceded. Miller wrote Attorney General James Speed (a fellow Kentuckian): "My son in law Charles S.D. Jones of Dubuque, Iowa, was so unfortunate as to be Seduced into the Rebel Army. He has returned a penitent man, and ... deeply sorry."[150]

Ambassador Jones, though, denied that Charles had been seduced. The ambassador explained:

My sons were both of mature age—were well educated—formed their own opinions and acted accordingly; and without fear or the hope of pecuniary or other reward, as privates, tendered their services to the side in which they put their faith, and breasted the storm of battle for that side.[151]

Charles was pardoned on September 25, 1865. He moved to Missouri to run an insurance business with a friend. He then moved with Annie and Josephine to Sioux

City, Iowa, to run his father's properties. Charles, Annie, and Josephine then moved back to Dubuque where he practiced law.[152]

Charles probably had an easier time settling in Dubuque than elsewhere, given the high number of Peace Democrats who had supported negotiations—and not war—to bring about reconciliation with the South. Dubuque was also more receptive to Charles because many Dubuque residents still respected his father.

Four years after Appomattox, Robert E. Lee wrote a letter to George Wallace Jones, noting their common friend from the Black Hawk War, General Charles Gratiot. Lee restated his political record, extended an invitation, and offered a prayer for Iowans who wore gray. Lee wrote in March 1869:

> I was not in favor of secession and was opposed to war. In fact, I was for the Constitution and the Union established by our forefathers. No one now is more in favor of that Union and that Constitution, and as far as I know, it is that for which the South has all along contended; and if restored, as I trust they will be, I am sure there will be no truer supporters of that Union and that Constitution than the Southern people.
>
> But I must not wander into politics, a subject I carefully avoid, and return to your letter.... When you next come to Virginia, I hope that you will ... come to Lexington. We shall be very glad to see you, and I hope that you will be repaid for your journey by the pleasure which you will see your visit affords us....
>
> Please present my kindest regards to every member of your family, especially to your brave sons who aided in our struggle for States' rights and Constitutional Government. We failed, but in the good Providence of God, apparent failure often proves a blessing. I trust it may eventuate so in this instance...
>
> With my earnest prayers for the peace and happiness of yourself and all your family, I am with true regard, your friend and servant.
>
> R. E. Lee[153]

In 1877, Charles and Annie divorced, and she took their five children back to Sioux City. Charles attributed the divorce, in part, to Annie's being "rather a bigoted Protestant, unreasonable in her extreme prejudices against Catholics."[154]

He had endured eighteen years of periodic relapses of Chagres fever, with resulting episodes of depression and personality change. In March 1877, Charles was incarcerated at the Iowa Hospital for the Insane at Independence, his first of several visits.[155] He said he experienced "the harshest and severest lessons of adversity."[156]

In between incarcerations, Charles lived with his parents. He worked as a miner because he could not practice law. He dug a mine shaft by himself, 25 feet deep, outside of his parents' house in Dubuque County, where he also lived. He called this a time of "abasement and humiliation." His mother was "overwhelmed with grief."[157]

Twenty-five years after Appomattox, Charles wrote a pathos-filled letter to Jefferson Davis. He recalled his first visit to Davis's office in 1862 in shining terms. Then he told Davis, "If you should be told that I am 'hopelessly and incurably insane,' don't be troubled. Jesus of Nazareth was called 'mad.'"[158] Veering further into unreality, he asked Davis to nominate him as Democratic candidate for President of the United States. Charles also described "the alternate joy and sorrow, intense exhilaration & exaltation, and deep dejection and 'heaviness'" that he felt ever since he unsuccessfully tried to join Jefferson Davis's fleeing cabinet in Danville, Virginia.

Charles died of pleurisy at the Iowa Hospital for the Insane on January 28, 1890.

Be Careful What You Write:
Agonies of a Double-talking Democrat

This story, featuring Charles S.D. Jones's shadow image, sheds light on the intense battles within the Iowa Democratic Party during the great secession winter of 1860–1861.

Lt. Herman H. Heath, 1st Iowa Cavalry, galloped through the Civil War, defeating Rebels and earning promotions, but he had a pre-war secret. He might have done well to remember the words of Jesus, "Whatsoever ye have spoken in the darkness shall be heard in the light."[159]

Heath had started a Southern-rights newspaper in Washington, D.C., before coming to Dubuque. He then befriended Iowa U.S. Senator George Wallace Jones. As a "Jones man," Heath became postmaster of Dubuque.[160]

The Jones machine supported the spread of slavery into the Territories. Most Iowa Democrats disagreed, and Jones lost his senate seat. President Buchanan appointed Jones to be minister (ambassador) to New Grenada, South America, but Heath lost his political patron and his postal job.

After Abraham Lincoln was elected president, Heath offered Jefferson Davis his services in the Confederate military or government. Davis never responded.

Five days before Fort Sumter, Heath wrote to an official at the Confederate Postal Service:

Although a Northern Man by birth, [I] have never been anything but Southern in my feelings.... Had I the means to support myself and wife for one year South, I would not remain out of the Southern Confederacy one day longer....

There are tens of thousands of loyal hearts at the North ... they will never pull a trigger against the South.... Before I would march against my brothers of the South, I would suffer myself to be hanged on the first tree before the eyes of my own wife.[161]

Five days later, the war began. A month or two later, Heath enlisted in the 1st Iowa Cavalry and organized a company. Ambassador Jones's eldest son, Charles S. D. Jones, wrote his father: "Your pusillanimous friend Heath has turned Black Republican and gone to the war as 1st Lieut. of Fitz Kenny Warren's Iowa Cavalry.... I loathe & detest and despise a man who has hitherto pretended to be a democrat."[162]

Josephine Gregoire Jones, the ambassador's wife, wrote her husband about Heath:

> If he was not so busily engaged in going to fight for abolitionists (though he says for the union that is gone forever) he would be put in jail.... He is not made of the right material for an honorable man. I told you that long ago.[163]

Lt. Heath became colonel and brevet general. After the war, he became Secretary of New Mexico Territory. In 1870, President Ulysses S. Grant nominated Heath to be Marshal of New Mexico Territory. The Senate released Heath's pro-Confederate letter. Admitting his Democratic past, Heath defended himself: "The sin [of that letter] has certainly been wiped out by my blood, shed upon the field of battle, in the Union army, [and] the sacrifice of my only child, who was killed in the Union service, and an untarnished Republican record."[164] The Senate rejected this explanation. President Grant withdrew the nomination, and Heath faded from public life.

Hell Hath No Fury like an Irishman Scorned

This story reflects the emotional tenor of wartime Iowa, although its subject didn't necessarily live in Iowa for two years before the war.

Postal clerk P. J. Kelly was also a captain of the Iowa City Artillery. Unlike other militiamen, he had ten years of experience serving His Royal Majesty's artillery.[165] Kelly probably never imagined he would serve both sides in a civil war.

In 1859, young Iowa men had a "martial spirit" and formed paramilitary companies in many towns. Besides practicing drills, the companies formed a social group that held balls and marched in parades.

In 1859, Kelly became captain of the Iowa City Artillery.[166] The next year, he left (or lost) his job as a postal clerk. Kelly moved to job-plentiful Memphis in late 1860 with his wife and their one-year-old son. Shortly afterwards, voters elected Republican Abraham Lincoln as President.

Voices in the Cotton South and even the Upper South expressed concern and outrage about the "Black Republican" (supposedly abolitionist) President-elect Lincoln. After the firing upon Fort Sumter, President Lincoln called up 75,000 troops to put down the rebellion. Border-state Southerners feared that soldiers would cross their states to reach the Confederacy. A week later, the *Dubuque Daily*

Times (a Republican paper) quoted the Memphis *Daily Argus* that P. J. Kelly, "late Captain of the Iowa City Artillery," was raising troops for the "Southern Rights Home Guard."[167]

Kelly placed a notice calling for every native Irishman in to stand "against the attacks of the Black Republican despot of the North!" He explained: "The Irishman is celebrated for his devotion and loyalty to whatever flag he fights under. If we are called to defend our newborn and infant flag, let us show ourselves no less patriotic and faithful than the Irish at Bunker Hill."[168]

The Constitution, according to Kelly, "has been usurped and overthrown by the black-hearted infidels of the North." He called for his "fellow countrymen in free States not to take up arms to aid Lincoln and his black-hearted band to lay waste a fair country, and murder a liberal and generous people."

With a nod to the Know-Nothing roots of many Republicans, Kelly claimed that Lincoln "stands at the head of a political party whose history is full of the grossest hostility to Irish adopted citizens in particular."

In early June 1861, Kelly became first lieutenant of artillery, basically serving as a recruiting and mustering officer. He enlisted as many as fifty men a day. He later wrote:

> This made more enemies for me in the North, so much so, that they erected a Gallows, for me in Iowa City, to give to the first Regiment who left there for the South & ordered them when they arrived in Memphis to hang me.... They had another at Cairo & detained several men of my name there for many days, thinking they might get me.[169]

Perhaps Kelly had only heard a rumor of a gallows in Iowa City. Nonetheless, it reflected the prevailing sentiment in Iowa.

On August 5, 1861, Lt. Kelly enlisted in Co. "K," 1st Tennessee Heavy Artillery, commanded by Capt. Andrew Jackson Jr. A month later, Kelly had a serious run-in with Captain Jackson, so Kelly wrote their commanding general, Leonidas Polk:

> I would like to see Jackson [Kelly's superior officer] come out nobly & acknowledge his very ungentlemanly conduct towards me.... I am disgraced in the eyes of the people.... I would put a stain upon my honor, my position & my character, to remain quietly in the same command with a man that greatly insulted my Person, character & worth in the most debasing & scandalous manner. I would feel thankful to him if he shot me thru the heart at once.[170]

Kelly floated the possibility of resigning and being reinstated at a different command. In late October 1861, he moved to Fort Pillow, Tennessee, waiting for Captain Jackson to apologize or be rebuked. Nothing happened, and Kelly submitted his resignation in March 1862.

While Kelly waited to hear that he was out of the Confederate Army, he groused to General Polk:

> I am being sick in body and mind to think after raising so many soldiers in Memphis I had not the happiness of being present with them at any of our engagements.... God will, I hope, attend to those who are wrongfully oppressed. I consider myself one of this number ... I have a family to support. All I have in the world is gone in defense of this country. I am only eighteen months in the South.[171]

Within a month, Kelly left the Confederate Army, blaming his troubles on "a few petty enemies," but he wanted another commission. He told a staff officer, "It seems that my services are not needed in this country.... Should the Yankees find me here, I will be badly off as I am only sixteen months out of their service."[172]

On July 13, 1862, the *New York Times* reported that Union authorities were organizing an artillery company in Memphis. The authorities planned to raise 15,000 troops in Tennessee to suppress "guerrillas and home traitors."[173]

The *Times* noted: "Several of the most powerful and experienced men in the state are at the head of this most excellent movement.... Capt. P. J. Kelly has also been commissioned to raise an Artillery Company."[174]

Kelly explained his new job in the Union service:

> I accept the above appointment that I may have an opportunity of wiping out the stain that lies on my very soul in taking part in this unholy rebellion.... Everyone remembers the horrible treatment I received from Jailor JACKSON and his mob on the public streets of Memphis....
>
>   No man, poor or rich, but will acknowledge that I have been badly treated for no reason whatever. I call upon all oppressed to rally to the support of that Government which always protects its subjects alike, let them be poor or rich, of native or foreign birth; let us return to our allegiance with a determination never to wrong, by word or deed, that noble country, which is now like a kind and indulgent parent, with hands stretched forth to receive and forgive his offending children.[175]

"No Rebel in our Hallowed Ground!": A Casket Returns Home

Ten Confederates from Iowa did not survive the war. One died as a prisoner of war; his life and burial reveal emotions on the home front.

Tennessee-born Albert H. Newell moved to Mount Pleasant, Iowa, as an infant. According to family tradition, they had a slave named Tom who would not leave them.[176] Tom came to Iowa and remained with Albert's family as a freed servant.

When Albert was five, the family moved to Danville in Des Moines County. Albert's father was a farmer and an itinerant preacher in the Methodist Protestant denomination. He was financially comfortable.

Sometime around Fort Sumter, Albert went to Clarksville, Tennessee, to work for his uncle who produced flour and lumber.[177] Union troops invaded Tennessee in 1862. Two of Albert's cousins enlisted in the Confederate Army, and he did, too. On October 8, 1862, Albert enlisted in Woodward's 2nd Kentucky Cavalry.[178]

He went on furlough in late December 1863. Captured while returning to his unit, Albert wrote a cousin:

I am sorry to say that I have been made a captive. After getting [within] a mile and a half of Dixie, I was betrayed into the hands of the Yankees. I had after many hardships gained the banks of the Tennessee River, stopped to warm my frozen feet [and] ears. But oh, unhappy stop. You Know my dread of prison. I am in the hands of very kind captors. They vow to be my very best friends of all, allow me almost anything I ask.[179]

He became a POW at Fort Delaware, where he became sick and died on May 29, 1865. Union authorities buried his body on the New Jersey shore. His sister, Fredonia, traveled to New Jersey to bring Albert's body back to Danville.[180]

Emotions were inflamed toward Iowa Confederates. For example, one Iowa woman, whose husband was in Sherman's army, believed it "right and Christian-like" to be eternally hostile to "all rebels, North and South." She wrote, "I can never forget that they killed my brother Barton and now our dear old President. The time to be conciliatory is past. I am bitter, bitter!"[181]

Iowa's Lieutenant Governor Enoch W. Eastman, a Republican, thought that retribution was "a holy cause." He wrote President Andrew Johnson, "The people of Iowa do not thirst for blood."[182] But he hoped that Jefferson Davis and all other congressmen and West Point graduates who served the Confederacy, would "be hanged."

Stories have been passed down in Albert's family about his burial and his grave. According to family tradition, when Fredonia arrived with Albert's body at the train station, no one would load his casket onto a wagon.[183] Then a gentleman helped. (A lady should not have to manhandle a casket.)

Albert and Fredonia's parents were seemingly out preaching, so she handled the burial arrangements, but the cemetery committee told her, "No Rebel in OUR Hallowed Ground." She finally buried his body just outside the cemetery fence.

Family tradition relates that the cemetery expanded to include Albert's grave. Years later, when feelings had begun to soften, the most decorated grave was Albert's.

Flashpoint of Civil Liberties in Madison County, Iowa

U.S. Marshal H. M. Hoxie began arresting Iowa Democrats in August 1862, a little over a year after Lincoln began restricting civil liberties. Hoxie arrested some thirty-six men, including Dr. Gideon S. Bailey. Dr. Bailey was a former Iowa State Representative from Van Buren County. Someone had accused him of saying that married men should not have to serve in the army.[184]

The pot began to simmer ominously in Madison County, southwest of Des Moines. Many residents had already left to enlist in the Union Army. A large portion of remaining residents had Southern roots, and most were Democrats. Some Democrats referred to soldiers as "Lincoln's hirelings."[185] This insulted resident Caroline Murray.

Years later, Murray described "the hatred we then felt for our foes and the Southern sympathizers living in our midst, whom we spoke of as Butternuts, Copperheads, and Rebels." She described them as "undesirable citizens" and "a constant annoyance in all that pertained to the war." She wrote: "We really felt more bitter toward them than we did toward the Southern rebels. They were constantly stirring up strife and insulting our patriotism." Some local anti-war Democrats met privately and vented their feelings. George Rose, a resident (and former gun-smuggler), spied on them for Marshal Hoxie.[186]

Rose made the men sound subversive, and Hoxie now had the opening he desired. In September 1862, he led rifle-bearing troops to Madison County and arrested seven Democrats. For example, soldiers came looking for William Evans. When his father opened the door, a soldier wounded the father with his bayonet.[187] During the melee, an officer reportedly fired a shot into the house. Next on the list was William Evans's brother, former sheriff Joseph K. Evans. Soldiers marched him out of his house at bayonet point. Hoxie ordered the soldiers to shoot anyone who tried to escape. The marshal took the prisoners to Camp McClellan, near Davenport.

Never officially charged, the prisoners never received a trial, and they were released in December 1862. Some 200 Winterset residents gave them a joyous welcome and elected one prisoner, David McCarty, chairman of the county board of supervisors.[188, 189]

Muscatine Courier editor Edward Thayer spoke for local Democrats when he wrote: "We plead for the old order of things—for freedom of speech—freedom of the press—the preservation of individual rights—the re-establishment of civil power—and the overthrow of military tyrants."[190]

A month after joyful Madison County Democrats greeted the seven released prisoners, President Lincoln signed the Emancipation Proclamation in January 1863, freeing slaves in Confederate-held territory. Locals remembered that Lincoln had said the war was to restore the Union, not to free the slaves. Many doubted Lincoln's word.

As the pot began to boil, a Union Army recruiter set up shop in Winterset.

The next month, February 1863, about 100 armed men came to Winterset to publicly oppose the war. They were Peace Democrats. Their desire: persuade the Southern states to come back into the Union. They risked jail time when they resolved that the Confederacy should be recognized at once; they would oppose the draft; and they would oppose paying taxes if the war continued. One speaker also criticized the Lincoln administration.[191]

The new Union Army recruiter, Lt. G. A. Henry, heard the resolutions. Some Peace Democrats spoke heatedly. Someone said he would tear down the U.S. flag if Lt. Henry dared to raise it. Lt. Henry responded, he would shoot anyone who touched the flag. Rumors ran wild about the Peace Democrats' evil intentions.

The local Republican newspaper editor and other "loyal Union men" assumed the worst. They begged Gov. Kirkwood for 100 rifles and ammunition to defend themselves from the Peace Democrat "nullifiers."[192]

Lt. Henry briefed Marshal Hoxie who also assumed the worse. Hoxie believed informant George Rose that 800 Madison County men belonged to the Knights of the Golden Circle.[193] Supposedly, they met secretly and wanted to overthrow the Union. Hoxie wrote, "The public mind is in a feverish state."[194]

Hearing from Hoxie, Gov. Kirkwood also assumed the worst. The governor sent an army captain and ten troops to guard Lt. Henry's recruiting station in Winterset. Kirkwood also sent fifty muskets and ammunition to the "loyal Union men."[195]

Local Republicans Lt. Henry, Marshal Hoxie, and Gov. Kirkwood all jumped to conclusions about the local Peace Democrats. They thought that Peace Democrats were ready to help the C.S.A. gain its independence. They accepted George Rose's false report of 800 K.G.C. members in Madison County. They feared that the bitter war in Missouri might spread into southern Iowa.

Decades after the war, resident Caroline Murray remembered that a Peace Democrat came inside a Winterset store with a butternut symbol pinned to her waist.[196] A Mrs. McNeil, whose husband was a Union soldier, tore the butternut off the other woman's dress. Murray recalled: "A lively fist fight was on, but the bystanders separated them, and thus spoiled what promised to be the liveliest female battle of the war."

For the rest of the war, there were no other arrests, but the hard feelings continued. Murray recalled:

> It is hard for us now to realize that the much loved, martyred President, Abraham Lincoln, was so thoroughly hated and constantly abused in language, not only by the Southern rebels, but equally as much by our home ones....
>
> At the time of his assassination, an ignoramus was heard to say, "I would like to have a stone as large as I could carry and drop it on him as he is put in the grave."

Today, 150 years later, most of the stories are dim memories, but some people still associate Madison County with the Knights of the Golden Circle. However, no "unimpeachable evidence" supports this belief, according to historian Frank L. Klement.[197]

Escaping the Long Arm of the Law

William V. Burton watched a distant cloud of government power, as small as a man's hand, grow in size and speed and reach his small town. He was frightened that a federal dragnet could snare him.

Born in 1841 in Bentonsport, Van Buren County, Iowa, William V. Burton's father was a Kentucky native and a Black Hawk War veteran.[198] William's mother was born in Ohio. By the time William grew up, his father had a moderate amount of land and money.[199]

William attended an academy in Bentonsport. He was twenty years old when the Civil War began. The following year, 1862, twenty-one-year-old William worked on the family farm.[200] That same year, President Lincoln signed the Militia Act of 1862, effectively the nation's first conscription law. Within a month, on August 8, 1862, Secretary of War Edwin H. Stanton set up a national mechanism to suppress dissent against the war.[201]

Five days later, on August 13, 1862, Stanton ordered the arrest of any draft-eligible man, between eighteen and forty-five, who left his town or state in order to evade his "military duty."[202] William "wanted to get off the farm and go fight," according to his great-granddaughter, but not for the Union.[203]

About two weeks later, on August 29, William and a companion, Otto Ding, were enrolled for a future draft; they bolted for Missouri later that day. The local deputy marshal, John D. Sandford, asked the Provost Marshal in St. Louis to arrest William and Ding. Sandford explained:

> It is believed here that they are aiming to get to St. Louis. Ding's Father lives in St. Louis and is a rebel. The two older Brothers were in the Rebel ranks at Camp Jackson and there paroled. Otto was sent here that he might not share a similar fate.[204]

William spent the winter of 1862–1863 in St. Louis. He headed to southwestern Arkansas and, sometime after October 10, 1863, he joined Captain Lesueur's battery of Price's army.[205, 206] William saw action in southern Arkansas and Louisiana with this artillery unit, serving through the end of the war. His unit surrendered at New Orleans on May 26, 1865.

"William Valentine [Burton] was proud of his uniform, sword and other memorabilia from the Civil War. He kept everything until he died," great-granddaughter Barbara Wells said.[207] William moved to Mississippi, where he "operated an extensive [cotton] plantation ... and amassed considerable wealth ... only to have his entire holdings wiped out by the high waters of 1882."[208]

He headed to St. Louis. William the entrepreneur saw a need for an inexpensive hotel for working men. He parlayed this idea into nine hotels and a fortune of $250,000. He married two times, had two sons, and died on May 9, 1922.

The St. Louis United Confederate Veterans chapter eulogized William's "courage as a soldier in the hour of battle, when, as a member of Lesueur's Battery ... he so heroically served his guns while death and destruction swept by."[209]

Heart in the Confederacy, Body in Iowa

The smuggler's rowboat glided in the darkness, carrying a passenger. John F. Henry listened to the oars dipping in the water, hoping that Yankee sentries wouldn't catch him. Scenes from Iowa filled his mind: Asking his father's blessing to join the Confederate Army; working in a bank while friends braved Yankee bullets; choking down tears while his heart told him to go South. In the black of the night, it all came down to a smuggler, rowing him to the Virginia shore.

John Flournoy Henry was an Illinois native who lived in Burlington, Iowa. He stayed in Des Moines County well into the Civil War. He had attended Beloit College prep school in Wisconsin and Cumberland College Law School in Tennessee.[210]

He came from a politically well-connected family. His father, a doctor, was a friend of David Davis, who conceived the strategy for making Abraham Lincoln the Republican candidate for president.[211] And there was another connection: Henry's uncle, Gustavus A. Henry, later became a Confederate Senator—and Fort Henry, Tennessee, was named after him.[212]

In June 1859, Henry passed the bar in Tennessee. He then panned for gold in Colorado, and worked in a mine in Granby, Missouri. After the Civil War started, he came back to Burlington and worked in a bank. Burlington was a city on edge.

In August 1861, a Burlington resident claimed that there were "twenty-one known secessionists" and fifteen "suspected secessionists" in Burlington, and a *Burlington Hawk-Eye* editor said that rebel sympathizers should "go where they belong, to the rebel states."[213, 214] The editor doubted that any man, known as a traitor, could be "safe."

A year later, in August 1862, Secretary of War Edwin Stanton authorized law enforcement officials throughout the country to arrest disloyal civilians and try them before a military commission. It was illegal to discourage enlistment "by act, speech, or writing."[215]

Henry had a dilemma because he said "his training, proclivities, and love of country were altogether in touch with Southern sentiment."[216] All around him, the public rhetoric heated up. Governor William M. Stone stated in his January 1863 inaugural address: "There is no longer any middle ground where loyal men can stand.... If treason is a crime, to sympathize with traitors is also clearly criminal."[217] Five months later, in June 1863, twenty-four-year-old Henry was enumerated for the draft.[218] He felt "harassed and worn out by the repeated calls for troops and the threatened drafts."[219]

Henry told his father, Dr. Henry, that he wanted to join his Tennessee friends and relatives in the Confederate Army. Dr. Henry advised against this move.

Henry had few options: if he stayed in Burlington, he could be drafted; if he paid for a substitute, he would be putting another soldier in the Union Army; but if he left Iowa and law enforcement caught him, he could still be arrested and put in the Union Army.

A month later, Burlington residents marked the Union victory at Vicksburg. They formed an exuberant nighttime procession with bells ringing, firecrackers exploding, and cannons firing.[220] Afterwards, the *Muscatine Weekly Courier* said that "rebel sympathizers ... should be compelled to leave," "take the oath of allegiance," or be hanged.[221]

Henry finally left Iowa to take up arms "in defense of his convictions."[222] He apparently used the cover story of seeking a job in Philadelphia or Baltimore.[223] He took a roundabout way of going from Iowa to the Confederacy. When he reached the Potomac River, separating Maryland from Virginia, he encountered a culture of cross-state smuggling that carried humans instead of contraband.[224] He safely entered Virginia on his second try, crossing the river at roughly the same spot later used by John Wilkes Booth.

Henry enlisted in Woodward's 2nd Kentucky Cavalry.[225] Two months later, in October 1863, he was wounded at the Battle of Farmington. He recovered and fought in Tennessee, Georgia, and South and North Carolina.

In the closing days of the war, Henry and about 2,000 other men, mostly Kentuckians, caught up with Jefferson Davis in Charlotte, North Carolina. They escorted Davis into South Carolina.

The story is told that, while in South Carolina, an elderly lady chewed out the soldiers. She said, "You are a gang of thieving, rascally Kentuckians, afraid to go home, while our boys are surrendering decently." One of them answered, "Madam, you are speaking out of your turn. South Carolina had a good deal to do in getting up this war, but we Kentuckians have contracted to close it out."[226]

On May 5, 1865, Henry and most of the Kentucky cavalrymen were dismissed at the Savannah River.[227] Henry was captured and paroled. He wrote his father that he was "tired of War and wishes to lead a peaceable & quiet life."[228] Henry had a hard time obtaining amnesty. His father contacted prominent Iowa Democrat Charles Mason, who interceded for Henry.[229] Eventually, he was pardoned.

After the war, he worked in business and banking in Louisville, Kentucky. He died on November 28, 1899.

The Murder of the Marshals

Amid mounting Union Army death counts in summer 1864, Iowa had its first draft. Three men didn't report for duty on October 1, so the provost marshal in Grinnell sent two deputy marshals to southern Poweshiek County to round up the draft deserters. Bushwhackers murdered the marshals. As the second marshal lay dying, he named the murderers. The killings occurred in an atmosphere thick with fear that could be traced back to the firing upon Fort Sumter.

Many Iowa Republicans and Democrats had enlisted after Fort Sumter, but many peace-minded Democrats feared a draft. Some conscription-eligible men considered moving to Canada.[230] As the war continued, outraged Republicans blasted Democrats who dissented against the war, President Lincoln, and (as the war progressed) emancipation. Congressional candidate J. B. Grinnell (co-founder of the town of Grinnell) worried about Iowa's southern border with slave-holding Missouri. He wrote Gov. Samuel J. Kirkwood in August 1862: "Secret Societies are being organized to defy the draft and collection of taxes. The traitors are armed. Our soldiers are defenseless. We want arms. Can we not have them?"[231]

In July 1863, thousands fell in hails of bullets at Gettysburg. The Lincoln administration quickly enacted a draft, but it did not yet affect Iowa (which had high numbers of volunteers). Conscription sparked several days of deadly race riots in New York City.

Outspoken editors of dissenting Democratic newspapers denounced the federal government's tactics. The *Muscatine Courier* wrote, "Let Mr. Lincoln withdraw his emancipation proclamation and there will be no more riots in New York or elsewhere, occasioned by resistance to the draft."[232] John Gharkey of the *Fayette County Pioneer* told Iowa men in September 1863: "You should resist the conscription with your rifles, your shotguns, or whatever weapons you get hold of. If you, young men, do not resist conscription, you are unworthy to be called American citizens."[233]

Words turned violent outside of South English, Keokuk County, Iowa, on August 1, 1863.[234] Gun-toting Peace Democrats, led by Rev. Cyphert Talley, passed through the heavily Republican town. Fiery words flew, gunfire erupted, and Talley dropped dead. His supporters rallied at the Skunk River, some 16 miles away, drawing friends from Poweshiek and other counties. Gov. Kirkwood sent in six militia companies, and the mob disappeared, ending "Talley's War."

The next governor, William M. Stone, responded to Talley's death (and the New York City draft riots) by calling in January 1864 for "loyal men" to "preserve the peace of the state."[235] Volunteer militia companies in every county were "promptly organized ... of loyal and substantial citizens." This action later bore deadly fruit in Poweshiek County.

As the war continued, Democrat fears of a growing war machine—and opportunities for African-Americans—became a reality. On February 1,

Congressman J. B. Grinnell introduced a resolution to encourage African-Americans to enlist in the Union army.[236]

President Lincoln told Grinnell: "I am glad that Congress has endorsed the policy of actively enlisting black men.... It is a great day for the black man when you tell him he shall carry a gun ... it foretells that he is to have the full enjoyment of his liberty and manhood."[237] Lincoln concluded: "Now, tell your people in Iowa ... the time has come when I am for everybody fighting the rebels. Let Indians fight them; let the Negroes fight them; and if you have got any strong-legged jackasses in Iowa that can kick rebels to death, they have my hearty consent." Southern-sympathizing congressmen described Grinnell as being "drunk with blood." Grinnell retorted that Democrats were "in league with slavery and the Devil."

In early May, Union troops entered the Wilderness Campaign. Turning his face like flint toward Richmond, Grant said he would "fight it out on this line if it takes all summer." Over the next six weeks, more than 60,000 Union soldiers died, were wounded, or went missing. Meanwhile, Sherman's troops moved toward Atlanta.

The war came home to Grinnell when Provost-Marshal James Mathews quietly announced a draft. Grinnell Republican men formed a militia and began to drill. Mathews, located in Grinnell, "spoke of the necessity of dealing with severity with the rebel sympathizers at the North."

Men formed a militia in Sugar Creek Township, 14 miles south of Grinnell. That part of the county had most of its Southern-born population.[238] Elizabeth D. Williams, wife of a Union Army soldier, said the neighborhood "contained numerous sympathizers with the South," and she said they harassed her, killed their cows, and destroyed other property.[239]

The Sugar Creek militiamen called themselves the "Democratic Rangers."[240] Said to be Democrats, its members took an oath to support the United States Constitution and the State of Iowa, but with a twist; they reportedly "would resist the draft ... shoot any Marshal or officer who would come for them ... and assist the rebels if they should come into Iowa."[241]

The fifty or so Democratic Rangers drilled twice in September 1864. Many of them carried arms. In mid-September, Provost-Marshal Mathews issued draft notices to three of them, requiring them to appear in Grinnell by September 30.[242] One draftee, Joseph Robertson, said that if he were forced into the army, he would "shoot the officers."[243]

Democratic Ranger Michael Gleason, a native of Ireland, said he was "not in favor of forcing men to fight in a nigger war." He bragged that "if the Marshals came to Sugar Creek Township to take men, he was ready to help kill them" and he "had plenty of backing."[244]

The draft deadline passed, and on October 1, Provost-Marshal Mathews sent Deputy Marshal John L. Bashore and Special Agent Josiah M. Woodruff to locate and arrest three draft deserters.[245] Bashore and Woodruff rode a buggy into Sugar Creek, unaware that the Democratic Rangers planned to drill that afternoon. The marshals began looking for draft-deserter (and South Carolina native) Samuel A. Bryant. Two brothers, John and Joe Fleener, rode up to the marshals, opened fire, and killed one instantly. A third bushwhacker, Michael Gleason, ran up and started hitting the surviving marshal in the head with a rifle. Someone shot Gleason in the leg during the melee.[246] The Fleeners rode away, never to be seen again. A local man found Gleason and Marshal Bashore. The dying marshal identified his killers (and Gleason as an assailant), and he said bushwhackers (who "had sworn resistance to the draft") had come directly from the drilling site.

Provost-Marshal Mathews suspected the murders were planned and that all Democratic Rangers were accessories to the crime. He called up militias from Grinnell and Montezuma and asked Governor Stone for help.[247] Mathews set up roadblocks into Grinnell, and he sent militiamen to capture the Fleeners, Gleason, and the draft-deserters.

Three days later, Governor Stone arrived, passing out new Springfield rifles to the militiamen, who rode off to arrest the remaining Democratic Rangers. Grinnell militiamen bagged six Colt revolvers, a pistol, a horse pistol, fifteen rifles, eight shotguns, and ammunition. They also arrested sixteen men.

The editor of the *Burlington Weekly Hawk-eye*, a Republican paper, assumed the worst. He wrote, "The Unionists of Poweshiek are naturally a good deal stirred up, and if the long-threatened Copperhead war is now to begin, they are ready."[248] He also demonized leading Democrats as being "armed and ready, with murder in their hearts … but waiting the opportunity to deluge the country in blood. Our safety is in their cowardice and want of opportunity."

The *Montezuma Republican* editor made political hay, calling Poweshiek County Democratic leaders "more guilty in the sight of God, and more deserving of punishment, than the three men who committed the murder[s]."[249]

The evidence suggests that the Fleeners murdered the marshals to keep their uncle, Joseph Robertson, from being impressed into the U.S. Army. Gleason, on the other hand, was a Democratic Ranger who expressed drunken bravado (about the marshals) to the Fleeners. He unwittingly stepped into a nightmare that spun out of control.[250] The Democratic Rangers as a group just happened to be drilling the day of the murders.

By 1867, authorities had released every Democratic Ranger except Michael Gleason, who was tried and sentenced to death by hanging. President Andrew Johnson commuted his sentence to life in prison, where Gleason died in 1875. The Fleeners escaped justice.

Tempers and emotions had dissipated by 1911, and Sugar Creek Township's odious Copperhead reputation faded. Poweshiek County historian Leonard F. Parker wrote that the former Democratic Rangers "were evidently misled. We are glad to accord them an honorable place among good citizens since that unfortunate hour in 1864.… The war is over. Neighborly relations have been restored."[251]

Dubuque:
Home of Twelve Confederates

Romantic Conflict in the Shadow of the Confederacy

James couldn't help smiling as he mounted the horse and waved goodbye to his comrades. Another trip into town. He was eager to buy food and supplies for the men, and sign up recruits. Once he was finished, he was free! He knew just the right place to pick a bouquet of flowers for lovely Miss Cora, she with the enchanting voice.

James H. Williams grew up in a slave-owning family in the Shenandoah Valley in Virginia.[1] His father was a county clerk and a Virginia legislator.[2] James loved hunting, playing games, and spending time with ladies.[3] He graduated from the University of Virginia Law School, came to Dubuque, and joined his future brother-in-law in a thriving law practice.[4] James had an aptitude for litigation and excelled in the courtroom. Not surprisingly, he prospered and had high hopes for a successful career in Dubuque.

Life was enriched by spending time with male friends and calling on ladies. His Dubuque circle included some powerful local Democrats and their sons. James befriended or was acquainted with eleven Dubuquers who later served the Confederacy.

Politics loomed large as an enticing stage for his gifts. He ran as an independent Democrat and served two terms in the Iowa General Assembly.[5, 6] He also became a correspondent for the Democratic Party organ, the *Dubuque Herald*.[7]

When the 1860 presidential campaign descended upon Dubuque, a Democratic stronghold, most residents favored Illinois Senator Stephen A. Douglas. A minority supported John Breckinridge, including James, who served on Breckinridge's local campaign committee.[8]

After the war began, Iowa Governor Samuel J. Kirkwood called for Iowa volunteers and then a special legislative session.[9] Republicans suspected state representative James H. Williams of disloyalty because he was a native Virginian. Even more damning, James's legislator-father had called for Virginia to secede.[10]

One of Williams's constituents, Dewitt C. Cram, confronted Williams in a public letter on May 3, 1861. Cram asked Williams:

1. Are you a believer in the Constitutional right of secession, as distinguished from the right of revolution, and as maintained by Southern Statesmen of the Jeff. Davis order?
2. Does a citizen of Iowa owe superior allegiance to the general Government?
3. Does a citizen of Iowa, born and bred in another State, owe any allegiance of any sort to the State of his birth, as against the State of Iowa or the general Government?
4. Will you sustain the State or general Government in any measures adopted … to maintain the Union by force if needed, and to put down the Southern rebellion?
5. If you deny the right of secession, as a remedy for alleged grievances, found in the Constitution, and place this rebellion upon the right of revolution, is it your opinion that the Seceding States have so far exhausted all Constitutional and peaceful remedies?[11]

A week later, on May 10, Cram stated:

So far, no answer has appeared … [I] have a right to know the opinions of him who represents me....

If Mr. Williams be a believer in the doctrine of secession as a constitutional right, and that the State of his birth has superior claims upon him as against the State of Iowa, or the general Government, then he ought not to take a seat on our Legislature.[12]

Iowa Governor Samuel J. Kirkwood called for Iowa volunteers and then a special legislative session. James wrote in his diary: "12 May 1861. Started for Des Moines this morning.... I go most reluctantly to the legislature. Want to be home, to get ready to go to Va. & espouse her cause."[13]

After the General Assembly convened, a bill came up to "prevent rendering aid to rebels."[14] James proposed an amendment requiring Iowans to enforce the Fugitive Slave Act; his bill would have made it illegal to help fugitive slaves escape or avoid arrest. Republicans strongly disapproved, and the issue was tabled.[15,16]

James's bill likely reflected his beliefs. Six months earlier, using the penname "Lex," James reportedly wrote:

The abolition of slavery [should depend] upon more than the wish of the slave. The best interest of society, of both races, enter[s] into the right to be free. Their superior condition in slavery [as compared] to freedom in the North must enter into it.[17,18]

James next resisted a bill to allow soldiers in the field to vote in state elections. He moved to postpone the bill until 2065.[19] Some legislators called James a "rank disunionist," and the legislature adjourned on May 30.[20] About this time, James's father, Samuel Croudson Williams, organized a company, the Muhlenberg Rifles, and was awarded the rank of captain.[21]

When James returned to Dubuque, he re-entered the fray in the editorial pages of the *Dubuque Herald*. He criticized President Lincoln for suspending the writ of *habeas corpus*. This meant that citizens could be arrested and jailed without a trial by jury. James H. Williams said that suspending the writ violated the Constitution.

Former Iowa Congressman Lincoln Clark argued that the president had the power to suspend *habeas corpus* without congressional approval. James disagreed, stating:

You justify the President in his stab at the personal liberty of the citizens, in his annihilation of that ancient, and almost sacred writ of *Habeas Corpus*, in his conflict of military power ... against the Courts....

Your cry that the "King" (the President) can "do no wrong" is strangely out of harmony with the instrument that placed so many restrictions on the Government. If it be disloyal to cry out against usurpation, wicked to complain of breaches of the Constitution, let us burn that sacred instrument ... and serenely recline our heads on the footstools of tyranny.[22]

Clark retorted:

You say I "justify the President in his stab at the personal liberty of the citizen"—I say no such thing—but only that the traitor is entitled to no such liberty in a time of rebellion. If you ask who is to determine whether he is a traitor or acting in aid of the enemy? I answer, for the time being, in the existing state of things, the President, and he alone....

It is understood that you sympathize with Virginia in her secession ... that you have often stated that if Virginia seceded, you would go back and fight for her.[23]

James responded:

I am a citizen of Iowa; I have not gone back to Virginia ... I have written nothing to favor violations of the Constitution in any quarter ... I thought I had the right to call attention to unconstitutional acts at home.... It may be that no one has a right to question the acts of this Government.[24]

His intentions were evolving. James later reflected, "I was impelled to sacrifice all that I had acquired to take an active part in sustaining our cause."[25]

Events moved quickly. On July 16, a crowd threatened to destroy the *Dubuque Herald* offices.[26] James showed up with horse pistols to help guard the paper.[27] Six days later, on July 22, he learned about the First Battle of Bull Run (Manassas). He wrote in his diary, "About 3 1/2 o'clock, the News [of] the glorious victory was received. Took the biggest drink of brandy &c."[28]

He realized the time had come to leave Iowa for Virginia. He caught a 5 a.m. train on July 24, destination Richmond.[29] Arriving on July 30, he "booked a hotel room, had hair cut & shampooed" and "called on Governor Letcher." The next day, he visited the Virginia State House (where his father was a legislator) and the War Department.

Ever-alert to the opposite sex, someone introduced him to Cora deMovell Pritchartt, a music teacher. "Think her pretty, and I am almost struck," he scribbled in his diary.[30] Ten days later, "She is a most interesting woman, plays splendidly and looks bewitchingly."

Whatever thoughts he might have had of immediately entering the Confederate service were put on hold while James dived into hunting and fishing, "big eating and sleeping," catching up with friends, and exploring a tantalizing new romance with Cora.[31]

On August 8, 1861, James wrote in his diary: "Pa fished & I hunted down to Old Mrs. Conner's. I had a rough time of it. Pa caught some fish. Only killed a quail.... The pure air & good water is enough to raise the dead."[32] The next day, he wrote: "One big fish. Out in the rain, wading in water up to my waist. Out until almost midnight. There is a pleasure & wild excitement about such scenes for me. I love the stream & wood, my gun & dog, the rod, & solitude."

On August 14, two weeks after arriving in Virginia, James "wrote to General Magruder about raising [a] Company among [the] militia."[33] Opening his diary again, "There must be something in love at first sight. Called on Miss Cora, played first game of backgammon with her."[34] Later, he wrote, "Why do I go every night? I scarcely know her."[35] Answering his own question, he wrote, "I do believe I am in love."

On September 2, he wrote, "More frequent grow my visits [to Cora] and more saucy my speeches. Segars [*sic*.] 15 [cents], sent flowers to Miss C."[36] Cora was not so sure about James's character, his intentions, and the speed of this romance. Two months into the pursuit, James wrote that Cora "acted coldly, yesterday. I shall not visit so often."[37]

He looked up Dubuque friend Junius L. Hempstead of the 5th Virginia Infantry, whose father had been Iowa's second governor.[38] James also visited three other Dubuque residents in the Confederate service, all in Virginia.

On November 2, Colonel Turner Ashby (James's future commanding officer) sent him a letter, "in reference to forming a Company and advising me to come down."[39] James noted, "With Miss Cora much of the day." Two days later, James and three other Virginians met with Col. Ashby to discuss how they might help defend Virginia; out of this meeting came James's future unit, Chew's Battery of Horse Artillery, 7th Virginia Cavalry.[40] Three days later, James wrote Cora, "If I can get fifteen or twenty men, I will get the position of Lieut. There is a company almost organized by two cadets of Lexington. I am working with them."[41] Cora responded, "Hoping you may succeed beyond your most sanguine expectations."[42]

Gradually spending more time "working among the militia," James made several visits to Cora.[43] He wrote on November 19, "Took the last farewell. I have won the prize I so much coveted."[44]

James and Cora seemingly were engaged in late November 1861. Looking back at his decision to forsake his legal and legislative career in Iowa, James told Cora, "I felt as though I had lived for naught," but now he had met "the creature of my destiny." He continued:

> I loved you with all the strength of my nature. My impulses, the ardor of my devotion, the outrushing affections of my heart yearning for its counterpart....
>
> Perhaps the proudest and happiest hour of my life was when I learned that I could unreservedly claim your heart's affection. There was nothing so much coveted. There is now nothing save my own personal honor and respect from which I had not sooner be divorced.[45]

He continued: "I envy your quiet, philosophic way of taking life. I have watched you and have asked myself, how has she brought under control even the affections of a woman's heart." Cora responded: "I know I am determined almost to obstinacy, as much as I regret it."[46] James confessed, "I have had more influence over every lady I have been intimate with than yourself, and none as much over me."[47]

On the eve of joining Chew's Battery of "Horse Artillery," he wrote Cora: "Here I am, about to try the life of a soldier, to take a subordinate place, only hoping for something better, with everything to make, positions to win, even the means of subsistence to acquire, perhaps privations to undergo, wounded pride to endure."[48]

He confided to Cora, "The thought of waiting, of biding my time, of undergoing the drudgery of camp-life, of separations, of delays, grates upon the substance of being."[49] With remarkable self-awareness, James stated, "I instinctively shrink from responsibility. I feel most keenly the responsibility that attaches to my new position."[50]

Appointed quartermaster-sergeant, he recruited troops and gathered food and supplies. His non-traditional duties gave him unusual opportunities to visit Cora and his family. He wrote Cora, "My position exempts me from drill & service at the guns. I will drill for my own amusement & improvement & will take part with the men in any fight we may have."[51]

James asked Cora several times if she would like his photograph. She wrote, "About the picture, as long as you have baited for an invitation, I would love very much to have it."[52]

He was lighthearted about his first encounter with Union troops. He wrote on December 18, 1861: "Ordered off today to falling waters with two guns. Had quite a cannonading across the River. Made the Yanks run like good fellows. The first I ever saw of hostile firing & real war."[53] Cora had a more sober view; she wrote James: "When this dreadful conflict is over, it will be awakening from a long and troubled dream, never realizing until then, the many ties severed, some by distance, some by estrangement, but how many more by death!"[54]

Cora sometimes thought about James's commanding officer, General Thomas J. "Stonewall" Jackson. She wrote on March 26, 1862: "How did Jackson manage to be so gulled? This exceeds I think his terrible Romney trip.... I can find no excuse for such generalship. Write and tell me all about it."[55]

James got his first taste of hardship during the Shenandoah Valley campaign. He wrote Cora on June 21, 1862: "There is no rest for us. I have slept on my horse, gone for 48 hours with but one meal ... I captured a Yankee horse. Would give it a pet name, but she is so determined, not to say obstinate, and is a Yankee product."[56]

With love never far from his mind, James gave Cora flowers aplenty, and then he gave her a revolver. She wrote, "It is a pretty weapon, and just the right size. Shall retain it with pleasure, though you did not buy it."[57] He also wooed her with words. Cora chided any overstatement as "Jim's bombast."[58] He complained: "You would make a fine businessman. In a few lines you dispose of what cost me many thoughts. A 'list' for your 'thoughts,' why not say feelings? Is your heart an intellectual organ? I have never heard you speak of feelings."[59]

Cora admitted: "You were right, I don't always write as I feel ... I have so taught myself to think without speaking, and feel without acting, avoiding especially (when possible) all that can annoy or grieve."[60]

On December 26, 1862, James wrote Cora: "You ought to know that I mean to get through this war with as little needless fighting & exposure as possible as is consistent with duty."[61] He added, "I am afraid if opportunity offered, I should forget my resolve in eagerness to wipe out the disgrace of so many retreats."

On February 2, 1863, James boarded a train for a pleasant ride over a mountain. Fast asleep in the rear car, James didn't notice the track sliding over the edge of an embankment. The engine jumped the track, and the wheels ran outside of the rail, breaking several ties. When the train finally stopped, the rear car was suspended over "a frightful precipice" hundreds of feet deep. James relayed to Cora, "Can't help but feel profoundly grateful for such a deliverance."[62]

The next day, James marked his birthday, writing Cora, "Never have I so fully realized that one needs the consolations of a divine religion to bid us both beyond the grave to the abode of the immortal."[63] Six days later, James began an emotional rollercoaster when Cora, in the throes of grieving her brother's death, asked to be released from their engagement.[64]

James struggled to be sensitive to Cora's loss, support her emotionally, and clarify their relationship. He wrote:

Many a true heart, I know, has poured forth in silence its purest sympathy for you and yours in the deep bereavement ... I am happy to know, strength from on high is given you.... The longest, darkest night must yield to the sunshine, and the waters of grief subside from the land and the olive bloom again.[65]

A few days later, James wrote: "Has the drama closed, and no sequel yet to come? Why so suddenly? Is it final, irrevocable? Write me once more, tell me what you mean.... Did you not love me?... Pardon the excess of feeling."[66] Waiting two weeks to reply, Cora applied for a job in the Confederate Treasury Department. She explained that her only brother—a provider and protector—had died.[67]

Returning to James's letter, Cora wrote: "I had yielded to unhappy feelings until I lost all control.... Under present circumstances, annoyed, perplexed [in] thought and feelings. I was unwilling another should suffer by it. And so, constantly in this frame of mind, thought it more honorable to break it."[68]

James soon had his own trials. Halfway through the war, on June 9, 1863, Union soldiers killed his younger brother, George H. Williams, at Brandy Station, Virginia. It was the biggest cavalry battle of the war. James wrote:

We have just buried George here, he was killed in the cavalry fight just below Brandy Station, was shot in the forehead, rather between the eyes, they were engaged in a hand to hand fight at the time, was shot perhaps by one on foot. I only got here in time to see him deposited in his last resting place....

You may have heard I was taken prisoner ... barely escaped, but only by fighting.[69]

A week later, James wrote, "The floodgates of grief have been turned loose upon my soul.... This is the severest struggle I have ever known."[70]

Less than a month later, Lee's army moved into Pennsylvania. James's unit avoided most of the fighting at Gettysburg, but they watched the Confederate right flank and "had an engagement with Cavalry."[71] After the battle, James and the others began their long retreat. He wrote Cora: "This is the first hour of rest I have had for a week ... for the last three nights I have not slept except naps ... on the march.... The Gettysburg fight was a perfect fortress, why oh ever attack them."

He reflected: "How terrible a thing is battle. The killed are gone but the sufferings of the wounded, what an intensity they must endure, the moving, the rain, want of food & shelter &c. Never saw as much as in Md."[72]

Cora and James both pursued vocational opportunities. Her obstinacy came in handy at her new job of copying bonds in the Confederate Treasury Department. After a busy day in 1863, she wrote James, "You will wonder at this hand writing, but I am writing with a broken pen, and after numbering two hundred thousand bonds today, see only numbers before [my eyes]."[73] Although exhausting, she later wrote, "Indeed I was happy.... It gratified my ambition and kept me employed."[74]

James was gratified when, on furlough, he argued a case in a Virginia courtroom. This revived his heart's desire to practice law. He told Cora, "Trust the future has more in store for me."[75]

Word spread about his legal experience, and the army detailed James as judge advocate on a court-martial. In this role, James advised the court in matters of law and form, did stenography, and assisted the prosecution.[76] These duties were a great contrast to that of civilian attorney, engaged in battles of wit, eloquence, and emotion. He found judge advocate "a very boring business but will serve to kill time."[77] Not surprisingly, James also found picket duty to be boring.

Wounded at Raccoon Ford, Virginia, on September 14, 1863, James wrote Cora:

My arm is very stiff and rather painful. I have no use of it this morning. Was on foot at the time, a large piece of shell passed under my arm at same time, cutting my coat on the right side, and before I dashed away, my horse was struck on the foot, but no injury was sustained. I had just mounted my horse as the Yankees charged … I had a hard run to get off.…

You may have heard me speak of my dread of losing my right arm, when struck I thought my arm was broken, and all the consequences of the loss of it flashed across my might [mind], should then have had to write left handed letters all the time.[78]

Reflecting on his experience, James wrote: "I sometimes I fear I cannot survive this contest. I have made so many escapes. I am not rash nor reckless, in a fight, but cool & cautious, sensitive to danger, my aim is to do my duty."[79]

James changed his mind about being a judge advocate. He asked prominent friends to recommend him for an appointment. On October 15, 1863, James's former law professor from the University of Virginia, the noted John B. Minor, wrote a letter, recommending James for "the position of Judge Advocate, or member of one of the Army Courts."[80] Minor praised James's "capacity, learning, and high character.… The country could not be better served, I am persuaded, in either part, than by him."

One of James's references noted that he, as Iowa legislator, had "boldly denounced the proposed coercion of the Southern States, resisting manfully the raising of men or money to prosecute a war against the Confederate States."[81]

On December 28, 1863, James wrote General J. E. B. Stuart, applying for the position of judge advocate or member of a military court in Stuart's command. James stated a few motives for seeking an appointment. James mentioned the deaths of his father, his brother, and a brother-in-law, leaving him "the only male representative" and "protector" of his family (and extended family). James wrote: "Situated as matters now are, I am unable to give any personal supervision to affairs at home, make adequate provision for the provision of mother, Brothers and Sisters [and extended family]."[82]

James divided his time between quartermaster, lieutenant of his battery, and details as judge advocate. While waiting to hear about his application, James wrote Cora on February 3, 1864, "I am enduring once more the idleness and torture of camp life."[83] In late October 1864, he found time to hunt, bagging "two deer and a tremendous turkey."[84] He told Cora, "I begin to enjoy hunting again."

An "old Iowa friend" met James and said his brother had heard, by flag of truce, that James had been killed in the Battle of the Wilderness in May 1864.[85]

Less than two months before Appomattox, James was senior lieutenant and entitled by seniority to fill a vacant slot and be captain of his battery. However, his superior officer objected that James, who had spent more time as judge advocate and quartermaster than he had in the field, "displayed a distaste for field service."[86]

General Robert E. Lee solved the dilemma by recommending that James be promoted to captain and, at the same time, serve as judge advocate in a new, second military court for the cavalry of the Army of Northern Virginia.[87] This happened on February 27, 1865.

The war ended before James could fully enter this role. He was paroled about a week after Lee surrendered at Appomattox. About four months later, Cora wrote James: "So little did I dream, that it must end as it has, but it is all past, to speak the grief and disappointment of one, is but the expression of thousands, a feeling in sympathy, with a nation."[88]

Surrounded by wreckage and despair in the Shenandoah Valley, James took up farming. He bent his back and plowed, planted, cultivated, and harvested. He also practiced law when not exhausted. Cora eventually gave piano lessons.

Less than a year into Reconstruction, James observed in January 1866: "There is so much to discourage, so little to hope for, so much malignity and bitterness on the part of our enemies, so much zeal in securing our humiliation that I almost long for the clash of arms."[89]

James continued to assure Cora of his feelings for her. "You know I love you, that for years in the face of trials and difficulties and discouragements I have cherished the attachment. Have no hopes aside from it."[90]

Pausing his manual labor, he wrote Cora, "[I] love the excitement of the court house as the gambler loves the card table or the drunkard his cups, and am rarely weary of the strife."[91] In another letter, he said that politics "suits my temperament, feelings, habit, and mode of thought. Had a taste of it once and try to restrain the longing for such a life."[92]

Four years after Appomattox, and almost a decade after Cora broke their engagement, James felt her heart change. He wrote, "I sometimes think you have just learned to love me ... [I] know you don't mean to neglect me, and at last feel I have won you."[93] He concluded, "The future is our world. There is or must be no past. The present is a prison."

Cora and James married in 1871 They went on to have a daughter, Nannie. James flourished as a lawyer; he served as a Virginia representative in 1873; and he was appointed general in the Virginia militia.

James supported a new biracial coalition of African-Americans who had left the Republican Party and poor white Democrats. The new Readjuster Party shot upward like a rocket, headed by James's close friend, former Confederate General William Mahone. Historian Peter Rachleff writes that the Readjusters "made some impressive gains," including abolishing the whipping post as a form of legal punishment, expanding free speech rights, reducing the state debt, and hiring black principals and teachers.[94] Voters elected Mahone to the U.S. Senate in 1881, and some thought James would be the Readjusters' next candidate. However, the party fizzled after a race riot in Danville.[95]

More than thirty years after the war ended, in 1899, President William McKinley, a Union Army veteran, visited Civil War sites in the Shenandoah Valley. James shook McKinley's hand at Woodstock. Remembering his service with Chew's Battery at the Battle of Kernstown, James said, "I was one of those who shot at you. I am glad I missed you, and now I am glad to shake your hand."[96]

Late in life, James was known for his political brilliance, and his "inexhaustible supply of anecdotes, which made him extremely popular." James Harrison Williams died on December 7, 1903.[97]

In one of the odd twists of the war, James's former slave named John Jackson continued to work for James after the conflict ended. Jackson wrote a letter to *Confederate Veteran* magazine, years after the war ended. He stated:

> I thank you for putting my picture in your magazine. I am proud of my war record. I was given when a young man by my old master, Samuel C. Williams, who was a member of the Virginia Secession Convention, to his oldest son, who was then Lieut. James H. Williams, of Chew's Battery, and I stood by him and his brothers until the close of the war.
>
> I was taken prisoner twice, captured once with the watches and money of our boys and others of the Williams mess upon my person, given into my care when the battle began. I escaped and returned with watches and money all safe....
>
> Like the rest of the veterans, I am growing old; but I am with my people in Woodstock, where I was born.[98]

The day of James's funeral, Masons, Confederate veterans, and members of the bar stacked flowers atop James's casket and followed it to the Massanutten Cemetery. The obituary states:

> Immediately in rear of the hearse marched his old body servant, John Jackson, who had so faithfully followed him, from the time he entered the army till his famous battery fired its last shot. He carried the blanket with which he had so often covered his master when he lay upon the field of battle, and when his body had been deposited in the grave, he covered him for the last time.[99]

Cora survived another twenty-four years. She memorialized her service and honored James by helping found the Shenandoah Chapter of the United Daughters of the Confederacy. She died in 1927.[100]

Sometimes You Can Go Back Home Again

The Union cannons unleashed a horrific bombardment on Spanish Fort. W.J. Cantillon sniffed danger and opportunity, an ability that would serve him well.

Eight-year-old Irish native Cantillon sailed with his family to Boston in 1846.[101] Ten years later, in 1856, Cantillon and family settled in Dubuque. Working as a clerk, he studied law at night, and he was admitted to the Dubuque Bar at age twenty in 1858.[102] Rookie lawyers had a hard time finding clients. Cantillon cut his losses after a year and moved South for its business climate in 1859.

Around this time, Dubuque Democrats appointed his father, J. O'Hea Cantillon, to a minor political office. The local party was splintering, with most of the faithful supporting Illinois U.S. Senator Stephen A. Douglas. A minority of Dubuque Democrats backed former Iowa U.S. Senator George Wallace Jones (who supported pro-slavery measures in Congress).[103] J. O'Hea Cantillon steered between the two factions and entered the independent wing of the local party, heavily populated by Irish constituents.

During the 1860 presidential campaign, J. O'Hea Cantillon supported Douglas's unionist platform. Two months after Fort Sumter, W. J. Cantillon enlisted in Co. "A," Wise Legion's Artillery Corps, on June 21, 1861.[104] At the same time, back in Dubuque, father J. O'Hea Cantillon represented Dubuque County in the Iowa State Democratic Convention.[105]

The Republican *Dubuque Times* caught wind of W. J. Cantillon's Confederate service. A *Times* correspondent accused J. O'Hea Cantillon of being a Rebel and sending his son to serve the C.S.A. Denying the allegations, J. O'Hea Cantillon stated:

> My son, alone, is responsible for his own acts; having attained his majority according to our common law, he is his own master. The South has been his home for nearly three years past, where he is engaged in business, away from my control or jurisdiction, and in joining the Southern Army, he did so without consulting my feelings or wishes.
>
> I will further state that were he subject to me, I would not permit him to fight in the irrepressible conflict, with either side, believing this war to be the effect of Northern fanaticism on the one side, and ultra Southern retaliation on the other; it seems to be caused by men whose strongest desire is to imbrue their hands in their brothers' blood.[106]

W. J. Cantillon mustered out of Wise Legion on December 21, 1861. His whereabouts are unknown for the next year and a half. He next appears in Mobile, Alabama, on September 22, 1863, where he enlisted in the 22nd Louisiana Artillery (soon to be renamed the 22nd Consolidated Regiment, Louisiana Infantry).

He was detailed to the Conscript Bureau for a month, starting on January 15, 1864. Cantillon's regiment spent the next year guarding Pensacola and Mobile Bay. On March 27, 1865, Union troops began siege operations against Spanish Fort, across the bay from Mobile.[107]

Union artillerymen unleashed ninety cannons on Spanish Fort on April 8. Smoke filled the air, and the ground shook for miles around. Late that afternoon, the 8th Iowa Infantry broke through the northern Confederate lines, and that night, Cantillon and his comrades evacuated Spanish Fort, retreating to nearby Fort Huger. Four days later, they retreated again, heading to Mobile. Cantillon took advantage of the confusion to desert.

He returned to Dubuque in 1868. He was one of the few Iowa Confederates who had a successful post-war career in the state. His upward trajectory began with mining coal. Cantillon next practiced law, served as county attorney, became a Dubuque police officer, and later was a contractor. He married a native of Scotland, and they had two children.[108, 109]

In 1892, the Republican-leaning *Times* stated that Cantillon should not be elected Justice of the Peace because he had served in the Confederate Army, and he had often insulted the G.A.R. and old Union veterans.[110] Cantillon, aged fifty-four, confronted the *Times* editor on Main Street, spitting "extract of navy plug" in his face and on his shirt, and "cuffing him." Cantillon lost that election, but he had the satisfaction of winning the next two.[111]

Local Businessman Heads South

Living in a political family can sometimes yield benefits. Daniel O'Connell Quigley was born in 1830 in St. Louis, Missouri, to a staunch Irish Catholic family, and they soon moved to Dubuque where his father, Patrick Quigley, became a merchant, an early Dubuque mayor, and a close personal and political friend of U.S. Senator George Wallace Jones.[112, 113, 114] Patrick Quigley shared Senator Jones's pro-Southern, pro-slavery outlook.[115] These pillars of Dubuque society in the 1840s and 1850s rewarded their "friends" with job recommendations and appointments.

Daniel O'Connell Quigley may have traveled to California to make his fortune in the Gold Rush of 1849.[116] In 1858, Daniel had a wife and a daughter, and he worked as a merchant in Dubuque. Scores of local businesses were struggling; merchants found it hard to operate since people no longer had specie (gold and silver coins), and more ominously, much paper currency (from some states and territories such as Nebraska) was worthless. Leading Dubuque bankers asked the Dubuque Harbor Company to issue notes.[117] This worked for a while, but even this local currency failed. Daniel's father (a Dubuque alderman) flexed his political muscle, helping his son become a Dubuque City auditor in 1860.[118]

As the national political battles intensified, Daniel told his friend Charles S. D. Jones (eldest son of former senator George Wallace Jones) that he thought about serving the Confederacy. A couple of months after Fort Sumter, Daniel enlisted in Memphis, Tennessee, as a private in the First Regiment Missouri Volunteers P.A.C.S.[119] That same day, July 1, 1861, Charles S. D. Jones wrote a letter, introducing Daniel to the commander of Hunter's Louisiana Rifles. Jones wrote: "Dear Hunter, By this I introduce to you my friend, Daniel O.C. Quigley, of this town, and bespeak your kindness and attention toward him. I believe he will prove himself worthy of your friendship. With every wish for your prosperity and happiness, Your Friend, Charles S. D. Jones."[120]

Improbably, the letter ended up on the battlefield of Shiloh. A Republican reporter from Dubuque found the letter in the detritus of battle. He sent it to the *New York Times* in an effort to embarrass George Wallace Jones.

After a year of service, Daniel left the Confederate Army in July 1862, ostensibly due to a disability. He may have headed to Montana for the remainder of the war. He returned to Dubuque in 1870 after his eleven-year-old daughter, Katie, died.[121] Daniel O'Connell Quigley died a year later and was buried in Dubuque.

Cavalry Officer from Dubuque

One Iowa native became a Confederate cavalry officer. Serving in the furious Atlanta campaign, he was destined to lie in an unmarked grave.

Thomas Wilson Lewis was born in 1842 and grew up in a pro-Southern household, influenced by his father's Democratic political friends.[122] His father, Warner Lewis Sr. who had grown up with many slaves in Virginia and Missouri, held local, state, and federal offices.[123]

In a family of eight children, Thomas was the youngest son. His oldest brother, Charles, died in 1853 in a horrific prairie grass fire, while surveying for their father (Surveyor-General of Wisconsin, Iowa, and Minnesota).[124] Thomas was eleven at the time.

In 1856, aged fourteen, Thomas enrolled in Cornell College in Mount Vernon, Iowa.[125] That year, his older brother, Warner Jr., attended Western Military Institute in Nashville, Tennessee, where he received a Southern military college education. Thomas transferred to Beloit Academy in Wisconsin the next year.[126] He was 5 feet 10 inches tall, with blue eyes, light hair, and a light complexion.[127] Unlike his brother, Thomas never attended a military academy.

Three months after Fort Sumter, Thomas, aged nineteen, enlisted in the 16th Tennessee Infantry on July 20, 1861. A few months later, older brother Warner Jr. enlisted in the 5th Tennessee Regiment. Thomas transferred to "Capt. McBride's Company," McLemore's 4th Tennessee Cavalry, on April 10, 1862 and was appointed Third Lieutenant. Union troops captured both brothers in Tishmingo, northeast Mississippi, on May 30. Guards escorted them to Camp Chase and then Johnson's Island, Ohio.

Eager to report news of Dubuque Rebels, the *Dubuque Times* stated:

> The two sons of Gen. Lewis, of Dubuque, late of the Confederate Army, were captured by our troops at Corinth. Gen. Lewis is of course, a Vallandigham Locofoco, and his hopeful offspring take after him. Of such material is the party composed which promises, during the coming campaign, to wipe out Republicans in the State.[128]

Fellow Dubuquer and family friend, George R. G. Jones, was also a POW at Johnson's Island at the same time. In late November 1862, prison officials sent Thomas and Warner Jr. on a two-week journey back to the Confederacy. They (and 768 other POWs) eventually boarded the steamer *Charm* and were exchanged in Vicksburg on December 8, 1862.

Thomas returned to the 4th Tennessee Cavalry.[129] He served for the next year and a half until he was killed outside of Atlanta in 1864.

Lawyer in the Confederate Civil Service

The crowd sweltered in the humid April air of Culpeper. Gabriel S. Jones wiped his brow, strode to the lectern, and addressed the question, Would Virginia secede?

Gabriel S. Jones had attended the University of Virginia, where he became friends with fellow student and future colleague, John T. Lovell. Gabriel wrote in 1852, "Dear Lovell ... I feel that the bonds of friendship bind us, tied as with a gordian knot."[130]

Gabriel earned a law degree at Louisville Law School in Kentucky in 1854, and he practiced in Rockville and Terra Haute, Indiana.[131] He moved to Dubuque in 1858 to practice law with John T. Lovell and two other native Virginians, James H. Williams and William Wirt Bird. They skillfully filed motions, researched precedents, and made court appearances, but they also had a "high old time," going to balls and getting drunk, playing card games for money, fishing, riding boats, and smoking "segars."[132] The rollicking lawyers did very well for themselves, and Gabriel bought some land in Iowa.

After Lincoln was elected president, Gabriel headed back to Virginia, a state still in the Union. The day after Sumter surrendered, he attended a mass meeting in Culpeper, responding to Lincoln's call for 75,000 militiamen to maintain the Union by force. The enthusiastic crowd thought it absurd to preserve "public harmony by actual war." They underscored their past loyalty to the United States, "the most magnificent experiment in behalf of human liberty," but they opened the door for secession. Different speakers offered three resolutions:

1. The means and expedients for a pacific and patriotic solution of our national troubles are finally and entirely exhausted.
2. It is now the sacred duty of all our people ... to unite together and present an undivided and indivisible front in support of the interest, the honor, and the order of ... Virginia.
3. Virginia has no alternative but to reclaim all the attributes of her original sovereignty, and to ... seek such future affiliations as are most favorable and convenient to the interests and security of her own people.[133]

The official record states, "Mr. Gabriel Jones, lately of Iowa, though born and raised in Culpeper ... responded in the same spirit."

Two days later, he enlisted in the Culpeper Minute Men and was mustered into the 13th Virginia Infantry, for one year, on May 22, 1861, at Harpers Ferry. The following February 8, 1862, Gabriel wrote the Confederate Secretary of the Treasury:

I have the honor of applying to you for a position in your department.... About five years ago, I moved from Virginia to the State of Iowa where engaged in the practice of law. I remained until upon the breaking out of hostilities between the North and the South. I left just in time to join the first expedition gotten up in Virginia, that for the purpose of securing for the State and the South the Armory and arms at Harpers Ferry....

From that time, the 17th of April 1861, up to the 17th of January 1862, I was a private in our army on the Potomac at the entire sacrifice of everything I had in the world, as in leaving the North I had to leave everything I had behind me.[134]

Gabriel's one-year term of service ended, and he worked in the Second Auditor's Department. Three months later, on July 7, 1862, Robert Toombs (former U.S. Senator) wrote Secretary of the Treasury C. G. Memminger, commending Gabriel as "entirely worthy of your confidence and fully competent to the discharge of the duties he seeks to discharge."[135]

Gabriel's duties in the Second Auditor's Office included signing pay vouchers for deceased soldiers. Confederate authorities at the capital in Richmond formed governmental clerks into self-defense companies. Gabriel drilled alongside clerks from the Comptroller's, Produce, Loan, and War Tax offices. He signed up for as long as he lived in Richmond.

Three of Gabriel's former Dubuque law partners returned to Virginia and served the Confederacy. During the war, Gabriel saw his fun-loving Dubuque friend, James H. Williams, a couple of times.

After the war ended, Gabriel practiced law in Rodney, Mississippi, and in Beaumont, Texas, where he died.[136] In 1870, a Dubuque real estate agent wrote Ray B. Griffin, a realtor in Manchester, Iowa, about Gabriel. Griffin wrote:

> This Virginian by name of G.S. Jones could not get north or send north during the war & so lost his land as far as non-payment of taxes loses land. Tell me what there is about the matter, and what you give or take for title? I mean to do as well I can for my friend, but I do not want any contest with you. Let's fix it up equitably.[137]

Loving the Law and Virginia

College dreams of fame and fortune led William Wirt Bird and three classmates to Iowa. These University of Virginia *alumni* came to Dubuque in the mid-1850s. They picked well, because Dubuque was a growing political, economic, and legal powerhouse until the financial Panic of 1857. The city's reputation as a legal center rested on its large population (15,000 in 1856); the federal land office in Dubuque (a source of lawsuits); and diversified industries (that included mining).

Once Bird and the other Virginians arrived in Dubuque, they tapped into Iowa U.S. Senator George Wallace Jones's network of legal, political, and business friends. Democrats all, the *émigrés* found a sympathetic, pro-slavery atmosphere among the "Jones men." John T. Lovell was senior partner who brought into the firm his friends (Bird and Gabriel S. Jones) and his brother-in-law (James H. Williams). They enjoyed each other's company.

When Southern states seceded, all four Virginians considered returning to their home state. Three months after Fort Sumter, John T. Lovell spoke at a rally in Zwingle and said, "no power on earth, in heaven or hell could make him take up arms against his brethren in Virginia." As Lovell departed for Virginia, Bird stayed in Iowa, administering an estate in Delaware County.[138]

Bird eventually left his law practice in Dubuque and returned to Virginia. He enlisted midway through the war in the 7th Virginia Cavalry—James H. Williams's regiment—on August 8, 1863.[139] Bird last appears on a company muster roll in August 1864.

Two years after the war ended, Bird and James H. Williams were delegates to the Virginia Conservative State Convention. In 1869, Bird petitioned Congress for "removal of [political] disabilities" so he could run for public office. William Wirt Bird died six years later, on June 10, 1872, in Mt. Jackson, Shenandoah County, Virginia.

Divided Families/Relationships Across the Lines

Snapshot of a Divided Family

Rev. William Salter pushed aside a blood-sheet in the doorway of the Federal field hospital near Marietta, Georgia. Talking with pain-wracked Union troops drained Salter of energy and sympathy. He was surprised to meet Green Ballinger, a wounded Confederate from Iowa. Salter was a former conductor on the Iowa Underground Railroad. He generally opposed war, but he supported the Union. He was in Marietta on a mission of mercy with the Christian Commission.[1]

Twenty-four-year-old Green was seriously wounded in thigh and shoulder.[2] He told Pastor Salter of his home in Keokuk and his father's home in nearby Sandusky.[3] Green said he had been opposed to "the Rebellion" (Salter's words), but the "force of circumstance" led him into the Confederate army.

Green's family had roots in Kentucky and a kinship network throughout the South. His father, James F. Ballinger, had been a clerk of court and a slave-owner.[4] Because of his father's two marriages, Green had older siblings and half-siblings.[5]

Looking for economic opportunity, Green's father moved his family to Keokuk in 1854. So did Green's brother-in-law, Samuel F. Miller, a doctor turned lawyer.[6] Keokuk's economy boomed soon after they arrived. Congress passed the Kansas–Nebraska Act in March 1854. Samuel F. Miller was a Whig (unlike his Democratic in-laws), and he predicted that slavery would split the national Whig and Democratic parties. Miller wrote Green's half-brother in Texas, William P. Ballinger, of "a real danger that you and I shall live in different nations."

By summer 1860, Samuel F. Miller (now a rising member of the Iowa Republican Party), Green's father, and Green's older brother struggled to stay afloat in Keokuk.[7] The family sent twenty-year-old Green to Texas (where the economy was better) to visit relatives. They expected him to return. In late July 1860, Green visited his half-brother, William P. Ballinger (a prominent attorney), and brother-in-law, Benjamin A. Botts, both of whom owned slaves.[8] Green was still in Texas when the war began.

A former Confederate assistant surgeon wrote, "Nearly every Northern man was suspected of not being truly Southern if he had not enlisted in some sort of military company."[9] Brother-in-law Botts helped form Terry's Texas Rangers, and Green joined, too.[10] Half-brother William P. Ballinger became a Confederate sequestration receiver.[11]

It is not clear why Green enlisted. The "force of circumstance" could have been his Texas relatives' expectations, and/or his need for a job. Perhaps Green also got caught up in the local enthusiasm for war.

Green's father in Keokuk remained loyal to the Union, and his older brother enlisted in the Union Army.[12, 13] President Lincoln nominated Green's brother-in-law, Samuel F. Miller, to the U.S. Supreme Court. Green's mother, on the other hand, felt she could not support "war against her own children." She sympathized with the Confederacy.

In July 1864, Green was badly wounded in the Atlanta Campaign. Rev. Salter told Green he would contact his father in Iowa. Green died a month later.

When the war finally ended, Green's father and other family members wrote letters to their Confederate relatives. The letters expressed a "proscriptive vindictive Unionism."[14] Then Green's family had a small reunion. Looking his relatives in the eye, Green's father allowed that his kin could have served the C.S.A. out of "patriotism and devotion to principle."

The Last Confederate from Iowa to Surrender

Smoky campfires made Stephen M. Dicken's eyes water, as he walked among clumps of Confederate prisoners. If only he could find his big brother, James! It was the same fruitless search after every battle. The reunion between Stephen (14th Iowa Infantry) and James (33rd Arkansas Infantry) was destined to wait until after the war ended.

James, Stephen, and their siblings were born in Illinois. Their parents were natives of Kentucky. In 1855, when James was fourteen, his family moved to a farm in Bremer County, Iowa.

James later moved to Jackson County, Missouri. In June 1862, he enlisted in Captain Overstreet's Company, Grinstead's Regiment.[15] It became Co. "D," 33rd Arkansas Infantry. Stephen enlisted in the 14th Iowa.

On April 9, 1864, James was at Pleasant Hill, Louisiana. His skirmish line entered the woods in mounting darkness, heading toward Federal troops. The Confederates were ordered back. In the confusion, James was captured. Union guards were surprised to recognize a Confederate POW who used to live in Bremer County.[16] Stephen had no such luck, since James was soon paroled and rejoined his unit.

As the war was ending in the East, James was in Indian Territory (present-day Oklahoma). This was the site of the Confederacy's only allies: the Cherokee, Chickasaw, Choctaw, Creek, and Seminole nations. James served under a Cherokee, General Stand Watie. James was stationed in the Choctaw Nation.

In May 1865, the tribes learned that Lee had surrendered a month earlier.[17] Twenty-five-year-old James deserted and headed toward his Missouri home. Midway, he decided to surrender, so he headed toward Fort Scott in southeast Kansas. As James trekked, the Choctaw Nation surrendered on June 19, and Stand Watie followed suit on June 23.

James reached Fort Scott and surrendered on July 11—three months after Appomattox. He swore to "forever oppose secession, rebellion, and the disintegration of the Federal Union." He could not sign his name, so he left his mark.

After the war, James visited his family in Bremer County.[18] He moved to Paris, Texas, in 1873, and fades from the scene.

Loyalty and Friendship

John A. B. Putman was nearly done with the Texas bar exam, and confidence was growing that he would pass it. The judge said one more question: do you solemnly swear to uphold all the laws of the Confederate States of America? John scrambled for a reason, a justification to say "I do," but he found none. Biting down his frustration, he said, "No sir, I do not."[19]

Thus ended John's year-long study of law under his uncle, a Texas lawyer. John, his older brother, and the rest of the family had moved to Texas in 1860 after their father died, and John graduated from Cornell College in Mt. Vernon, Iowa.[20] The authorities drafted John in July 1862, three months after the Confederate Congress passed a conscription law.[21] He enlisted in the 23rd Texas Cavalry on July 10, 1862, and so did his older brother, C. V. Putman.[22, 23]

According to family tradition, John A. B. Putman tried to make the most of the situation, so he consented to being appointed junior second lieutenant.[24] He must have been well received because he was promoted to second lieutenant.

After an early skirmish, one of John's prisoners was a Cornell College *alumnus* and fellow member of the Amphictyon Speech Society. Family tradition states that John took him several miles from camp, gave him a horse, and started him for the Union lines. Reportedly, "Cornell loyalty and friendship proved stronger than official duty."[25]

After the war ended, John A. B. Putman practiced law in Texas.

Loyal Brother and Efficient Soldier

Walking by his little brother's side, they entered the Confederate Provost Marshal's office. Cornelius decided that his newly drafted brother, smart as he was, shouldn't enter the army alone.

Cornelius V. Putman was born in New York in 1836, and he moved to Iowa Territory in 1846 with their parents and his younger brother (and future Confederate officer) John A. B. Putman. By 1856, they lived in Mount Vernon in Linn County, Iowa. Cornelius got a job as a postmaster, and his father died. After Lincoln was elected in November 1860, but before his inauguration, Cornelius, John, and their mother moved to Texas to join an uncle who practiced law.[26] Cornelius got a job as a laborer.

A year after the war began, Cornelius entered the Confederate service by way of the draft and solidarity with John. The Confederate Congress enacted a conscription law on April 16, 1862, ten days after bloody Shiloh.[27] When authorities drafted John, Cornelius walked with him into the provost marshal's office. They both enlisted as privates in Co. "F," 23rd Regiment Texas Cavalry (Gould's Regiment), July 10, 1862.[28,29]

He had a persistent fever for a few months in 1863, spending a month in north Texas to recuperate. Promoted to fifth sergeant on January 1, 1864, Cornelius participated in the Battle of Mansfield, Louisiana (Sabine Crossroads), helping stop Union General Nathaniel P. Banks's advance up the Red River.[30] The next year, the 23rd Texas Cavalry surrendered in June 1865. Comrade J. M. Wester recalled that Cornelius was an "efficient soldier."[31]

Cornelius began a new chapter in his life at age fifty-five, marrying thirty-four-year-old Nancy. They had a twenty-five-year-run together until he died in 1914. She received a Texas Confederate Widow's Pension until she died in 1931.

From Iowa Wesleyan to the Battle Lines: An Old Friend Says, "Thank You"

This soldier hadn't lived in Iowa for two years before the war, but his story illustrates the power of relationships that transcend time and space.

We never know where friendships will lead us. A Methodist preacher's son from Mississippi, George Carson Leavell, was to discover that friendship "gladdens the heart, and makes the face to shine."

George came to Mount Pleasant, Iowa, in early 1861 to attend Iowa Wesleyan University's prep school. He reportedly had Iowa relatives.[32] Sometime after Fort

Sumter, he returned to the South. George enlisted in late June 1863—midway through the war—in the 60th North Carolina Infantry.[33] He served as *aide-de-camp* to Col. James M. Ray at the fierce Battle of Chickamauga.[34]

During the Atlanta campaign, less than a year later, Confederates captured a number of Union soldiers. George discovered among the POWs an old friend from Iowa Wesleyan. His friend, Hiram Thornton Bird, tells the story:

> On our arrival at Atlanta, we, with other prisoners, were drawn up in line in the woods at East Point.... After the [Confederate] officer had taken our names and regiment and what valuables we had in our pockets ... a Confederate soldier stepped up and said, "I heard you say you are from Iowa. Do you know anybody in Mount Pleasant, Iowa?"
>
> I at once recognized the voice and features of my old college chum George Leavell. But he was so thin and wan ... that it took a second look to recognize him. But here in War Country was my chum sure enough, though it seemed like a fairy story to find him.
>
> When the Civil War broke out, George Leavell was a student at our Iowa Wesleyan University from Jackson, Mississippi....
>
> At the breaking out of the war, he had called his friends together and had told them he would have to return to the South and go with his people. We all shed tears and bade him good bye, hoping that "when the cruel was over," he would return to Iowa Wesleyan University.
>
> My meeting with him was the only time he was ever heard from. The first question he asked me was concerning his sweetheart at Wesleyan. It was indeed hard for me to tell him that she had been married a short time before. He looked very sad....
>
> He put question upon question to me, all about his College life; the war was not mentioned—his heart yearned for his College friends at the old school.
>
> Then he said, "Now Thornt, we are on the battle line, and they will become suspicious if we talk too long. What can I do for you? Would you like something to eat?"
>
> He was in charge of some supplies for the sick and wounded, and he took my haversack and filled it full of good things, and as I had had nothing to eat for more than a day, it showed his good will as nothing else could have done at that time. And then we said good bye forever....
>
> My friend looked very ill, almost like death, for he had been on the sick list for some time....
>
> Through the years, since that day in Atlanta, I have held in sacred memory the meeting with George Leavell. I draw from it the lesson of the bigness of College Friendship, of the trueness of those ties formed in youth. We met as friends, not as enemies of war, the ties of friendship were first and dearest—all else was small, insignificant, and forgotten.[35]

Soon after their meeting, George was discharged from the Confederate Army for "paralysis." After the war ended, he moved to Ocala, Florida, and became a Methodist minister.[36] He died on February 14, 1879.[37]

From Confederate POW to Officer in the Spanish–American War

Returning to Davenport, Iowa, after the war, Spier Whitaker Jr. remembered his teenage friendships and the path that led to his freedom.

Spier Whitaker Jr. was born in 1841 in North Carolina.[38] When he was thirteen years old, his father, prominent lawyer Spier Whitaker Sr. moved their family to Davenport, Iowa. His father sent Spier Jr. back to North Carolina to attend a prep school the following year. In 1857, Spier Jr. enrolled in the University of North Carolina.[39] He came back to Iowa during school breaks.

Spier Jr. was in his final year of college when the "rage *militaire*" swept North Carolina. Three of his brothers enlisted in the Confederate Army, and he joined a company assigned to the Bethel Regiment.[40] General Ambrose Burnside's troops captured Private Spier Whitaker Jr. on March 14, 1862, while attacking New Bern.

Judge James Grant (his cousin and a Davenport notable) tried to arrange for Spier Jr. to be paroled and exchanged. Judge Grant asked former congressman and fellow Davenport resident James Thorington to intervene:

> Noble Tyner, adjutant 14th Iowa, was taken prisoner by the enemy at Pittsburg. Lt. Spier Whitaker Jr., son of Spier Whitaker of Chapel Hill, N.C., was taken prisoner by our forces at New Bern, N.C. These men hold the same rank. Their fathers and families are intimate friends. They desire to get one exchanged for the other. If you can get Spier Whitaker Jr. paroled, I will be responsible for his exchange at any time and place required.
>
> If you will get a letter to his father at Chapel Hill, N.C., he will go and find Tyner if he is alive. You and I know him and know that he has influence, wherever he lives. He was formerly a resident of this place [Davenport], and I believe Jr. and Tyner were schoolmates in this town.[41]

In spite of Judge Grant's best efforts, Spier Jr. spent four months in a POW camp before rejoining his unit.

Spier Jr. had a fresh promotion to second lieutenant when he joined Lee's army on the eve of invading Maryland. He was in the Battle of "Antietam and most of the struggles of 1863 and 1864."[42] Spier Jr. sheathed his sword at Appomattox, and he returned to Davenport, Iowa, and studied law under his accomplished father.

The next year, 1866, Spier Jr. moved back to North Carolina, where he began climbing the public ladder. After becoming solicitor, he entered the state senate, practiced law, became a Superior Court Judge, and resumed practicing law.[43, 44]

Spier Jr. was later commissioned as major with the Sixth Regiment, U.S. Volunteers, during the Spanish–American War. He drilled with his men in Knoxville, Tennessee, and departed for Puerto Rico, but the war ended before they saw active duty.[45]

Spier Whitaker Jr. died at his home in Raleigh, North Carolina, on July 11, 1901.[46] A caretaker shrouded his body in a Confederate battle flag, according to his wishes.

"Love Will Keep Us Together"—Or Will It?

John and Nancy Shipley had great hopes and dreams on their wedding day.[47] They married amid the gloomy financial Panic of 1857.[48] The twenty-five-year-old groom and the nineteen-year-old bride thought the best was yet to come.

John and Nancy headed to Memphis, Tennessee, a town that was fairly booming.[49,][50] Companies were engaged in construction as well as steamboat manufacturing, repair, and reconditioning.

Nancy conceived and came back to Muscatine, Iowa, to deliver their son, William Everett Shipley, born in June 1860. Nancy and the baby rejoined John in Memphis. Nancy felt their marriage was "happy and contented."

After Lincoln was elected president, John sent Nancy and five-month-old William back to her parents' home in Muscatine. She supposed it was "because of the political troubles."[51] Nancy's parents supported her and the infant.

Nancy missed her husband, so she returned to Memphis five months later, in April 1861, around the firing upon Fort Sumter. John immediately sent her back to Muscatine, saying she "might find it difficult to get back."[52] A few weeks later, John enlisted in the Tennessee Infantry.[53] He stopped sending letters, and he did not send any child support.

Nancy's father went to Confederate-held Tennessee the following spring of 1862. He saw John's "manner and action" and thought "his affections were entirely alienated from his wife and child."[54] His conclusion? John was devoted to "the Southern confederacy."

Mutual friends said that John had been promoted. He was now a captain and Acting Commissary of Subsistence, providing food to soldiers. Despite his promotion, he still didn't send money to support Nancy and their son.[55] Of course, John was paid in Confederate dollars that Nancy couldn't spend.

The *Muscatine Journal* reported on April 18, 1862 that John was in the Confederate Army, and had been captured at Island Number Ten. (In fact, he had not been captured.)[56] The *Journal* also stated that the 11th Iowa Infantry lost half of their officers at Pittsburgh Landing. Local passions burned against rebels and their families and supporters.

The next year, on January 14, 1863, Nancy filed for divorce, claiming "desertion and abandonment of her and their child."[57] Her lawyer said that John was serving "a nefarious cause." She believed that John had sent her back to Muscatine in order to "free himself" from his responsibilities, and to aid the Confederacy. Nancy obtained a divorce on June 1, 1863, while John was in Shelbyville, Tennessee. She soon married another Muscatine man.

John's motives are a mystery. Shipley family tradition implies that John's drinking was a factor in the divorce.[58]

Two years later, Robert E. Lee surrendered, and Jefferson Davis fled Richmond, heading for the Deep South. In the manhunt that ensued, Union Brigadier General W. J. Palmer captured John near Athens, Georgia, on May 8, 1865.

After the war, John returned to Muscatine and worked as a bookkeeper and insurance salesman.[59] In 1893, he was elected to one term as Muscatine City Treasurer.

Dedicated Leadership

Years in the army, long years of bloodshed, horror, and hardship, hadn't prepared him for losing his wife and a baby in childbirth. In the grief that followed, William M. Smith wondered whether he should leave the sunny South and return to Iowa.

William M. Smith had been a fatherless lad with eight siblings when his Virginia-born mother moved the brood from Indiana to Illinois and finally Winterset in Madison County, Iowa, in 1852.[60] William farmed for a year before heading to northwestern Missouri in 1858.[61]

He married Margaret Davison in 1859 in Andrew County, where one of every fifteen people was a slave.[62, 63] Fear and outrage related to abolition and slavery occasionally led to mobs and violence.[64] After Lincoln was elected, residents divided into pro-Union and pro-Southern factions. After Fort Sumter, many men entered military service on one side or the other. Some stayed home.

Months passed, and the December chill settled on tense Andrew County. Twenty-four-year-old William saddled up, leaving behind Margaret and their newborn daughter, Mary Ellen, to enlist in Gates's Regiment Missouri Cavalry, part of the Missouri State Guard. Back home in Iowa, two of his brothers enlisted in the Union Army.[65]

William moved up from private to third sergeant after Elk Horn (Pea Ridge) and Farmington. A wound at Corinth was followed by promotion to second sergeant. William entered the crucible in 1863, fighting at Bakers Creek (Champion Hill) and Vicksburg. Attrition in those battles probably contributed to William's promotion to second lieutenant. At the same time, the 1st Missouri Cavalry was consolidated with the 3rd (Samuel's) Missouri Cavalry Battalion.

Even plow-horses need to rest, and William asked for his first furlough in late 1863, so he could visit relatives in Montgomery, Alabama.[66]

Returning perhaps a bit fresher, William fought with the Army of Tennessee throughout the Atlanta Campaign, and he rode with General John Bell Hood in Tennessee. William experienced some of the heaviest fighting of the war when Confederate troops attacked the Union line at Franklin, Tennessee, on November 30, 1864. Union troops captured William and whisked him to frigid Johnson's Island, Ohio. He sat out the rest of the war and signed an Oath of Amnesty on May 13, 1865.

William returned to Margaret and young Mary Ellen. Margaret soon delivered another baby, but they both died.[67] William rejoined his brothers in Cass County, Iowa. He probably attended the ordination of brother Jackson Clay Smith, who had served throughout the war in the 1st Iowa Cavalry. William built a log cabin, improved three farms, married two more times (first to Martha, who died, and then Elizabeth) and had four more children. The date of his death is unknown.

Divided Family

It should have been easy to approach the Federal pickets. Instead, one spotted William P. Cresap and fired. He crumpled with piercing pain as the minie ball hit his thigh. Comrades managed to drag him back to safety.

Farmer William Price Cresap was born in Maryland. At age ten, in 1851, he and his family moved to Danville Township, Des Moines County.[68] By age sixteen, he farmed, and so did his fifteen-year-old brother, James.[69] They lived next door to a future Iowa Confederate, Albert H. Newell.

In April 1861, when William was twenty-one, he enlisted as a private in Clark's Regiment, Missouri Infantry.[70] This unit later became the 9th Missouri Infantry. Wounded in November 1862 at Crooked Creek in Arkansas, he was captured a month later on the White River. After being paroled and exchanged, he participated in the Battles of Boonville, Pleasant Hill, Jenkins Ferry, Cypress Benn, and Gaines Landing.[71] William surrendered on May 26, 1865, in New Orleans, Louisiana. He was paroled two weeks later in Alexandria, Louisiana.

The Cresap family was divided during the war. William's younger brother, James, enlisted in the 8th Iowa Infantry.

After the war, William stayed in Missouri. He married Julia D. Porter in 1870 and worked as a carpenter. In 1913, he received a Missouri Confederate Pension. He died on July 20, 1914, in Humansville, Missouri.

In Footsteps of German Military Tradition

The sound of saws and hammers was peppered with complaints. Frederick von Ende and others didn't want to build fortifications. They longed to attack, raid, or even ride patrols. Brigadier General Albert Pike, commander of the Indian Territory, called his Texas troopers "even more worthless and troublesome together than I had supposed."

Frederick's family was steeped in German military tradition. Three uncles had been Hessian soldiers under Napoleon Bonaparte; two of them fell in battle.[72] Political upheaval caused Frederick's father to leave his judgeship in Hesse and move his children, including nine-year-old Frederick, to Burlington, Iowa, in 1852.[73]

Eight years later, in spring 1860, older brother, Charles, and Frederick left home together. At Hannibal, Missouri, they parted ways. Charles hoped to discover gold in Colorado, and Frederick headed to a job as clerk for a wealthy uncle in Greenville, Texas.[74, 75]

Charles's gold-mining expedition did not pan out, so he returned to Iowa.[76] Five months after Confederates fired upon Fort Sumter, in September 1861, Charles enlisted in Co. "F," Fifth Iowa Cavalry.

A total 600 miles southwest, Frederick rode through the December chill into Fort Washita, Chickasaw Nation (present-day Oklahoma), on a horse (and rigging) worth $160. He enlisted as a private in Co. "D," Taylor's Regiment Texas Mounted Rifles, 22nd Texas Cavalry.[77] The 34th Texas Cavalry joined the 22nd and moved to Fort McCullough, also in Indian Territory. Frederick's comrades engaged in building fortifications.[78]

The 22nd Texas dismounted and spent the rest of the war in Arkansas, Louisiana, and Indian Territory. They joined General Richard Taylor's army and helped defeat Federal forces in the April and May 1864 Red River campaign.[79] The following year, Frederick's regiment was back in Texas. It disbanded in May 1865.

Frederick went back to work for his uncle, Fred Ende, in Greenville. About fifteen years after Appomattox, Frederick began a prosperous insurance agency. He married Clara in 1892, and they had a daughter two years later.

At some point, Frederick met his older brother Charles and swapped stories. Throughout the war, Charles had not known that his little brother wore Confederate gray.

Comrades Through Marriage and Service

Julia Douglass shifted the toddler onto her hip and glanced back at Fort Smith. Shortly after her husband and her brother-in-law enlisted, the Federals arrived, and everything changed.

The fort wasn't the Garden of Eden, and she wasn't Eve, but an armed bluecoat prevented her from returning as surely as the angel with the flaming sword.

Brothers-in-law James M. Collier and Moses S. Douglass were farmers and Tennessee natives. James was the first to bring his wife and children to Madison County, Iowa, in 1855, at age twenty-eight. Moses (with wife Julia) followed suit.[80] During the late 1850s, James and Moses eked out a living, doing better than many Iowans.[81]

In early 1861, James and Moses and their wives moved to Arkansas. A year after the Confederacy instituted a draft, Julia Douglass had a baby boy.[82] She and Moses were in Fort Smith, close to the Indian Territories, when Moses and James enlisted in Co. "C," 1st Arkansas Cavalry (later known as Gordon's Regiment Arkansas Cavalry), on June 17, 1863.[83, 84]

Federal troops rolled in, capturing Fort Smith.[85] Julia Douglass took her children to Choctaw Nation, Indian Territories. Adrift in a strange land, Julia died in March 1864.[86] Her now-motherless young son died there the following October.[87]

During this time, the 1st Arkansas Cavalry seemed to constantly forage. In April 1864, they tried to capture Union supply wagons at Poison Spring and Marks' Mill (where one of every five of their comrades were injured).[88] In August 1864, Gordon's Regiment joined General Sterling Price's bold invasion of Missouri.[89] Ultimately unsuccessful, James, Moses, and their comrades began a demoralizing, exhausting retreat to the Indian Territories. About a month after Appomattox, the 1st Arkansas Cavalry disbanded.[90]

Moses married Charlotte a year after Lee surrendered.[91] The newlyweds joined brother-in-law James and his wife, Mary, in Sebastian County, Arkansas. Moses died first, in 1892, followed by Charlotte. James died in 1901, and his wife, Mary, received a $100 Arkansas Confederate pension from 1908 until she died in 1910.[92]

Tennessee Roots, Divided Family

Moving forward the third time under murderous cross-fire was the hardest. Bursting shells, screams, and bullets were the violent reality as James Nathaniel Cobb plunged toward the ridge and Sherman's headquarters. When the smoke cleared, sixty-one percent of his comrades were killed, wounded, or missing, and James was gone.

James was born in Tennessee in 1839.[93] His North Carolina-born parents had ten children. Most of the family moved to Iowa in 1855. James, however, temporarily stayed behind in Tennessee with some brothers.

Three years later, he travelled to Iowa by way of Missouri where he met a belle, Mary King. They got married in Putnam County, Missouri, on May 19, 1858, and moved to Lucas County, Iowa, where he worked as an engineer.[94] Their first child was born in Iowa in May 1859. Their second child was born in Chariton, Lucas County, Iowa, on March 7, 1861.

Mary and the children likely came with James to Tennessee so he could join two of his brothers (to whom he was especially close) in the Confederate Army.[95] James and his older brother, George L. Cobb, enlisted in Co. "F," 2nd (Robison's) Tennessee Infantry, on May 1, 1861.[96] Another brother, Jacob Sidney Cobb, enlisted in Co. "E," 4th (McLemore's) Tennessee Cavalry. James enlisted for twelve months. In early December 1861, he re-enlisted for two years or the duration of the war.

Five months later, the 2nd Tennessee saw heavy action at Shiloh.[97] On Sunday, April 6, 1862, the third day of battle, Colonel William Bates tried to dislodge the 70th Ohio (a regiment in General William T. Sherman's division) from a ridge near Shiloh Church. The 2nd Tennessee advanced three times under "murderous crossfire."[98] The third attempt gained the ridge and Sherman's headquarters but at a huge cost. Confederate authorities declared James a deserter, but brother George remained on the rolls.

Yet another brother made a choice that would sunder the family. Almost two years after James deserted, their younger brother, Ephraim, enlisted in the 3rd Iowa Cavalry.[99] Their brother-in-law, Charles Jones, served in the same unit. Ephraim was still a green recruit when Confederate troops captured him after a skirmish at Ripley, Mississippi, on June 11, 1864. Ephraim died in hellish Andersonville Prison on September 26, 1864.

After the war ended, James farmed, and he deserted Mary. He later married Paulina Willingham in Calhoun County, Alabama. James N. Cobb died on May 18, 1912.[100]

The Brothers' War

Dipping his pen into the inkwell, Charles O. Musser, 29th Iowa Infantry, critiqued his big brother, William, a Confederate in a POW camp.

The Musser family had moved from Ohio to Pottawattamie County, Iowa, by 1853.[101] William A. Musser, born in 1841, was two years older than Charles. By 1860, nineteen-year-old William had a valuable apprenticeship at the *Council Bluffs Nonpareil*.[102] Charles, in contrast, was an unskilled farm laborer. He enlisted as a private in the 29th Iowa Infantry on August 9, 1862.[103] Promoted to sergeant, Charles frequently wrote their father in Council Bluffs, Iowa, about the rigors of a Union soldier's life and the war.

Older brother William entered the Confederate service on September 20, 1862 (almost a year and a half after Fort Sumter) in Co. "D," Hunter's Battalion (later known as the 3rd and then the 11th Missouri Infantry).[104] Two days later, twenty-two-year-old William became a "government printer" and an "army printer" in

General Thomas C. Hindman's headquarters. He labored in this position until he was captured in September 1863 in Bolivar County, northwest Mississippi. Federal troops whisked him to Camp Morton POW Camp in Indianapolis, Indiana.

William had rigors of his own at Camp Morton. The population more than doubled in size after he arrived in September 1863, putting a strain on its cramped hospital. Many prisoners were "profusely verminous."[105] A medical inspector stated: "The ratio of mortality is unwarrantably large.... This camp is a disgrace." He added that there were not enough latrines, and those that existed were never cleaned.

Winter arrived early at Camp Morton. The barracks in November 1863 were unfloored, badly heated, and poorly ventilated.[106] Prisoners kept pouring in, many of whom lacked drawers, socks, and shirts. Prison officials doled out shoddy clothing, including short blue coats that lacked buttons (so no one could mistake prisoners for Union soldiers).

Later that month, Charles wrote their father about William: "If it is in your power to help him, do so.... I hope he has seen the errors of his ways.... And he is still my Brother [even] if he is a rebel."[107]

William's life became harder on New Year's Eve as the temperature plunged to 20 degrees below zero.[108] Furious, swirling snow blew through the crevices of dilapidated barracks, huts, and tents. Woodstoves could not cope with the punishing conditions, and sleeping was an ordeal. Prisoners typically lay huddled in groups of three, on long shelves, with a little straw and one blanket beneath them, and one or two blankets stretched across all three men. Lice and fleas—hardy even in this weather—proliferated. Men with no change of clothing washed their only garments and bathed in teeth-chattering cold. Freezing temperatures pushed many weakened Confederates to their deaths.

Charles urged their father on January 17, 1864 to forget about his brother's choice to serve the Confederacy.[109] But the longer William remained in prison, the more Charles hardened his attitude. On May 20, 1864, Charles advised, "If he does not relent, let him suffer the penalty of his misdeeds."[110]

The Lincoln administration in mid-summer cracked down on Confederate prisoners in retaliation for widespread malnutrition in Andersonville Prison. Camp Morton officials cut rations and doubled the prison population.[111] When prisoners stepped outside to relieve themselves, they encountered a massive, noxious latrine with swarming mosquitoes. Unbeknown to them, the mosquitoes carried pestilent malaria. Wells and cisterns dried up during a drought. Sick POWs overflowed the hospital, and no one had enough fruit and vegetables. Hungry men sometimes caught and ate rats. Prisoners took vengeance upon a miserly sutler by eating his dog.

Compared to William's woes, Charles was having a good summer. He crowed to their father about his good health.[112] In October 1864, Charles was building snug winter quarters. He paused to write their father. Striking a note of patriotic indignation, Charles stated: "Let him [William] suffer the consequences. Or let him adjure his Traitorous principles and become a man again."[113]

William survived the winter and was released on March 14, 1865, after taking an oath of allegiance to the Constitution.[114] He remained in Indianapolis, working as a printer at the *Herald* and then the *Journal*, rather than returning to Council Bluffs.[115]

Charles wrote their father on April 1, 1865, that he wanted to see William and hoped he was doing well.[116] It is doubtful that William was eager to see Charles, given his brother's ire toward "Rebs." After the war, William hoped to find joy in his new marriage to an Iowa woman. He wrote their father: "The sufferings and hardships of the war, and prison life, have left their effects on me. I can never forget the treatment of prisoners at the hands of the Federal authorities."[117]

In the years after Appomattox, William remained distant from his family, and he ended up living at the Union Printers Home (a residence for "invalid, aged, or infirm printers") in Colorado Springs, Colorado.

Principled Commitment to C.S.A./Southern Loyalty

"True son of Virginia": Hints of Southern-Defined Honor

Smoke poured into the yard from the burning house. John ran in from the cornfield, shouting for his wife Lucy. He plunged into the blast, looking for his wife in room after room. One door remained. He opened it, scooped her up, and stumbled outside.

Breathing raggedly, John and Lucy sat in the yard as the roof fell in. Reflecting on it later, John was reminded of the wreckage of the Confederacy.

Ambitious lawyer John T. Lovell had moved from Virginia to the boom-town of Dubuque, Iowa, in the mid-1850s.[1] He joined the practice of his brother, Judge William Y. Lovell. Like several other Virginians, they tapped into U.S. Senator George Wallace Jones's network of legal, political, and business friends.[2, 3]

Born in 1832 in Culpeper County, Virginia, Lovell enrolled at Delaware College (predecessor of University of Delaware) in about 1849.[4] Lovell transferred to the University of Virginia to study law.[5]

He wrote to Gideon B. Waples, a friend from Delaware College, about himself and other "sons of Virginia": "Our state … is soon destined (as she ought) to be the first State in the Union … Virginia will be the "bright particular star" and rise superior to all the rest. So mote it be."[6]

Lovell studied intensely and constantly. He began having "hemorrhages from the lungs," leaving him pale and emaciated. His father worried about Lovell's health, stating "that I would fall a victim to my ambition, in trying to excel others in the pursuit of that bauble called 'honor.'"[7] Lovell withdrew from school in 1851 to recuperate. His early lung problems were a sign of things to come.

During the interim, he tutored children of gentlemen, and he followed the presidential race of 1852. Being a Millard Fillmore man, he wrote: "Mr. Fillmore … [is] a lover of this invaluable Union—and is as true to Southern interest as 'the needle is to the pole.'"[8]

In summer 1853, he visited his brother, William Y. Lovell, in Dubuque.[9] The next year, 1854, Lovell was initiated into Delta Kappa Epsilon at the University of Virginia. He graduated in 1855 and joined his brother's thriving law firm.

Dubuque was good for Lovell. He blossomed as a lawyer, and he dipped his toe into the water of politics. He wrote Waples:

My own success both professionally and pecuniarily is unparalleled and even more than I ever anticipated, even in the green, sportive days of boyhood. I made last year over $10,000.

This fall, I made some dozen speeches in different places in behalf of Buchanan and the Union and established quite a reputation as a "Stump speaker." I am henceforth a Democrat ... now we march with the only party that keeps step "to the music of the Union." Buchanan is our next President, and we have buried "Black Republicanism" so deeply that the hand of resurrection will never reach it.[10]

In late 1857, Lovell returned to Virginia to marry Lucy Ann Williams. The bride and groom returned to Dubuque.

Historian Goodspeed writes: "By 1858, Dubuque had a powerful bar—one of the most powerful in all the West ... lawyers who then and afterwards made themselves famous."[11] Three other native Virginians joined Lovell's law practice, including one of Lucy's brothers, James H. Williams. All were Democrats. They found a sympathetic, pro-slavery atmosphere among Senator George Wallace Jones's political and business friends. In fact, Williams became an Iowa state representative. Prospects were bright for legal success.

On September 7, 1859, Lovell gave a speech on behalf of local independent Democrats. He noted in his diary that he "pleased the natives."[12]

During the 1860 presidential race, Lovell's practice continued to prosper. He owned an impressive $10,000 of real estate, including fifty-two lots in Manchester, Iowa.[13]

When Lincoln was elected president, Lovell asked Waples: "Who is responsible for the overwhelming defeat which the Democratic party has met, and which causes patriots everywhere to fear for the continuance of our Union beyond the 4th of March 1861 [Lincoln's inauguration]?"[14]

Lovell shared his thoughts:

To my mind, Judge Douglas has contributed more to the election of Lincoln than all the Black Republican orators together ... I cordially voted for Breckenridge and Lane but did not make an active canvas in their behalf, for the reason that I wished Douglas to carry Iowa if he could over Lincoln, and thus aid Breckenridge.... Give up Douglas and join again an organization which can alone preserve the Union, *viz.*, the Breckenridge democracy.

Affairs look equally in the South. I believe she is right, however, and unless she can have equality and independence in the Union, then she must and will have them out of it.

I recognize in its broadest sense "the right of a State to secede."... If a dissolution of the Union comes, and I now think it probable, my destinies will be cast with the South, whose honor and interests I hold sacred, and stand ready to sacrifice my life in defense of them ... I am getting a good practice in the law but am regarded as an ultraist in my political opinions.[15]

In June and July 1861, a few months after Fort Sumter, Dubuque Republicans accused Lovell's brother-in-law, state legislator James H. Williams, of disloyalty.[16] Lovell showed his colors at an Independence Day celebration in nearby Zwingle. He stated, "No power on earth, in heaven or hell, could make me take up arms against my brethren in Virginia." Audience members silenced him. The *Dubuque Weekly Times* editor opined, "We have some very bold rebels in this county."[17]

Williams soon returned to Virginia, and Lovell followed him two weeks later.[18] The next month, September 1861, Lovell and Williams visited their mutual Dubuque friend (and former governor's son), Private Junius L. Hempstead, 5th Virginia Infantry. They "talked over Iowa matters."[19]

In the summer of 1862, Lovell networked with University of Virginia friends, trying to find a civil service job. One such friend was Robert Garlick Hill Kean, who supervised clerks for the War Department in Richmond. Lovell stated:

I am a refugee from Lincoln's despotism and have sacrificed in my return to Va. $15,000 or more and have nothing but my personal exertions to depend upon now for the support of myself and my family.

My lungs are in the opinion of physicians too much diseased to permit my entering the ranks of our noble army, where I would delight to be, if I could go with safety to my health.[20]

Kean scrawled on the letter:

The writer is a very estimable gentleman and a great man of business. He left a prosperous business in Dubuque, Iowa, on the breaking out of the troubles to cast his lot with his Mother State: Virginia. He is a native of Shenandoah Co., is well known there, and would make an excellent enrolling officer for that section.

Lovell "tried active service" in spring 1863, but he coughed up blood.[21] He worked as a clerk in a quartermaster's department and then as an ordnance agent for Warren County, Virginia. In November 1863, Lovell hauled muskets, rifles, bayonets, and cavalry sabers from Front Royal to Staunton.[22]

He visited his in-laws from time to time. After a brother-in-law, George Williams, was killed at the Battle of Brandy Station, Lovell located George's body. Lovell found James H. Williams (who also fought at Brandy Station), and they arranged to bury George.

Civil government continued to function in war-torn Virginia. In November 1864, Lovell became an agent in the 10th Congressional District of Virginia. He considered and paid claims for "property taken or irregularly impressed for the use of the Army." In February 1865, two months before Appomattox, the Confederate Comptroller's Office paid Lovell $904.60 (including expenses) for three months work.

In February 1866, their house burned.[23] Lovell wrote lawyer and land speculator Ray B. Griffin of Manchester, Iowa: "In leaving Iowa, I lost all my property there and that I owned here by the war and hence I am very poor ... I really stand in need of every cent I can get."[24]

He later wrote Griffin: "Federal soldiers captured my Book of Land Entries whilst I was in your State.... I am farming at present—but when the 'Stay Law' expires in 1868, I expect to resume the practice of law somewhere in Va."[25]

Lovell wrote Griffin on April 1, 1867:

Now, as we are in "District No. 1" (once the noble Commonwealth of Va.) will be required by our Military Dictator to register as Voters and take the prescribed oath ... I am too good a Democrat and "Rebel" to be willingly deprived of the privilege of voting at elections, even where the ignorant Negroes are for the first time in this oppressed section of the country allowed the right of suffrage.

By the way, let me tell you, that the Radicals will not find as much strength politically given them in the South by their recent legislation as they anticipate, for their "American citizens of African descent" are still under the influence of their former masters and know, too, their real friends.[26]

Three years later, Lovell tried to make a fresh start out West, hoping to join his brother, William Y. Lovell, a probate judge in Montana Territory. Lovell, Lucy, and their two young daughters made it as far as St. Joseph, Missouri, where Lucy had a relative.[27] On July 15, 1871, Lovell was away on business when tragedy struck. The *St. Joseph Gazette* described a "terrible storm" that hit the three-story house where Lucy and their daughters lived:

When the storm commenced, Mrs. Lovell was upstairs in a back room, reading the Bible to her little daughter. The windows of the room having been blown open, she took her children, ran down stairs, passing from the hall into a bedroom, put the children on a bed and kneeled at the bedside. In this position the lightning struck her, causing instant death. Mr. Blakemore [another tenant] was in the hall and the same bolt killed him.... The two daughters with whom she was kneeling in prayer, are aged respectively nine and six years. They were uninjured.[28]

Lovell later served as sheriff, clerk of courts, state senator, and editor of the *Warren Sentinel*.[29] He became paralyzed from a stroke in May 1899. John T. Lovell died on February 10, 1900.

A writer memorialized Lovell's post-war activity:

Throughout the desperate days of military occupation and political slavery, Judge Lovell along with other valley newspapers and leading men openly discussed measures of resistance and denounced oppression. And no man labored harder to restore the government of Virginia into the control of her own people.[30]

From Officer of the Court to Officer with a Sword

Bending over a map, Lt. Colonel Spier Whitaker Sr. softly ordered soldiers to search for Confederate deserters in Randolph County, North Carolina. Long experience in Iowa and North Carolina had taught Spier that authority need not be loudly expressed.

Spier's resume included lawyer, North Carolina legislator, and Attorney General of North Carolina from 1842 to 1846. In 1854, when Spier was fifty-six, he moved to Davenport in Scott County, Iowa, with his wife and a couple of children. Spier joined an active law practice with his nephew, Judge James Grant, and he retired from practicing law in 1860.[31] Spier was well to do, having real estate valued at $10,000 and a personal estate of $50,000.[32]

In April 1861, Spier believed civil war was inevitable. At age sixty-two, he left his home and belongings in Davenport and moved back to North Carolina. One son remained in Iowa, practiced law, and lived in his parents' home.[33]

A Scott County attorney thought Spier left Iowa because "he was a Southern gentleman with Southern sentiments."[34] According to Spier's daughter-in-law, he believed slavery could only survive in the Confederacy. She explained: "He returned to North Carolina to share the hardships of war and assist in defending his native State from an invading army."[35]

North Carolina seceded shortly after Spier arrived. He visited the governor, offering his services to the state military forces. According to family tradition, "Governor [Henry Toole] Clarke replied that Colonel Whitaker had sons enough to represent him in the field."[36] However, the governor appointed Spier as *aide-de-camp* to advise him on military affairs. Spier had the rank of lieutenant colonel.[37]

The *Richmond Times* marked Spier's appointment, noting "Col. W. was formerly Attorney General of the State, and ranks high as a gentleman, a jurist, and a patriot."[38]

Dissent against the Confederate government and the war heated up in historically Quaker north-central North Carolina. Governor Clarke on March 4, 1862, issued a proclamation against disaffection and disloyalty in Randolph County. Reportedly, residents said they would resist drafting militia members into the state military service (where they could enter the Confederate Army). The governor stated: "They [Unionists] denounce our State and Confederacy ... and desire to effect a union with a government at war with us now invading our soil; and in various ways, by word and deed, giving aid and comfort to the enemy."[39]

Neighboring Davidson County also erupted in "treasonable conduct and threatened violence." Gov. Clark sent Spier to investigate the situation and, if possible, capture weapons. Clark authorized Spier to use 300 volunteers and two companies of troops. The governor added, "If any force is used, we desire it to be effectual."[40]

Historian William T. Auman states: "On March 14, Colonel Whitaker noted that all the dissidents from Randolph County had been rounded up, including three of their leaders by the names of Rush, Kindly, and Hill, who had either been drafted or had 'volunteered.'"[41]

Spier explained, "Their families and farms are sureties against desertion.... Two-thirds of the drafted men from Randolph have volunteered; more will volunteer."[42]

Spier resigned at the end of Clark's term, on August 5, 1862, after fourteen months of service. Spier's daughter-in-law later recalled, "In after years, Governor Clark took occasion to express in emphatic terms his appreciation of Colonel Whitaker's marked ability and service."

While Spier dealt with dissenters, four of his sons served in the Confederate Army, and three of them died.[43] After the war ended, Spier Whitaker Sr. returned to Davenport and resumed practicing law. He died four years later, on December 2, 1869. The Scott County Bar mourned his loss. The *Davenport Daily Gazette* stated: "Colonel Whitaker was a man of fine personal presence, resembling very much the great Kentuckian, Henry Clay. His manners were agreeable, courteous and winning.... He was essentially one of the old school gentlemen, cultivated, refined, and abounding in a high sense of honor."[44]

The Architect of Andersonville Prison: A Son's Quest to Clear his Father's Name

Mass imprisonment and poor supplies at Andersonville led to horrible cases of starvation. The War Department publicized photos of emaciated soldiers, giving Andersonville an infamous and enduring reputation.[45]

Historian Arch Fredric Blakey wrote a biography of Confederate General John H. Winder, who was later blamed for Andersonville. Blakey writes, "To rescue a villain from history—to overturn a historical myth—is a difficult task."[46]

William Sidney Winder ("Sidney"), one of General Winder's sons, spent years trying to rehabilitate his father's name. Sidney grew up in a slave-holding military family in various Southern towns.[47] After attending Columbian College near

Washington, D.C., Sidney practiced law in Keokuk, Iowa, from 1857 to fall 1860, and then he was an attorney in Baltimore.

Sidney's family divided as war loomed. His father, a career military officer, wavered between remaining in the U.S. Army and serving the Confederacy. Sidney intended to fight for Southern independence, and his older half-brother remained a captain in the U.S. Army.[48]

After North Carolina seceded, Sidney's father, John H. Winder, resigned his U.S. Army commission "with great regret" and became a brigadier general in the provisional Confederate army.[49] Sidney also joined the Confederate forces.[50] He was promoted from first lieutenant to captain and assistant adjutant general, eventually serving on his father's staff.

General Winder became inspector general of prisons in the Richmond area. When hungry housewives broke into shops, General Winder helped President Jefferson Davis put down the Richmond Bread Riot.[51]

Late in 1863, the prisons in Richmond were seriously overcrowded. General John H. Winder sent Sidney to Georgia to locate a prison site for Union POWs. That order led to the infamous Andersonville Prison. Sidney and his father tried to build and operate a prison that was spacious and relatively healthy, unlike the horror that Andersonville became. However, they failed.[52]

Conditions worsened when, in December 1864, the North refused to resume the cartel (the exchange of POWs). Prison populations continued to increase, in spite of insufficient resources to feed, clothe, and care for them. General Winder proposed that the Confederates parole POWs and send them home without exchange. That would have alleviated the problems at Andersonville, but his superiors rejected the idea, calling it "worse than evil."[53]

On January 26, 1865, General Winder informed his superiors in Richmond that prisoners were starving and "suffering very much for want of clothing." He added, "I would be glad if the attention of the Federal Government were called to the fact." General Winder died about a week later.[54]

Sidney went to Richmond, planning to resign, but instead he was charged with guarding the Confederate treasury and archives after the fall of Richmond. Sidney and eight other officers eventually reached the David Levy Yulee plantation in Florida on May 22, 1865—twelve days after Jefferson Davis was captured. Author Blakey writes: "The group decided to bury the archives on the Yulee grounds [and allotted] one-fourth of the gold to support of Mrs. Davis and her children; the rest they divided equally among themselves. Each officer received gold sovereigns in the amount of $1,995." The nine officers surrendered and were paroled. Sidney eventually resumed his law practice.[55]

Even before Appomattox, historian Marouf Hasian Jr. writes, "Northern presses were filled with lurid tales of lurid tales of victims of dysentery, scurvy, and gangrene" at Andersonville and other prison camps. Author Susan Sontag writes that "photographs of skeletal prisoners held at Andersonville inflamed public opinion."[56]

Since General Winder was dead, the logical person to blame for Andersonville was commander Captain Henry Wirz. Captain Wirz was given a military tribunal and hanged.

Sidney maintained that he and his father had never been cruel to prisoners. He and an uncle struggled to clear his father's name. However, Union officials who controlled the captured Confederate archives did not cooperate. Without original documents, it was impossible to refute Union accusations that General John H. Winder was a cold-blooded mass murderer.

Sidney spent more than ten years in a quixotic quest. His health deteriorated, and he eventually withdrew from the world, dying on February 25, 1925.

Desertion

Leaving Together the Way They Came In

Black, sooty smoke belched from the steamboat chimney as the vessel pulled up to the dock. The Talty brothers joked as they walked down the ramp and stepped onto dry ground.

Four years earlier, the four Irish immigrant brothers had moved to Davenport, Iowa, in 1856. The two oldest brothers (Patrick and Simon) were stonemasons, the third brother (George) was a laborer, and the youngest (fourteen-year-old John) had no job. Patrick and Simon married two Irish lasses. After the Panic of 1857, the Talty brothers moved to Memphis, the "biggest inland cotton market in the world."[1]

Irish immigrants to Memphis "found jobs as laborers on railroad construction crews, on levee construction gangs, and on the steamboats and docks," according to historian Robert A. Sigafoos. Historian Ella Lonn, author of *Foreigners in the Confederacy*, writes that Irish immigrants dug ditches, cleared land, chopped down trees, and repaired levees. Lonn explains that some plantation owners preferred to use Irish workers instead of slaves, because they would suffer financial loss if their slaves died.[2]

During the lead-up to the Civil War, Tennessee remained in the Union until Fort Sumter fell, and Lincoln called up 75,000 militiamen to restore the Union. A month later, all four Talty brothers enlisted in Captain Bankhead's Company, Light Artillery, on May 20, 1861.

Lonn comments that Irish immigrants, "governed by the place of their residence, enlisted with equal readiness in both armies." She states that, "as a race, they held no positive convictions for or against slavery or secession." However, "once in the fight, they gave themselves with their usual warm ardor to the cause they were espousing."[3]

The brothers did not see much action at Columbus (Kentucky); New Madrid; or *en route* to Corinth (Mississippi)—perhaps the work did not agree with them. Just as likely, they reacted to being paid inconsistently. Around their one-year anniversary of enlisting, the four brothers went back to Davenport. Confederate authorities called all of them deserters except for Simon, who had been working in detached service in a hospital.[4, 5, 6, 7]

A year later in Davenport, George, Simon, and John Talty were working as laborers when the federal government enumerated them for the draft in June and July 1863.[8] None of them were called up to serve in the Union Army.

Two years later, the war ended. Patrick delivered beer as a drayman, and then he worked as a stonemason. Simon worked as a stonemason and then as a stone cutter. These two brothers moved their families to Atlantic, Iowa, where they died, Patrick in 1910 and Simon in 1919. All four brothers are buried in the Catholic cemetery in Atlantic.[9, 10, 11, 12]

"Against My Consent": Confessions of a Disillusioned Irish-American

William O'Day shivered in his prison cell. His threadbare Confederate jacket barely held his body heat. He scarcely noticed the approaching footsteps. Someone called his name and a key unlocked the cell door. William braced himself to see the Union commander of Camp Defiance.

In the late 1850s, engineer William O'Day left Iowa and got a railroad job in Mississippi. Irish native O'Day enlisted in Co. "B," 17th Mississippi Infantry, after the war began. His unit was near Richmond, Virginia, in summer 1862. After being hospitalized for illness, he rejoined his unit and was captured on November 6, 1862, in Hampshire, Virginia. O'Day gave the following statement to Union authorities:

> I was born in Ireland. I am twenty-six years old. I enlisted with Captain John McGirk of the 17th Mississippi Infantry Co. B and remained with him for the period of seventeen months.
>
> My reason for enlisting was because I was out of employment. I belong to Iowa and my Father lives near West Union, Brama [Bremer] County, Iowa. I had to leave home to obtain a living.
>
> I served seventeen months in the Confederate Army against my consent. When I left them, they were stationed between Winchester and Front Royal. Colonel Holder now commands the 17th Mississippi Infantry, numbering about 700.[13]

Union officials moved O'Day to three different prisons: Atheneum (in Wheeling, Virginia, present-day West Virginia); Camp Chase, Ohio; and Camp Defiance, Cairo, Illinois.

He was slated to be exchanged—and returned to his Confederate unit—but it never happened. O'Day presumably convinced Union officials to let him take the oath of allegiance to the U.S. government. His Confederate company roll call listed him as a deserter.

After his release from prison, his trail runs cold. Some fifty years later, on August 11, 1910, William O'Day died and was buried in Bremer County, Iowa.[14]

You Can't Outrun the Long Arm of the Law

Governments on both sides of the Mason-Dixon Line had an insatiable desire for military recruits. Pennsylvania native Samuel H. Bulger found this out during the Civil War.

Samuel had moved to Clinton, Iowa, when he was twelve. At age eighteen, in 1857, he and his family moved to Texas, where Samuel worked as a laborer, and his father raised stock.[15]

Texas seceded in 1861. A year later, twenty-two-year-old Samuel enlisted as a private in Co. "E," 6th Texas Infantry.[16] The infantry was an unpopular choice. A Confederate recruiter wrote: "[I] find it hard to get Texans to go into infantry companies. They say they will go mounted, but no other way. That is, a majority say so."[17]

Years later, Samuel said he had been "pressed into the rebel service."[18] He was not drafted, but he may have felt pressured to enlist by his Texas peers, his neighbors, or his employer.

His younger brother, Philip, enlisted in the same company a few months later.[19] Samuel's troubles began to mount. For starters, he received no pay for eight months.

Their regiment was sent to Fort Hindman, also called Arkansas Post, on the Arkansas River. Union commanders considered Fort Hindman a stepping-stone to Vicksburg. In early January 1863, Union troops and gunboats moved in, outnumbering Confederate troops six to one. Admiral David D. Porter's gunboats began shelling the Confederate positions. The Confederate infantrymen retreated to rifle pits outside of Fort Hindman. Intense shelling lasted for a day, and the Confederates surrendered on January 11.[20]

Union troops hustled them onto steamboats. Soaking wet from rain and snow, Samuel, his brother, and other POWs suffered terribly, heading up the Mississippi. The Bulger brothers and their fellow POWs went to Camp Butler in Springfield, Illinois. After a month and a half of captivity, in March 1863, Sam took the oath of allegiance to the U.S. Dozens of his comrades did, too, including his brother, Philip.

Historian James M. McCaffrey notes, "Other prisoners referred to this oath taking as 'swallowing the puppy,' and called those who took the oath 'razorbacks.'"[21] Samuel returned to Clinton, but he could not escape the war. He was enumerated for the draft that summer.[22]

Conflicting information creeps into the story. Samuel claimed to have served the Union Army for three months, which would have made him a 100 Day Man.

However, no record of this has been found. His brother, Philip, clearly was a 100 Day Man.[23]

Samuel claimed to have been drafted the following year, in 1864, so he scraped up enough money to hire a substitute to take his place.[24] He also married Alice D. Stockwell. They later had four children and moved to Appanoose County, Iowa.[25] In 1890, Samuel and his wife moved to Guadalupe County, Texas. He died on August 28, 1893.

Limited Dedication to the Cause

Desertion and conscription seemed like reasonable options for the Wainscott brothers. Their stories illustrate the difficulty of retaining Texas troops for duty in the Trans-Mississippi Confederacy.

Their parents, Southern-born Christopher and Hannah Wainscott, moved their growing family to the Iowa Territory in 1842.[26] Christopher was a farmer (and one-time judge) in Decatur County, southern Iowa; he owned more land than he could plow and plant, and the family moved to Texas in late 1860.[27, 28]

Seventeen-year-old Iowa native Benton Boone Wainscott rode a $115 horse (and carried a $35 gun) to Montague County, Texas, along the border of the Indian Territories. He enlisted in Co. "F," Johnson's Regiment Texas Mounted Volunteers, on January 8, 1862.[29] The regiment moseyed to Dallas a month later and became part of the 14th Texas Cavalry. After a year in Confederate gray, Boone joined Co. "A," 2nd Regiment Texas Cavalry, Texas State Troops, on January 27, 1863. He deserted on September 1, 1863, at Camp Stonewall in Collin County. Boone died in Texas in 1918.

Jefferson Straton Wainscott, age twenty-eight, travelled to Fort McCullough in the Indian Territories to enlist in Co. "B," 34th Texas Cavalry, on June 27, 1862.[30] He started out strong, but problems began piling up. The high point was the victory at Newtonia, Missouri, but things went downhill after they retreated into Arkansas.[31] There were new commanders; the regiment dismounted (and officers took his horse); and he went six months without pay, mileage for enlistment, or reimbursement for using his own weapons. Jefferson's patience apparently ran out, and he deserted.

About six months later, authorities caught up with Jefferson. He received amnesty by joining the Brush Battalion. Formed on November 8, 1863, the Brush Battalion consisted of the following men:

> Deserters, conscripts, and militia, who had taken to the brush in order to escape arrest by the conscript officers and who have been collected upon the promise that they would be pardoned and utilized on the frontier as a protection from Indians who were hostile.[32]

Jefferson's date of death is unknown.

Wilson Hunt Wainscott, age twenty-seven, traveled to Fort McCullough a couple of months after his brother, Jefferson. Wilson enlisted in Co. "A," 5th Regiment Texas Partisan Rangers (also known as Martin's Regiment Texas Cavalry), on August 5, 1862.[33] He deserted seven weeks later. Authorities eventually caught up with Wilson; military service seemed a better option than sitting in jail, so Wilson returned to the 5th Regiment Texas Partisan Rangers on May 1, 1863. He lasted eleven days before his commanders shipped him to an artillery company. After the war, he moved to Arizona where he died in 1919.

Charles Franklin Wainscott was conscripted into Johnson's Regiment Texas Mounted Volunteers.[34] He was detailed to work for some type of government contractor. His date of death is unknown.

Money Making Man on the Move

Donating a large cemetery plot, he decided, would help the town and bring him well-earned recognition. All he asked in return was to name the cemetery after him. George Washington Swailes was shocked when the ghost of his Confederate service returned, swaying the cemetery board against him.

At ten years old, George had realized the value of a good job when his father died in 1845. The family moved to Illinois and then Henry County, Iowa in 1856. He grabbed the golden ring in 1856 with a job at the Chicago, Burlington, and Quincy Railroad, making trips to Texas, Louisiana, Kentucky, and Tennessee.[35]

While local residents were embroiled in controversies over slavery and state's rights, George grappled with timber and iron trestles, pilings, and tracks. He toiled as Confederates fired on Fort Sumter. Five months later, sharp-eyed recruiters induced men to join the 16th Louisiana Infantry. Family legend says that someone told George to "join or hang."[36]

He enlisted on September 29, 1861.[37] Improbably, officers made him drive a hospital ambulance and then work as a teamster. He rejoined his leather-soled comrades in time for Shiloh on April 6 and 7, 1862. George next grabbed a shovel to dig fortifications at Corinth, Mississippi, but he had had enough; he deserted to the Union lines during the siege of Corinth on May 29.

Now George had a new problem: how could he convince the commanding Union officer to release him? Family legend says that George never fired on Union soldiers. This is unlikely unless George was ill during battles; or "shirked" (avoided fighting); or deliberately fired above Union soldiers' heads. However, this pacifist story may have quickly sprung George out of captivity.

He lit out for the Colorado Territory, but romance called him back to Henry County, Iowa. George married Nancy Dougherty on March 1, 1864 and returned to railroad work.[38] He became quite successful and touted his image as a self-made man.

Late in life, George made the generous cemetery donation. The town fathers—loyal men, all—rejected his tale of Confederate service as a pacifist, and so they refused to name a cemetery after him. George Washington Swailes died in 1916.[39]

Refusing to Return to Confederate Service

Joseph Collins Brownfield risked the ire of his fellow POWs when he said he wanted to swear allegiance to the United States. Even worse, he asked to return North to family and friends. Authorities denied the native Pennsylvanian's requests. Instead, they sent him to Fortress Monroe, Virginia. Three months later, Brownfield was exchanged and sent back to Dallas to rejoin Stone's Partisan Rangers, 2nd Texas Cavalry. But he wanted out.[40]

Joseph Collins Brownfield was born near Pittsburgh, Pennsylvania, in 1820 to Pennsylvania natives. The oldest son in a large farm family, he attended Uniontown College, taught school, and married Pennsylvania native Martha Schipp in 1846. He moved to Iowa in about 1853.[41] He lived four years in Clayton County, teaching school and buying and trading land. In about 1856, he moved to Missouri and did the same things. He accumulated enough money to buy 560 acres of undeveloped Texas land in 1859. He moved to Dallas the following year.

On November 1, 1862, Brownfield entered the Confederate service as a private in Stone's Partisan Rangers, Second Texas Cavalry. He served in Louisiana and was captured on June 23, 1863, after the Battle of Lafourche Crossing, Louisiana, on the Mississippi River. Brownfield was sent to New Orleans with about 700 other prisoners.

Six days after his capture, Brownfield failed in his attempt to take the oath of allegiance. Placed in an "unpleasant position," he was exchanged and sent back to Texas in August 1863. Brownfield refused to return to the Confederate armed forces, enduring several arrests and a death threat. Finally, the authorities left him alone, but his neighbors considered him a Yankee for a time.

After the war, Brownfield remained a large landholder. He and his wife, Martha, had nine children. Brownfield died on May 2, 1905, in Tarrant County, Texas.

Professional Service in the Confederacy

Chemist for the Confederacy

Leading his mounted troopers out of the timber, Captain George S. Laswell saw blue coats and shouted, "Charge!" Spurring his steed forward, Union riflemen opened fire, hitting the horse mid-stride. Laswell tumbled off, momentarily dazed. He scrambled up, looking for another horse to mount and rejoin his men.

George S. Laswell was a twenty-four-year-old druggist.[1] He was a Kentucky native and had attended West Point for a short time.[2] He lived in Ottumwa with his father, a banker. Laswell was a captain of the Ottumwa Guards, a paramilitary unit, in March 1857.[3]

Laswell wrote, "I left my home and relatives ... in Iowa and came to Arkansas in the spring of 1861." Union authorities confiscated George's property while *en route* to Arkansas. This left him penniless, with a family to support. In April 1861, he said he was offered a colonel's commission in the Union Army, but he rejected it and entered the Confederate Army as a private. Laswell stated that he was "branded by them [Northern friends] as a traitor and am forsaken by my dear relatives [in Iowa]."[4]

According to one rumor, Cyrus Franklin (an Ottumwa lawyer and former Iowa legislator) persuaded Laswell to serve the Confederacy.[5]

Laswell later became a captain of the 1st Arkansas Mounted Infantry.[6] In August 1861, he helped lead a Confederate charge at the Battle of Wilson's Creek. The next month, when the dust settled, Captain George Laswell helped organize a military ball in Neosho, southwest Missouri, held on September 3, 1861. The ball featured a "brass and string band to add to the festivities of the evening." The program included a cotillion, a quadrille, and a waltz.[7]

The following summer, in June 1862, Laswell wrote the Surgeon General of the Confederate Army, offering to manufacture chemicals and pharmaceutical preparations. He suggested building a laboratory for the army in Jackson,

Mississippi. The startup of a lab would be easier since he had his own equipment.[8] Laswell wrote his commanding officer that sick soldiers needed "proper medicinal and chemical preparations with which to treat their diseases," and most surgeons could not obtain them. Laswell proposed to "manufacture pure chemical and Pharmaceutical preparations … I think I can aid our glorious cause more in this way than I could by remaining in the field."[9]

A month later, Laswell was detailed to "manufacture chemical and medicinal preparations" for the Confederate Army. He resigned his commission at that time, stating: "My health is too bad to remain longer in the line. Being a practical chemist and Pharmaceutist, I believe I would be of more service in the medical dept. than I could be remaining longer in the field."[10] However, Laswell reappeared on the rolls in mid-1863, and he was promoted to major. On January 12, 1864, Laswell wrote President Jefferson Davis:

> Love for my helpless family alone induces me to apply to you … I have served the Confederate states honestly and faithfully for nearly three years … while thousands of Southern born citizens have placed in our gallant army substitutes to battle for their homes and property. Now when our bleeding country needs their assistance, they are trying to dispose of their property and desert their country in this her hour of trial.[11]

Mentioning that his little boy had died after he enlisted, Laswell worried that his "little family," behind enemy lines, were forced to "bear the cruel taunts of the insolent foe"—without his protection and financial support.

Hoping to be reunited with his family, Laswell asked the president for an appointment as colonel of artillery for ordnance duty in the Trans-Mississippi Department. Laswell explained: "They are needing large quantities of Nitric Acid in the Trans Miss. Department for manufacturing Percussion caps. I can manufacture this acid in sufficient quantities to meet the demand." This offer caught Davis's attention. Davis later reflected:

> My early attention was given to the organization of military forces and the procurement and preparation of the munitions of war. If our people had not gone to war without counting the cost, they were, nevertheless, involved in it without means of providing for its necessities.[12]

Laswell received the ordnance appointment and ended the war in Galveston, Texas, in the Trans-Mississippi Department.

The "Traitorous" Fiddler with a Connection to Jefferson Davis

An incoming shell exploded, killing most of the gun crew nearest George R.G. Jones. River water rose and seeped into Fort Henry. The newly minted lieutenant urged his battery to keep reloading until Confederate soldiers could evacuate. He tried to ignore his cold, waterlogged boots. He kept noticing Union gunboats coming closer, closer up the river, picking off Confederate guns. When the last Rebels left the fort, General Lloyd Tilghman raised the white flag. A gunboat silently mocked the defenders, splashing through the front gate into the fort.

Multi-talented George R. G. Jones wanted a career in the Confederacy. His dream became a reality through education and a few well-placed family friends.

George was born in 1837 in Wisconsin Territory, across the Mississippi River from Dubuque. He was the second son of George Wallace Jones, the lifelong friend of Jefferson Davis. When George was three years old, his family moved to Dubuque, in northeast Iowa. They brought three slaves—and one black freedman—with them.[13] (The family freed the slaves two or three years later.) When George was eleven years old, his father was elected U.S. Senator from Iowa.[14]

At age fifteen, George enrolled in Western Military Institute (WMI) in Kentucky. The school aimed to become the Virginia Military Institute of the West. He re-enrolled at ages nineteen and twenty. George made friends from "some of the best families" of Tennessee, and he became proficient at infantry tactics and drill.[15]

After he graduated from WMI in 1858, George attended schools in Germany and returned to Dubuque. His father was in South America after losing his senate seat and being appointed minister (ambassador) to New Grenada, present-day Columbia.

In early 1861, George, age twenty-three, bumped into one of his father's friends in Galena, Illinois. George said "he was going to Dixie to see his sweetheart," and gave a "Significant Smile."[16] His "sweetheart," however, was not a lady—it was the Confederacy. George also told his father that he would fight to defend the rights of the Southern people.

Two weeks after the war began, George was in Nashville, Tennessee, drilling newly recruited soldiers.[17] That summer, his mother wrote his father, Ambassador Jones: "We hear occasionally from George who is in Nashville or thereabouts. He says he is perfectly happy & will not move from there until the war is over & then only to visit for that is his adopted country."[18]

George became a drillmaster and a lieutenant with the Provisional Army of Tennessee on July 30, 1861.[19] While he drilled soldiers, U.S. Secretary of State William Seward spied on George's father, suspected Ambassador Jones of treason, and recalled him to Washington.[20]

The news of Ambassador Jones's arrest reached Tennessee. George wrote the Confederate Secretary of War that he wanted to be a career Confederate officer. George attached letters of recommendation from General Bushrod R. Johnson and Ambassador Jones's Southern political friends.[21] Unsurprisingly, George received a commission.

In early February 1862, Captain George R. G. Jones was at Fort Henry, Tennessee, commanding an artillery battery, expecting an imminent attack. Fort Henry was in a very poor location, on low ground between a slough and the Tennessee River. Rising water flooded the fort as Union gunboats attacked. General Lloyd Tilghman ordered sixty-some men, including Captain Jones, to hold off the enemy while the other soldiers escaped. The Confederate guns fired accurately until General Tilghman surrendered. The general praised George and the other officers for "their consummate devotion."[22, 23, 24]

A *New York Times* reporter called George "a renegade Northerner, a resident of Dubuque, Iowa, and a son of Honorable Geo. W. Jones." The reporter continued:

He has always lived North, has been supported by the North (through his father), and turns against the country which has fed him.... A large number of his fellow townsmen are here, who became so indignant at finding this young ingrate, in this place, ready to train his guns upon his former associates, that they discussed the propriety of shooting him. Wiser counsels, however, prevailed, and he is left to enjoy his infamy undisturbed.[25]

The *Davenport Daily Gazette* stated, "We presume young Jones will be sent to sympathize with his father at Fort Lafayette. An unfortunate family, those Joneses."[26]

Iowa Union soldiers who met George were more sympathetic. E. M. Van Duzee, a Dubuque resident and captain of the 12th Iowa Infantry, stated: "He said he was a citizen of Tennessee, and had been for several years. He was quite cheerful, and I think was quite willing to be taken prisoner."[27] C. S. Sumbardo stated: "I had a short talk with George Jones at Fort Henry. He stated that he was through with fighting, and would like to take a tour through Europe, where I think he would be more warmly received than at Dubuque."[28]

George spent the next seven months in captivity at Johnson's Island, Ohio. The prison, located on Lake Erie, held Confederate officers. A fellow prisoner, Maj. Joseph Barbiere, described George as "elegant." Barbiere stated:

Captain G.R.G. Jones, of the artillery, is a son of George W. Jones, late Senator from Iowa, to the United States Congress. Jones deserves credit for espousing the cause of the South, yielding his prospects for place and preferment, to take up arms for his adopted State, Tennessee; he is an accomplished gentleman, and a versatile genius, being one of the best musicians in prison.[29]

On September 1, 1862, George was paroled and sent to Vicksburg. Two months later, he was in Richmond, seeking an appointment as ordnance officer in General Tilghman's brigade. General Tilghman stated: "I deem him one of the most valuable men we have ... sacrificing Home, Property and friends, he has now proven himself an able and zealous soldier." Jefferson Davis commented: "Capt. Jones as the son of my early and valued friend has to me special interest and I rejoice to find that his merit as a soldier has proved equal to his zeal for our cause."[30]

In spring 1863, George left Vicksburg "to join Johnston's forces." Thereafter, U.S. Grant began his siege. When Confederates surrendered Vicksburg, a company of the 21st Iowa Infantry captured George's trunk. The *Dubuque Daily Times* announced: "Besides several articles of clothing and an excellent fiddle, this trunk contained letters of the most treasonable character, from several residents of Dubuque."[31]

George served the rest of the war in western Alabama and eastern Mississippi. After the war, he practiced law in Memphis. He got married and was awarded patents for a fan rocking chair and an inkstand.[32, 33] George died on January 2, 1905.

Ramblin' Man: An Impatient Iowan in the Confederate Navy

Twenty-year-old Midshipman William H. Wall was grinning the day he resigned from the U.S. Naval Academy. Dreaming of success in business, he went home to New London, Iowa, in 1858. He became a clerk as local businesses failed.[34] Gloomy men walked the streets, and Wall became alarmed. Facing the ugly truth, Wall knew he had made the mistake of his life.

After a year in New London, he tried to regain his place at the naval academy. No luck: the vacancy had been filled.[35] Wall went to Mississippi in summer 1860.[36]

Wall quickly made political contacts in Sardis. He enjoyed "the full confidence of the entire community" in less than a year. In spring 1861, before the war started, local residents asked President Jefferson Davis to appoint Wall a Lieutenant in the Confederate Army. The men stated, "You will greatly oblige your friends."[37]

But Wall did not wait for an appointment. Instead, he enlisted as sergeant in the 12th Mississippi Infantry. The unit was too late to fight at Bull Run, so they returned to Mississippi. Wall served as adjutant in Col. Henry Hughes's partisan cavalry.

Back in New London, Wall's younger brother, Charles—an Iowa native—enlisted in the Sixth Iowa Volunteer Infantry.[38]

Wall told Confederate Senator A. G. Brown that he was determined to be a career officer. Wall's first choice was a commission in the army, his second choice, the navy.[39] He was quickly appointed to serve on the gunboat *Atlanta*, outside of Savannah, Georgia.[40] The *Atlanta*'s commander, William McBlair, complained: "The lieutenants I have now are from civil life, miserable sticks. I would not give a penny for a cord of them."[41]

Wall moved to Charleston, South Carolina, serving two years aboard the ironclad *Chicora*.[42] The next stop was Richmond, Virginia, where Wall commanded the gunboat *Drewry* until Union artillery destroyed her in January 1865.

Wall and his superior officer, Capt. Charles W. Read, headed across the shrinking Confederacy for Shreveport, Louisiana. They had a bold plan; they hoped to run the gunboat *Webb* down the Red River, past New Orleans to the Gulf of Mexico, "to be used as a privateer."[43]

The Union Navy controlled the Mississippi River. Federal gunboats lined its banks "every ten to fifteen miles." Wall and Read crossed the river into northern Louisiana and found the *Frank Webb*, a side-wheel paddleboat, docked in Shreveport.[44]

They loaded the *Webb* with firewood and coal, and used 190 cotton bales as armor to protect the machinery. The *Webb* bristled with weapons: a 30-pound Parrot gun, two 12-pound howitzers, and five torpedoes, one of which was "projecting from the bow, supported by a long pole."

On April 7, 1865, the *Webb* left Shreveport, northwest Louisiana, chugging toward Alexandria in the center of the state. Two days later, Lee surrendered at Appomattox. By late April, the future of the Trans-Mississippi Department was in doubt, and Louisiana residents were increasingly demoralized.[45]

On April 23, under a murky pre-dawn sky, the Webb shoved off from Alexandria, disguised as a Federal boat. Slipping past a squadron of Union vessels below Simmesport, it entered the Mississippi River. The *Webb*'s crew cut telegraph lines as they traveled.[46, 47]

Federals identified the *Webb* as Confederate outside of Donaldsville, but she faced no opposition until she approached New Orleans. Raising a U.S. flag, she went full speed ahead (25 miles per hour) past the city. Dodging cannon balls from Union picket boats, she took three minor hits. Pursued by a Federal gunboat for 20 miles, the *Webb* raised the Confederate flag.[48]

Practically tasting freedom, the *Webb* sailed within range of the Federal steam sloop *Richmond*. As the *Richmond* opened fire, Capt. Read headed back north but was trapped between the two Federal vessels. Battered by shells, Capt. Read ran the *Webb* aground on the east bank of the river. Read and Wall set the *Webb* on fire. Captured later that day, April 25, they were sent to Fort Warren in Boston Harbor. Wall took the oath of allegiance to the U.S. government on June 13, 1865, and returned to Mississippi.[49]

Thereafter a Mississippian, Wall married, had children, and worked in business and banking.

A Worthy Challenge

The explosion rocked the horse. Shying to get away, it dumped James Ramsey Moore onto the ground. Intense back pain took his breath away. Staggering to his feet, James hobbled after his horse, grabbed its reins and walked back to his unit.

Born in 1835, James Ramsey Moore didn't stand out among the ten children in his strict Presbyterian family in Pennsylvania. He was a lackluster student at Washington and Jefferson College, where he managed to graduate in 1858. His parents farmed him out to his successful uncle, Dr. Joseph C. Hughes, dean of the College of Physicians and Surgeons in Keokuk, Iowa, where James enrolled and apprenticed in his uncle's private hospital.[50]

Every aspect of this life was new: the grueling studies, ministering to patients amid blood and gore, and even the freedom of being away from home. James finally had a challenge worthy of his sweat and tears, and he began to flourish. Family and friends remarked that James's "character rapidly developed, and he became studious, self-reliant, manly, and strong in principle and purpose."

Buried deep in his work, James little noticed the political turmoil embroiling the country. He might have stayed in Keokuk and completed his medical degree, but an enticing opportunity appeared: he could practice medicine in Mississippi, where his oldest sister and her husband lived.

Around the time of Fort Sumter, James alighted to Natchez, Mississippi, a community known for its intelligence and culture. Putting up his shingle, he examined three partially paralyzed patients—a landscaper, a stone mason, and the African-American foreman of a plantation—who had not responded to other physicians' treatment. Under James's care, they returned to work.[51]

This news spread fast. The Mississippi State Hospital hired James, and he encountered diseases new to him. Hungry for knowledge, his supervisor allowed James to take a leave of absence and study at the New Orleans School of Medicine. He needed to learn about diseases fairly prevalent in the South, including malaria, yellow fever, pellagra, and hookworm.[52]

While James attended lectures and visited New Orleans hospitals, back in Iowa, Governor Samuel J. Kirkwood appointed James's uncle to be the state surgeon general. Dr. Hughes organized and supervised the army hospitals at Keokuk, which treated as many as 2,000 sick and disabled soldiers at a time.[53]

While his uncle cared for Union soldiers up North, the Confederate Army came calling for James. A professor of surgery recommended James as an assistant surgeon, and he enlisted in May 1862 in Conner Battery, 1st Mississippi Artillery.[54, 55]

The soldiers appreciated James's professional demeanor. Chief surgeon Boyd said, "He is a remarkable man, both in professional ability and powers of endurance. If he don't break down, he will have few equals in the army."[56]

His unit went to Grand Gulf on the Mississippi River, where the Union Navy engaged Confederate troops. James mounted a horse, secured his leather medical bag, and headed for the front line. Hearing shouts, James saw a Confederate cannon fire at a Federal gunboat.

The gunboat lobbed a shell that exploded near James, throwing him off the horse and onto the ground. Severely bruised on his back, James went to Port Gibson for medical treatment. He moved into a home to recuperate. The bruise turned into a carbuncle, probably infected with staphylococcus bacteria.[57] The almost non-existent knowledge of germs meant doctors could not help him, and the wound festered. Sweating mightily, James unknowingly guzzled contaminated water and contracted typhoid.[58]

Headache, lack of energy, and dry coughing led to high fever and gastro-intestinal distress. James's older sister and her husband tried to comfort him. Bedridden for the third week, James became delirious. The gifted physician could not heal himself, and a Presbyterian elder came calling. In moments of lucidity, James turned to the Great Physician, asking Jesus to save his soul.

Up in Keokuk, his mentor-uncle, Dr. Joseph C. Hughes, helped wounded and disabled Union soldiers. Hundreds of miles south, in a shaded room choked with sweltering heat, James Ramsey Moore died on August 1, 1862. His comrades buried him in an unmarked grave in Natchez.[59]

In the Shadow of an Older Brother

Having famous doctors in the family—not just an uncle, but also a brother—makes it hard to find one's own path. Benjamin William Dudley tried to step out of two long shadows. At age fifteen, the Kentucky native attended Western Military Institute. He and his family moved to Keokuk, Iowa, in 1855.[60, 61]

His father may have owned the Dudley House hotel in Keokuk. Benjamin began studying medicine at Kenyon College. He next studied at the College of Physicians and Surgeons in Keokuk. Sometime around Fort Sumter, he graduated.[62]

Benjamin seemingly lost no time heading to Kentucky. He was appointed Assistant Surgeon of the 2nd Kentucky Infantry in September 1861, but the Dudley family was divided. Benjamin's half-brother Ethelbert left his teaching position and recruited a company of Kentucky Union troops. Ethelbert died early in the war.

On January 28, 1863, the Confederate Medical Department ordered Benjamin to transfer to General George B. Cosby's staff. Benjamin wrote Major General John C. Breckinridge: "I am sorry that I am thus separated from you and my friends from Kentucky, but I have been placed in as pleasant a position as I could be, separated as I am from my friends and relatives."[63]

Benjamin served as General Cosby's *aide-de-camp*. After the war ended, Benjamin W. Dudley practiced medicine in Ohio, New York City, and Lexington, Kentucky, where he died on July 3, 1884.

A Doctor with a Hand in Politics

Critics abound in the typical life of public service. Some complaints are warranted, and some wounds are self-inflicted. J. B. Edelen fit this pattern and gained a checkered reputation. Maryland native J. B. Edelen served on Maryland University's faculty and taught medicine in Washington, D.C., in 1848, at the age of twenty-four.

Four years later, at twenty-eight years old, Dr. J. B. Edelen did contract medical work with the U.S. Army, in New Mexico Territory.[64] He moved to Burlington by 1856. He advertised his medical practice on the front page of the *Burlington Weekly Hawk-eye*, and he got busy in local Democratic party politics.[65] He gave a speech at the Fourth of July celebration in 1857.[66] Shortly before he arrived, Congress had established a marine hospital in Burlington, completed in 1858.[67] It was "handsomely located" upon a bluff.

The federal government spent $200 to recruit a surgeon and doctor at the marine hospital. They selected Edelen. A rumor suggested that he was chosen because powerful local Democrats had pulled strings in President Buchanan's administration.

The marine hospital caused a ruckus. Republican critics called it a boondoggle, a political sop thrown to then-majority Democrats. It was a small building, and Republicans claimed "When the physician, and his steward, and servants get in, there will be no room for anybody else. It will always be full without a single patient." It was alleged that Edelen actually engaged in full-time political work for the Democratic party.[68, 69]

The critics were eventually proven right: the marine hospital treated only five patients before it was shuttered and sold in 1867.[70, 71]

Notwithstanding rumors by Republicans, Edelen worked with the Des Moines County Medical Association, starting in 1860. He served with Dr. John F. Henry, father of another future Des Moines County Confederate.

About three months after Fort Sumter, Edelen, age thirty-seven, enlisted as a private in the 2nd Kentucky Infantry.[72] He later served as a hospital steward, similar to a chief administrator. Historian Michael A. Flannery explains:

> Hospital stewards would implement the prescriptions of physicians from materials supplied by purveyors, all of whom were groping to understand the nature and cause of invisible enemies—*pneumococcus, streptococcus, staphylococcus, E. coli, Entamoeba histolytica, Vibrio Cholerae,* and many others—decimating their comrades worse than the cannon fire of their adversaries.[73]

Edelen also needed enough pharmacy knowledge to run the dispensary. His skills included reading prescriptions in Latin and keeping track of medicines.

Edelen later became an assistant surgeon at a hospital in Bowling Green, Kentucky. Next, he transferred to General John Hunt Morgan's Kentucky cavalry in February 1862. Edelen served as assistant surgeon, and then surgeon.[74]

At least one Union Army soldier from Burlington recognized Edelen after the Battle of Shiloh. The *Burlington Hawk-eye* reported: "Doctor Pendleton, the Democratic nominee for Clerk of Des Moines county, and Doctor Edelen, Physician and Steward of the Marine Hospital at Burlington ... are both in the rebel army and both fought against us in the Battle of Pittsburgh Landing."[75]

The newspaper made a mistake: Pendleton was actually a lawyer, not a doctor. Edelen took on the extra duties of medical purveyor for Morgan's headquarters in June 1862. Medical purveyors were responsible for ordering and distributing all medicines, and assuring their quality.

While Edelen served in the field, Burlington Republicans complained about Iowa Democrats who, supposedly, sympathized with the South. The *Burlington Hawkeye* editor stated:

> If these men would go South where they belong, it would be a great gratification to all honest people. If they would imitate Pendleton and Edelen, of this City, who thought the South was right, and accordingly went there and engaged in the war in behalf of the rebellion, we should give them credit for a little manhood, though our admiration for their intelligence and their patriotism would not be greatly magnified.[76]

In early 1863, Edelen was on detached service as a surgeon and as purveyor. While his compatriots joined Morgan's Great Raid into Kentucky, Indiana, and Ohio, a Confederate provost marshal arrested Edelen for drunkenness. He was relieved from the position of medical purveyor of Joseph Wheeler's Cavalry Corps. It is uncertain whether he drank in response to the pressures of performing surgery under discouraging conditions, or in response to high mortality rates. Historian Herman Norton comments:

> The South's drinking problem was acute. A good portion of the estimated 64,000 gallon daily output of ardent spirits undoubtedly reached army personnel, and officers, especially surgeons, were accused of drinking much more than their share. The lowly soldier escaped the charge of drunkenness, mainly because his supply was cinched by his alcoholic superiors.[77]

Edelen was apparently tried and transferred to the 4th Georgia Cavalry (which later became the 12th Cavalry), where he practiced surgery. Edelen was also appointed major.

At the end of the war, he surrendered and was paroled on May 3, 1865, in Charlotte, North Carolina. He traveled to Nashville, Tennessee, and took the oath of allegiance later that month.

After the war, Edelen lived in Louisville, Kentucky, and worked as a doctor for the municipal government.

Even the Smartest Can Fall

Stomach pain was the first sign that something was wrong. As it developed into acid reflux, vomiting, and gas, Dr. Philip Van Patten searched for a cure. Then depression hit, sapping his confidence and mental sharpness. Self-doubt, dismay, and dread battled for supremacy inside the physician who couldn't heal himself.[78]

Intellectually inclined Philip Van Patten was a New York native. Born in New York State in 1827, his father died when he was thirteen, so Philip, his mother, and his two brothers moved to Davenport, Iowa.[79] Father Pelamourges, a distinguished Catholic priest, taught Philip the classical languages Latin, Greek, and Hebrew.[80] Philip enjoyed doing mathematical proofs every morning.

For a man of Philip's ability, medicine seemed a good career. He enrolled in the College of Physicians and Surgeons in Keokuk, Iowa, and he apprenticed under Dr. Asa Morgan in DeWitt, not far from Davenport. Philip was a newly minted M.D. at age twenty-six.

He intended to teach future doctors at the Keokuk medical school, but he changed his mind and moved to Arkansas. This was to be a new stage of life in every way. Twenty-seven-year-old Philip soon proposed to Mary Miller, who had a young son. Philip married into a politically active Arkansas family. His father-in-law had been a Democratic presidential elector in 1836 and 1840, and his brother-in-law, William Read Miller, became Arkansas's twelfth governor after the Civil War.[81]

While practicing medicine and raising a family, Philip discovered an interest in politics. Voters elected him as Arkansas state representative in late 1860 and early 1861. He earned a little extra money by serving as acting surgeon of the 16th United States Infantry at Little Rock. After Arkansas seceded, Philip entered the Confederate service.

He became a physician employed under contract, and eventually he was appointed surgeon of the 13th Arkansas Infantry on February 17, 1862.[82] Less than two months later, on April 8, the 13th Arkansas entered the crucible at Shiloh, enduring "heavy and dangerous fire."[83] Philip and his tiny medical staff struggled to treat the seventy-three wounded men in their regiment. Some of the wounds were severe.

Confederate surgeon B. W. Allen stated:

> No one could imagine fully the labor required ... the "wear and tear" of both mental and physical energies, both by day and by night; the tainted atmosphere in spite of ventilation and disinfectants; the want of proper medicines; the lack of necessaries and comforts upon the sick and wounded; the moans of the dying—all were calculated to break down the strongest Surgeons....
>
> I have often wondered how, with comparatively nothing, we the Surgeons, who went through with it all and always saw the darkest side, ever got along as well as we did.[84]

In the aftermath of Shiloh, Philip could not cope with the emotional and physical stress. Three weeks after the battle—and one day before the regiment was reorganized—he resigned. He cited dyspepsia (digestive problems) and general ill health.

Philip took a break from practicing medicine, and he reentered politics. In November 1862, Philip served a second term in the Arkansas General Assembly. After the war ended, he practiced medicine, tended to inmates at the state penitentiary, and served as U.S. pension agent, and every day, he delighted in reading the classics for half an hour.[85]

Word drifted back north to one of Philip's Davenport classmates that he was "a member of the Arkansas legislature, an ardent abolitionist but a bitter secessionist during the war."

Dr. Philip Van Patten died on July 20, 1890, in Forrest City, Arkansas.

Ministering in the Name of Jesus

Gripping the leather reins, Joseph S. Howard guided the horses up a bumpy road toward his parents' house. Praying for wisdom and grace, he wondered how his father and brother John—a Union Army veteran—would receive him.

A life marked by wanderlust started early, with infant Joseph shoe-horned inside a covered wagon, bumping along rutted trails, headed into the as-yet-unformed Iowa Territory. His father, a preacher, planted Cumberland Presbyterian Churches in that virgin territory in 1835. The preaching bore fruit, and the second congregation in Iowa met in the family's home in Lee County. The family later moved to Lucas County, Iowa.[86, 87, 88]

Joseph first preached to a group of Cumberland Presbyterians in Oskaloosa, Iowa, in 1857. This experience must have suited him, because he enrolled in ministerial studies at McGee College in the "Little Dixie" area of northern Missouri. He married a local woman, Margaret Frances Hannah, whose parents reportedly owned slaves. Joseph impressed family members with his growing ability to speak several languages and read Sanskrit.

Margaret bore Joseph a daughter in 1861. After Fort Sumter, Joseph entered Sterling Price's Missouri State Guard as a recruiting officer and soldier.[89] (The Guard later entered the Confederate service.) He also served two months as a chaplain.

As Joseph experienced a soldier's life, his parents remained in Lucas County, and an older brother, John, enlisted in the Union Army in Kansas.

The following April 29, 1862, Joseph was in Rienzi, Mississippi, where he enlisted as a private in the 2nd Missouri Infantry. He engaged in the Battles of Farmington, Iuka, and Corinth. Joseph was appointed regimental chaplain on July 6, 1862, at the recommendation of his commanding officer, Col. Francis M. Cockrell.

History doesn't record how Joseph spent his time as chaplain. Many Confederate chaplains helped medical staff, but other military clergy picked up rifles and fought. Historian Herman Norton writes:

> The large majority of Confederate chaplains simply could not reconcile prospects of maiming and killing enemy troops with their sacred calling to render comfort and blessed assurance. They chose the dilemma's traditional horn, but—sensitive to the situation—seldom criticized their fighting brethren.[90]

Chaplains became part of the camp environment. Confederate Captain John Dooley, a son of Irish immigrants to Virginia, told a joke after seeing a Baptist chaplain "dunking" some new converts. Dooley wrote:

> Looking at those drenched Baptists reminds me of the village-countryman who one day, perceiving an old acquaintance of exceeding bad repute, undergoing a similar operation in the clutches of a Baptist minister, stopped his horse and sang out to the minister, "I say, mister, I don't wish to interfere with any of your religious ceremonies, but if you want to get all the sin out of that fellow, you'd better keep him under a thundering long time."[91]

Joseph's unit left Vicksburg in June 1863, prior to the Union Army and Navy's iron-grip siege. Joseph spent the rest of the year in Demopolis, Alabama, and Meridian, Mississippi. He saw his wife, Margaret, sometime in 1862 or 1863 because she bore him a second daughter in 1863.

Joseph served in the Atlanta campaign in 1864 as part of Cockrell's Brigade, French's Division, Stewart's Corps, in the Army of the Tennessee. He ended the war on May 4, 1865, when General Richard R. Taylor surrendered near Mobile, Alabama. Howard family tradition states that his father told him to not to come home to Iowa, but Joseph visited anyway, and his family warmly greeted him.

Joseph spent his post-war career in a South full of grieving people in a devastated land. He returned to Missouri, teaching Natural Sciences at McGee College, Macon County, from 1867 to 1874. He then became president of three successive women's colleges in Mississippi, Tennessee and Texas.[92]

Practicing the Arts of War: From Central Iowa to a Confederate Armory

The Spirit Lake Massacre got peoples' attention. Iowans were shocked to read that Chief Inkpaduta and his Wahpekute Dakota warriors had murdered whites of all ages and both sexes. A letter arrived, claiming that Chief Inkpaduta's band would raid Fort Des Moines. As alarm rose among nearby white settlers, the warriors grew to mythic proportions.

Men armed with hunting rifles and shotguns formed a militia. Captain John C. Booth took command and drilled four companies of these recruits. Polk County historian L. F. Andrews wrote: "The whole town was aroused with military spirit. For a week, pomp and circumstance of war, the fife and drum, kept enthusiasm at high pitch." Scouts galloped north and debunked the rumors. Andrews stated, "The incident ... disclosed the patriotism of the community."[93]

Booth was a Georgia native who had graduated from West Point in 1848. He was commissioned a brevet second lieutenant in Artillery. His postings included the Augusta Arsenal in Georgia and operations in Florida against the Seminole Indians.[94]

He resigned from the U.S. Army on May 1, 1856. He spent the next three years working as a civil engineer in Des Moines. In 1859, Booth took a job as clerk in the Illinois Central Railroad.[95]

On March 11, 1861, Booth offered his services to the Confederate secretary of war, calling it an "honor" to do so.[96] On March 29, Booth took command of the Baton Rouge Arsenal in newly seceded Louisiana.

After Virginia seceded, the federal armory at Harpers Ferry became a potential prize for the Confederacy. On April 18, Union defenders set the armory buildings on fire and rushed out. Virginia militiamen rushed in, doused the flames, and salvaged a great deal of equipment, arms, and components.[97] Three days later, North Carolina militiamen peacefully seized the arsenal at Fayetteville. It was quite a prize, containing an armory, gun carriage and caisson shops, and machine shops.

Booth assumed responsibility for the Fayetteville Arsenal on July 27. He started enlarging a building and converting flintlock muskets to faster-loading and more reliable percussion-cap weapons.

In the fall of 1861, machinery for making rifles (including rifles with sword-bayonets) arrived from Harpers Ferry. Thirty-six machinists and workmen came, too.

The Fayetteville Arsenal turned out about 500 rifles per month, along with small arms ammunition and carriages for heavy artillery (for sea coast defenses) and light artillery. The arsenal also produced two unique guns, the Fayetteville Pistol-Carbine and the Fayetteville Rifle.[98]

In March 1862, General Robert E. Lee formed plans for security of the North Carolina seaboard. Josiah Gorgas, ordnance chief in Richmond, ordered Booth to place obstructions in the Cape Fear River below Fayetteville.[99] Booth became sick, but he "worked incessantly."[100] A colleague wrote that Booth kept "growing weaker, until he was forced to take to his bed, and in a few short months he died."[101]

The colleague noted that Booth was "a splendid executive officer ... universally loved by the entire armory force." John C. Booth reportedly died of consumption (that is, wasting disease, possibly tuberculosis) on September 6 or 8, 1862.

Industrious Man

The smell of leather filled the tannery. Ambrose Key worked hard, knowing that Texas soldiers needed him to make all-important leather. The state actually needed more entrepreneurs like him.

The Texas State Library and Archive Commission states:

> At the dawning of the war, the South had almost no industry. What little did exist—sawmills, flour mills, cotton gins, wagon makers, bakeries, distilleries—was of a small-scale and served agricultural needs. For the most part, manufactured goods had always been imported from the North or overseas. Now the South would have to scramble to catch up under wartime conditions.[102]

Unlike many Confederate states, Texas was largely peaceful during the war. Many troops remained in the state and saw little combat. William H. Neblett, a soldier in the 20th Texas Infantry, called it "an extremely monotonous and tiresome life."[103] State and Confederate officials seized the opportunity to address wartime shortages. They developed factories (to produce military goods) staffed by civilians and soldiers on detailed duty.

Ambrose Key was born in Ohio in 1829. At age nine, his family moved to Louisa County, Iowa. He ran a business in Wapello, Iowa, in 1856, and he bought eighty acres of land. He moved to Texas two years later, where he bought a sash, door, and blind factory; ran a general store; bought a sawmill; and started a tannery. In 1859, he traveled up to Missouri to marry "an intelligent and accomplished lady." Ambrose and Mary lived in Washington County, Texas.[104]

After the war began, Ambrose's father, George, came to Texas and never returned. While Ambrose lived in Texas, four of Ambrose's brothers enlisted in Iowa regiments. An Iowa regimental history states that their father, George, had been drafted into a Texas unit, but he was too old to be drafted at sixty-six years of age. George reportedly died in Texas in 1864.[105]

Ambrose's skills were a good fit for Texas. The Texas State Library and Archives Commission states that the Confederate Field Transportation Bureau had factories in seven locations. The factories tanned leather for shoes and made harnesses, saddles, and wagons.[106]

Ambrose was detailed to work in a tannery in Falls County, Texas.[107] A tannery in San Antonio was "processing 2,500 sides of leather per month, and converting a good proportion of the hides into boots, brogan, belts, and horse equipment" by March 1864, according to historian Kerby.[108] Nonetheless, the Confederacy continued to be plagued by shortages of factories, manpower, and goods.

General Edmund Kirby Smith surrendered his Trans-Mississippi Department forces on June 2, 1865, but Ambrose's 20th Texas did not surrender until a month later, on July 6.[109] The following year, Ambrose returned to Louisa County, Iowa, to settle his father's estate.[110] Until he saw his family members, Ambrose may not have known that his brother, David, had died at Shiloh.

Ambrose bought out his siblings' interest in their father's estate, and then he moved his wife and children from Texas to Missouri and lastly to Kansas. He was involved in a freighting business, and then growing fruit. Ambrose Key died in 1908.

Farm Laborer in the Cavalry

When a man cannot use his legs, he realizes how much he depends on them. Lying immobilized, Miles Ramay had time to remember the excitement of joining the 4th Missouri Cavalry. So much had happened in that month before the fateful Battle of Pea Ridge. Miles had earned the respect of other men; he was elected 4th Corporal; and he rode a horse! It was a long way from the dusty road he had walked as laborer on his father's rundown farm.

Miles was born in Ohio in 1838 to a father from Virginia and mother from New Jersey. The family moved to Louisa County, Iowa, in 1845 when Miles was seven.[111] At age eighteen, he worked as a farm laborer, possibly helping his father run his farm.

Miles moved to Cooper County, Missouri, in 1860 and worked as a farm laborer.[112] He left behind his parents, four sisters, and a younger brother. Five months after Fort Sumter, Miles was a private in the Missouri State Guard.[113] He rang in the new year by joining Co. "A," 2nd Missouri Cavalry, as a fourth corporal. He enlisted for the duration of the war.

A slight wound early in the war paled in comparison to being "severely wounded in the legs" at the Battle of Pea Ridge, March 7–8, 1862. It took six months to recuperate. He next attended company muster roll in September 1862.

The 2nd Missouri Cavalry served under the overall command of numerous generals, including Nathaniel Bedford Forrest. Miles's comrade, Sergeant James T. Ellis, evokes the near-constant movement of the 2nd Missouri Cavalry. Ellis wrote in his diary: "25 Dec. 1863, Christmas morning. Christmas gift—we will spend this Christmas in the saddle. We crossed the river in ferry-boat and took the Sardis road. Passed through town at three o'clock and camped six miles northeast of town."[114]

Miles was promoted to fourth sergeant in March 1864. The following month, Miles fought in the Battle of Fort Pillow, Mississippi. A year later, just after Lee surrendered at Appomattox, Miles was promoted to sergeant. This short-lived promotion ended when the 2nd Missouri Cavalry, under Lt. Gen. Richard Taylor, surrendered to Maj. Gen. Edward R. S. Canby at Citronelle, Alabama, on May 4, 1865.

In about 1873, Miles married a Mississippi belle and farmed in what is now Panola County. Miles and his wife, Martha, had nine children.[115] When his father died, Miles received a $10 inheritance.[116] Miles reportedly did not talk much about his Iowa family.[117] In 1923 at age eighty-nine, Miles Ramay died.

Blue Collar Brothers in Texas Units

Dividing the chores between them, brothers Charles and George stroked the horses' flanks with currycombs until they gleamed in the sunlight. The boys learned the soft-spoken ways of gaining a horse's trust. This knowledge would prove useful during wartime.

Charles Bernidot Harris and George Webster Harris drove horses as teamsters while living in their native Iowa. Their mother and father had been born in Maryland and New Jersey. When Charles and George were eighteen and sixteen respectively, they left Jackson County and moved to Texas with their father in 1853.[118, 119, 120]

Charles got hitched first, marrying Sarah White in 1856. He worked as a teamster, took his bride to San Antonio, and they started having children. The young family moved to Sherman, Texas, near the Indian Territories, and George and his father joined them. George was a carpenter, and he wedded Mary Jane White. They had a baby boy in 1859.

The brothers went different directions during the war. George enlisted first, joining Co. "A," 11th Texas Cavalry, on October 12, 1861.[121] They fought at Elkhorn Tavern (Pea Ridge) on March 6–7, 1862. Thereafter, the 11th Texas Cavalry served as rearguard for the army. Later that year, Mary Jane was in Arkansas and gave birth to a son. George worked as a teamster for much of 1863, and the next year, Mary gave birth to a daughter in Arkansas.[122] The rest of George's service is unknown.

Charles waited two years to enlist. He and Sarah moved from Sherman, some 350 miles southwest, to San Antonio, and then Charles enlisted in Co. "A," Benavides Cavalry Regiment in April 1863.[123] The next year, Charles and his comrades drove back the 2nd Texas Union Cavalry from Brownsville in southernmost Texas.

Promoted to sergeant, he transferred to Co. "G" and surrendered with General Edmund Kirby Smith at New Orleans on May 26, 1865. Two months later, Charles was paroled at Port Lavaca, Texas.

Many years after Appomattox, Charles received a Confederate pension and died in 1919.[124] George was a laborer, and it is not known when he died.

Farmer Turned Confederate Pensioner

Planting, plowing, chopping wood, and flailing grain marked the days on the hardscrabble farm. Andrew Van Knight knew no other life. The grinding, unrelenting labor made for hard muscles, but sometimes a parched soul. In the fight for survival, at least he had his own horse.

Andrew spent his formative years in Iowa. Born in Ohio in 1841, he moved to Wapello County, Iowa, in 1845, where his father bought a farm. Andrew moved to Missouri during the presidential election of 1860.[125, 126]

The following year, six months after Fort Sumter, Andrew enlisted in a Missouri State Guard unit that became the 4th Missouri Cavalry, Confederate.[127] His horse was worth $80 and his equipment $5. In mid-1863, his unit dismounted. Late in 1863, Andrew had more financial troubles, going five or six months without pay. He transferred to Capt. Pratt's Battery, Tenth Texas Field Artillery, on February 1, 1864.

Andrew returned to Missouri in autumn 1864 as part of General Sterling Price's invasion. Price encountered stiff resistance and retreated along the Kansas–Missouri border. The Tenth Texas Artillery fought a rearguard action with Federal troops dogging them into the Indian Territory. Andrew's unit closed out the war in a way repeated by many Texas troops. After they heard that Lee surrendered, they lingered until they disbanded in June 1865 near Marshall, Texas.

In the decades after the war, Andrew married Delilah (an Arkansas native), had two children, and farmed.[128] He received a Texas Confederate pension from 1916 until he died in 1930.

Fortune Favors the Bold: From Iowa to Arizona, one Man's Tale

The slow journey in the covered wagon was bearable, if only because they were together. Day after day, Melinda Miller tended their two young boys while Winchester drove the mules. They stopped for a Texas roadblock. An official barred them from going West because war had broken out.

Their dream of finding gold in California crumbled to dust in a moment. They consoled each other, We just need to be patient. Surely, the war will end soon. And so they settled down in Texas, not knowing the challenges awaiting them.[129]

Winchester Miller and his wife, Melinda Young, started married life as farmers in Van Buren County, southeast Iowa, in 1857.[130] Melinda bore two sons, and Winchester eyed the lingering California Gold Rush.

Saying goodbye to both sets of parents, Winchester and Melinda left for California. They took the southern route through Texas. When Confederates fired upon Fort Sumter, authorities did not let the young family proceed further.

Winchester and Melinda settled in Texas. A daughter was born in 1862. Later that year, twenty-seven-year-old Winchester enlisted as a private in the 17th Texas Infantry.[131] He moved through the ranks, rising to third lieutenant and then second junior lieutenant. In 1864, Melinda became pregnant again. Nine months later, she died in childbirth, leaving three young children.

The war ended, and Winchester returned home. He could not care for his children alone. Winchester saddled up a horse and a mule for a 700-plus-mile journey to Iowa. He rode the horse with his small daughter in his arms. His young sons rode in "kayaks"—tough rawhide boxes draped over both sides of a mule.[132]

Once they arrived in Iowa, he divided up the children between his in-laws and his parents. Winchester then headed to California, again through Texas.

Discovering that the Gold Rush was over, Winchester moved to Arizona. He became Maricopa County Sheriff. Winchester later told a friend that "it was necessary" for him to hang two Native Americans. Some 250 fellow tribe members wanted to avenge their deaths, so they came looking for Sheriff Miller.

Winchester's friend shared the following tale with an Arizona historian:

> One day not long after he had given the two Indians their quietus, as Miller was standing in the yard near his house, his quick eye noted rising in the distance a great cloud of dust rapidly approaching.... Stepping into his house ... [he] took his rifle from its peg, buckled on two cartridge belts, stuck in a couple of six-shooters and a knife, and returned to the yard....
>
> As soon as they were in speaking distance, Winchester bellowed at the top of his lungs, "Now is a good time to begin the shooting!"... The moment one started forward, he was met with the cold muzzle of Winchester's gun. He watched every move and instantly checked the slightest show of advance, meanwhile constantly pouring at them at the top of his voice a string of epithets defying them to advance.[133]

Winchester claimed to have single-handedly held off the warriors for two days. Reportedly, "Ever afterwards, both Indians and Mexicans held Winchester Miller in great respect."

Winchester married a local woman, farmed, and had more children. One of his Iowa sons, at age fifteen, rejoined his father in Arizona. Active in Democratic Party politics, Winchester helped found Tempe, where he died on November 29, 1893.

Madison County Mystery: Hard-Scrabble Farmer Turns Dedicated Confederate Soldier

The Union doctors staunched the bleeding and cauterized his fingers and hand. After Napoleon Bonaparte Morgan healed, he was exchanged. Not really surprised that Confederate surgeons declared him "unfit for field duty," N.B. Morgan found other ways to be useful.

Napoleon Bonaparte Morgan was a Virginia native who had nine brothers and sisters. They moved to a farm in Madison County, Iowa, southwest of Des Moines, before the Civil War. Napoleon worked as a laborer on his father's farm, with no land and few possessions to his name.[134]

Five months after the war began, twenty-five-year-old Napoleon fought for the Confederacy at the Battle of Lexington, Missouri.[135] He had enrolled in the 1st Missouri Infantry (later to become the 2nd Missouri Infantry).

It is unclear why Napoleon entered the Confederate service; he may have simply needed a job. Once he donned a gray uniform, Napoleon climbed the ranks, being promoted fourth sergeant by August 1862.

The next year, on May 16, 1863, he fought at the Battle of Champion Hill, at Baker's Creek, Mississippi. He "lost [a] thumb and two fingers" of his right hand, and Union troops captured him. He was immediately released on parole, but he was exchanged (that is, declared legally free to fight) four months later. Back in his unit, Napoleon became a quartermaster.

The following year, 1864, he was demoted to private and became a "wagon master." On October 5, Napoleon was captured at Allatoona outside of Atlanta. He ended up in Camp Chase prison, Ohio. A month later, Napoleon applied to take the oath of allegiance, but the prison authorities held him until the war was over.

Apparently, Napoleon steered clear of Madison County for a few years and lived in Warren County. He ran a sawmill, and he still had no personal estate or real estate.[136]

Twelve years after the war ended, in 1877, Napoleon served as street commissioner for the brand-new town of St. Charles in Madison County. Two years later, he ran a hotel in town.[137] Thereafter, he fades into obscurity.

Teamster in Texas

J. Amos Burgoon's Grapevine Mounted Riflemen lacked rifles and pistols when he enlisted in June 1861.[138] This condition was common among Texas units throughout the war, according to historian Robert L. Kerby.

Joseph Amos Burgoon was born in Ohio in 1830. His father was an Ohio native, and his mother was born in Maryland. In 1847, when J. Amos Burgoon was seventeen years old, his family moved to Scott County, Iowa. They moved to Texas in 1853.[139, 140]

J. Amos Burgoon enlisted as a private in the Grapevine Mounted Riflemen in Tarrant County, Texas, on June 1, 1861.[141, 142] Six months later, J. Amos Burgoon enlisted in Co. "A," 9th Texas Cavalry on January 1, 1862. He worked as a teamster, driving wagons. Perhaps J. Amos, like most Texans, preferred to ride a horse rather than walk.

After the war ended, he married Minerva Milliken, and they had nine children. J. Amos Burgoon died in Texas on December 19, 1889.

Equine Trader Extraordinaire

The full moon watched in silence as Edward S. Flint rode his horse toward the huge Union supply train. On either side, comrades from the Five Sovereign Nations mingled with Texans, all waiting for a signal to attack. Confederate cannons opened fire, punctuating the war cries of Cherokee, Creek, and Seminole soldiers. By mid-morning, triumphant Confederates headed south from Cabin Creek with 130 Union wagons and 740 mules. The Federals couldn't let Rebels ride off with so much booty. Later that day, Col. James M. Williams's Second Brigade attacked the Confederates at Pryor's Creek. Historian Steven L. Warren writes:

> Fooling the Federal commander into thinking the train was being parked for the evening, at nightfall [Confederate General Richard M.] Gano ordered his men to light campfires and repeatedly drive an empty wagon across rocky ground. Then, under the cover of darkness, Gano rolled the wagons to the northwest and escaped with captured supplies valued at an estimated $1.5 million.[143]

Horse-riding skills came easily to New York native Edward S. Flint. Born in 1830, he ran away from the family farm and worked on the Erie Canal. His next job was clerk in a Chicago warehouse. As he entered adulthood, in 1850 he married Virginia native Margaret Nichols. Edward moved to Iowa in 1852 and bought a piece of land (probably with his older brother, Christopher, a land speculator).[144]

In 1854, Edward moved to Bell County, Texas, and began a lifetime of wheeling and dealing. He bought a farm on credit and made improvements on the land, but he could not make the payments. Next, he borrowed $4,700 to buy a half interest in a herd of mustang ponies. The business of raising and selling ponies was to be successful for the next twenty years, although he lost a lot of money after Confederates fired on Fort Sumter.

In July 1862, a year after the war started, thirty-two-year-old Edward enlisted as a private in Captain J. P. Morris's Company, 1st Regiment Texas Partisans.[145] Edward's horse was worth $200 and his equipment $25. His unit shortly became the 30th Regiment Texas Cavalry.

Edward's superior officers noticed his horsemanship and made him a messenger. Mainly he served in Indian Territory (present-day Oklahoma), Arkansas, and Louisiana. He later stated that he "had many narrow escapes from the [Union] Indians, [and] participated in several battles."

The Five Sovereign Nations in Indian Territory were all Confederate allies. Historian Charles D. Greer states that the 30th Texas Cavalry transferred into Brigadier General Richard M. Gano's Brigade in summer 1863—a move designed to protect the Indian Territory. In one raid into northwest Arkansas, 500 troopers from the 30th Texas burned 133 bales of Union-held cotton and destroyed two cotton gins.[146]

The 30th Texas Cavalry followed this feat a year later with the astonishing raid at Cabin Creek on September 19, 1864. Later that year, Edward ran his regiment's commissary department. In the spring of 1865, Texas troops melted away after the demoralizing news of Appomattox. Edward's final days in uniform occurred on the Red River, the border between the Indian Territory and Texas.

Business boomed in peacetime. Hitting the ground running, Edward parlayed seven ponies into a 320-acre farm. Land speculation was next, buying a half-league of land (about 2,200 acres) and parceling it out to seventeen families. Adding general contractor to his list, he built forty homes and improved many farms. Beyond all this, he farmed his own land and managed nine other farms. As his fortunes increased, so did his personal tribe, growing to eight children.[147] Edward S. Flint died in 1930.

Unanswered Questions

Bullets whizzing, clunking and whanging through the air riddled the battle flag. Urging the two brigades to hold off the Yankees, the colonel and lieutenant-colonel dropped dead. Amid the uproar, Maj. Seneca McNeil Bain was promoted to lieutenant-colonel.

Bain was born in 1833 to New York natives of Scotch descent. Bain graduated from Union College, Schenectady, New York, in 1854, and moved with his parents and siblings to Iowa. He was appointed land agent in Newton, Jasper County.[148, 149]

In 1857, Bain moved to Holmesville, Pike County, Mississippi.[150, 151] He began teaching and married a Pennsylvania native, Tillie. Bain was twenty-seven when Tillie gave birth to a boy, Eddie, on October 13, 1858. Joy turned to grief when Eddie died eight months later. That same year, Bain began studying medicine in New Orleans. In between semesters, Bain taught school in Holmesville. Tillie bore another son, O. G. Bain, in early 1860. Bain graduated from medical school in spring 1861.

Shortly after Fort Sumter, Bain stood alongside 107 Southern patriots in the Court House Square of Holmesville and enlisted in the Quitman Guards as a third lieutenant.[152] His unit became Co. "E," Sixteenth Mississippi Infantry, a month later, and they transferred to Virginia. Bain was elected second lieutenant and appointed assistant surgeon.[153] On April 16, 1862, he was elected captain. He may not have known that back in Iowa, his three brothers enlisted in the Union Army.

Bain's regiment supported Stonewall Jackson early in the Shenandoah Valley Campaign and participated in the Seven Days campaign before Richmond. At the Battle of Second Manassas, Bain's company engaged Yankees. They took casualties at Sharpsburg and repulsed repeated Union attacks at Fredericksburg, Maryland. After the battle ended on December 15, 1862, Bain's regiment quartered in the town of Fredericksburg.

"A cold, freezing blast howled through the camps of the shivering armies."[154] Short of firewood, blankets, clothes, and food, Captain S. M. Bain went absent without leave. When he returned in late December 1862, he was tried and court-martialed. Bain was suspended for six months, starting February 20, 1863. During that time, he received no pay and had to stay with his unit. Historian Jack A. Bunch comments that Bain functioned "as a man temporarily without power."[155]

Bain's unit participated in the Battle of Chancellorsville and played a supporting role at Gettysburg. Shortly after Gettysburg, Bain resumed command of his company.

The following year at the Battle of Spotsylvania Courthouse, on May 12, 1864, the Quitman Guards were part of two brigades that held off some 40,000 attacking Yankees. The 16th Mississippi's battle flag was hit by 250 bullets, and their colonel and lieutenant colonel were both killed. Bain received a battlefield promotion to lieutenant-colonel (later approved by the Confederate Congress).

On August 27, 1864, Bain was captured at the Weldon Railroad along with fifteen other Quitman Guards. Imprisoned at Old Capitol Prison, Washington, D.C., and then Fort Delaware, Bain was quickly paroled, exchanged, and returned to the Confederate service on November 15, 1864. This parole and exchange was unusually fast for that period of the war.

Bain's unit served Robert E. Lee's Army of Northern Virginia for the last five months of the war. Bain surrendered with Lee's army on April 9, 1865, at Appomattox Court House.

After the close of the hostilities, Bain returned to Mississippi and practiced his profession in Pike County, and then, in 1867, came to Coryell County, Texas. The next year, thirty-five-year-old Bain married fourteen-year-old Annie Bray. They had five sons. (It is unclear whether Bain's first wife, Tillie, had died, or they had divorced.) Annie outlived Bain who died in 1901. She collected a Texas Confederate widow's pension from 1909 until she died in 1929.[156, 157]

An Iowa county history says that Bain was "compelled to enter the Confederate service," but a Texas county history merely states that Bain, a native of New York, enlisted in the Confederate army. One of his former soldiers, Private Luke W. Conerly, stated, "A better soldier never served in the Confederate Army than Col. S. McNeil Bain."

Gifted Doctor, Unpredictable man

Death arrived innocently enough that sultry day. A blockade runner from Tampico, Mexico docked at Galveston, full of bantering sailors, cargo, and mosquitos.

Unbeknownst to the crew (or doctors, for that matter), the mosquitos carried the Yellow Fever virus of the Flaviviridae family. The first victim, a sailor named Graves, was the harbinger of many others as mosquitos spread through Galveston, depositing their infected eggs.

The second victim, a civilian named Warren, ejected black vomit before he died. Many residents panicked and fled. Many others (unable to leave) had redness of the whites of the eye, nausea, and vomiting.

Local doctors rose to the challenge as thirteen residents fell to Yellow Fever and three died. Dr. William H. Farner, on detailed Confederate service, thought people transmitted the disease to others. Nonetheless, he braved the danger, examining and comforting patients as the death toll mounted to 250 people.[158]

Farner's admirers stand out as exceptions in a controversial professional career.

He first practiced medicine and was active in the Liberty Party (later the Free Soil Party) in Wisconsin in 1848.[159] Farner moved his family to Lee County, Iowa, and practiced medicine.[160]

In 1856, he left medicine to edit a Democratic paper, *The Statesman*.[161] He also served on the Democratic State Central Committee.[162]

The next year, Farner rejoined the Free Soil Party, moved to Polk County, and co-edited a "Free Soil" Republican paper, *The Iowa Citizen*. He gave speeches across Iowa for John Fremont, the presidential candidate of the brand-new Republican Party.[163, 164]

Co-editor J. M. Dixon described Farner as short with a large mouth, sunken cheeks, and thin lips. Farner's clothes, wrote Dixon, "were of the most slovenly and dirty character." Dixon stated:

> [Farner] was a prodigious consumer of whisky. He drank early in the morning, and drank often [throughout the day].... [He drank] until every other man was under the table; and yet this little fellow ... was never known to be unsteady in his gait....
>
> He was a fine speaker ... [with] a bold, dashing, impromptu style, always supported by a native impudence.... He was the most remarkably sober drunkard.
>
> When on the street, he was always seen with three or four hunting dogs at his heels, for which he provided more liberally than for his six children and his patient, broken-hearted wife, who were suffering in a dreary shanty.[165]

The Iowa Citizen changed owners. By 1860, Farner's family was back to Wisconsin, and he worked as a doctor in Council Bluffs, Iowa.[166, 167]

Three months later, he took a load of pharmaceutical drugs to Denver. He was elected to the Denver City Council in April 1861, just before Fort Sumter.[168, 169]

Farner had a large medical practice among the 1st Colorado Infantry. This unit was formed to defend the territory against Rebels in the wake of Bull Run. The doctor was "a successful practitioner" among the soldiers.[170]

When the regiment left Colorado *en route* to New Mexico (to fight Confederate General Sibley), they impressed vehicles and livestock. Farner exposed their misdeeds in a letter to the editor of *The Rocky Mountain News*. The soldiers were furious.[171]

Farner quickly packed his bags and headed—where else?—to Texas to join Sibley's Confederate forces. One Colorado soldier hoped that Farner would be hanged "to purify the atmosphere from the taint of secession."

W. H. Farner became an assistant surgeon with Riley's Regiment, 4th Texas Cavalry, in April 1862.[172] He was stationed at Fort Bliss, Texas. A year later, Farner was captured at Bayou Teche, Louisiana, and paroled on May 11, 1863, below Port Hudson.

Farner bought twenty slaves (possibly as a broker) in Caddo Parish, Louisiana. Farner valued the slaves at $14,000, and "refugeed" them to Brazos County, Texas, far from invading Yankees.[173]

Now a slave owner (at least on paper), forty-two-year-old Farner married twenty-four-year-old Sallie Swindler in Brazos County. It is assumed that Farner and his wife, Mary, had gotten a divorce.

In 1864, Yellow Fever hit Galveston, making a "gradual, persistent, and fatal march from house to house." While Farner battled the disease, his son and namesake, William Henri Farner Jr. joined the Wisconsin Infantry Volunteers.

Farner surrendered with other Trans-Mississippi forces at Millican, Texas, in Brazos County, on June 26, 1865. Less than six months later, former slave-owner Farner worked for the Freedmen's Bureau in Millican. He served the Republican administration. His goal? To see that former slaves were paid and treated fairly.

Historian Dale Baum explains, "Farner was too sympathetic to the planters and often too quick to administer cruel physical punishment to the ex-slaves." Some freedmen complained that Farner punished them, stringing them up by their thumbs. In May 1866, military authorities ordered his arrest.[174]

Farner wanted to be appointed "District Judge, or Chief Justice of the County." He cited his "years of sacrifice & toil for the present dominant party." Farner listed his Republican credentials: "I started the first out & out Radical paper ever issued in the State of Iowa [and] canvassed the State for Fremont and Dayton.... Our efforts swept over the State like a whirlwind ... revolutionized the State and forever fixed it a brilliant satellite in the galaxy of universal freedom."[175]

He was not appointed to the bench, but he became a Radical Republican newspaper editor. In that role, he helped a former slave appeal for help from the Freedmen's Bureau. Thereafter, Dr. Farner moved to Illinois, practiced medicine, and died in 1878.

Farner's former co-editor Dixon recalled: "A sense of personal obligation never startled his conscience. He was without sympathy, and without affection, and without any grace which has its abode in the human heart; and yet he was hypocrite enough to seem to have them all in profusion."[176]

Diarist at Siege of Vicksburg

Union mortar boats, sloshing in the Mississippi River, face Fortress Vicksburg. A captain yells "Open fire!" and mortar shells ascend in beautiful curves over the Confederate bastion. They descend with fearful velocity, striking, pounding, shaking the ground. Concussions and tremors endanger civilians and sick and wounded soldiers. The firing ceases for a while. Two hours before daylight, Union cannonading resumes. No rest for the weary, including Samuel K. Fowler, son of a circuit-riding preacher.[177]

Born in Ohio in 1841, Fowler moved with his family to Lee County, Iowa, in 1850 and thence to Missouri in 1856 or 1857.[178, 179, 180] Fowler divided his time between working as a clerk and riding the preaching circuit with his father. Fowler joined the Missouri State Guard on December 8, 1861.[181] A month later, he and his younger brother, Greenfield T. Fowler were in Springfield, Missouri, a hub of Confederate activity. The brothers enlisted in Co. "F," Second Missouri Infantry (Confederate) on January 13, 1862.[182] Later that year, a third brother, James J. Jackson Fowler, enlisted in the 21st Missouri Infantry (Union).[183]

Samuel K. Fowler served throughout the Civil War, starting with Pea Ridge, Corinth, and Big Black River. Fowler wrote an unpublished 300-page diary, mainly focusing on the Vicksburg campaign. He often missed the brunt of meeting Union forces head-on, simply because his company was often kept in reserve. He expected that people would someday read his diary.

One afternoon in September 1862, Fowler wrote:

> I am very contentedly reclining upon the side of a precipitous slope, being a quiet retreat I gained by exercising due precaution in my descent.... Our Camp is established on the top, extending to the verge of this romantic declivity, at least 100 feet above its base. I am much pleased with the location as it affords me a place, where I can sit undisturbed and reflect upon the thousands of changes that have figured upon the vast theatre of war, and also indulge in an unbroken reverie of thought.[184]

The following month, Fowler's unit attacked Union forces at Corinth, Mississippi. They heard the "thunder of ponderous cannon and the bursting of prodigious bombs." Their colonel shouted and pleaded "ever onward," and they obeyed "through the double charges of grape and canister that showered like hail around us, at every step decimating our ranks." The "most athletic and daring" soldiers led an attack on the Union lines, opposed by "persistent cannoneers [who] stood to their posts with the tenacity of life itself." Their colonel shouted, "Onward my brave boys, one more effort!", and their unit captured some thirty pieces of artillery. But Fowler and his comrades were too far in front of other Confederate troops, and they retreated, leaving behind the hard-fought cannons. The larger picture was even worse, and General Earl Van Dorn ordered a retreat. Fowler noted, "Feeling considerably dispirited about the disastrous result of the battle."[185]

He describes the nighttime retreat:

> About sunset the rain began to descend and soon rendered the road exceedingly slippery and difficult to travel either by man or beast. Our march was much

impeded ... we were soon enveloped in deep, impenetrable darkness. The rain continued to pour in incessant torrents upon our devoted heads, thoroughly drenching us from head to foot. The earth beneath our feet was converted into a vast sheet of water, and in the road the depth attained in many places was near a foot. Move forward fifty or 100 yards and fall down, roll over once or twice, and up again only to repeat the performance, seemed to be the order of the night....

The darkness was so intense that the use of the eye was of no avail whatever.... Still on we went, splashing unceremoniously through mud and water, now and then being greeted with a boisterous explosion of laughter in front or near the convincing evidence that some poor unfortunate was prostrate in the mud.

We continued our march until about 11 o'clock p.m. when we were halted for the night. The rain had abated, and we rolled up in our saturated blankets and slept sweetly, however remarkable and strange it may appear to the casual reader, to those who have not experienced such exposures and hardship.[186]

Fowler discusses the difficulty of writing memories of war instead of keeping a diary of observations. He states:

Grasping and retentive indeed must be that memory, that in future months can thread the intricate labyrinth of the vast ocean of scenes of peace and happiness; of scenes of blood and carnage; of scenes of sufferings and sorrows; trials and turmoil; strife and revelry ... and unravel all the multiplied concomitants there ... and expose to light and reason the latent mysteries of ten thousand actual events once witnessed.[187]

Wounded twice in the foot in the siege of Vicksburg, he surrendered on July 4, 1863. Fowler and many others were paroled two days later.

He was promoted to fifth sergeant and served under General Joseph E. Johnston outside of Atlanta. Fowler later served under General Hood at Altoona Pass. Wounded at the Battle of Franklin, Tennessee, he was captured in Columbia, Tennessee, on December 22, 1864, and recuperated in the U.S.A. General Hospital in Nashville. Sent to Louisville and then Camp Chase POW camp in Ohio, he was paroled and exchanged in February 1865, in City Point, Virginia. Suffering from "debilitas" (weakness or feebleness), he entered the Jackson Hospital in Richmond before heading to Mobile, Alabama, to join Confederate troops.

The Union victory at Appomattox largely quenched the roaring fire of Confederate independence. Many exhausted and dispirited troops, including Fowler, left the ranks.

Later in 1865, Fowler taught school for three months. He then raised livestock in Knox County, Missouri, and he ran for county clerk. He married Martha A. Campbell, and they had four children. Samuel K. Fowler died in 1918 in Edina, Missouri.

Geography and the Influence of Southern Culture

"Not Afraid of any Damned Yankee That Ever Breathed!": A Belligerent Surgeon from Iowa

Marrying a local belle and buying two slaves, Dr. P. V. Whicher moved steadily away from his Iowa roots and deeper into Louisiana society. Patterson Venable "P. V." Whicher, long-time resident of Muscatine, Iowa, was the son of a well-known U.S. District Attorney for Iowa. P. V.'s father was a Connecticut Yankee, his mother a Kentucky belle.[1]

Born in Kentucky or Ohio in 1827, P. V. was named after his mother's family, the Pattersons and the Venables. Family tradition states that the Venables sympathized with the South.[2]

P. V. graduated from Tulane Medical School in New Orleans in spring 1851.[3] He sojourned in Iowa before entering Southern society. In 1854, he practiced medicine in Bayou Sara, Louisiana, and three years later married a Louisiana belle named Rosa Dashiell in St. Francisville, near Bayou Sara.[4]

P. V. acquired two slaves. He tried to purchase more slaves at an estate sale, but this effort was challenged in court.[5,6] Rosa gave birth to a son in 1859. After Fort Sumter, P. V. became assistant surgeon in the Second Regiment, 8th Brigade, of the Louisiana Militia.[7]

P. V. impressed Homer B. Sprague of the 13th Connecticut Infantry. According to Sprague, on May 23, 1863, P. V. was arrested in his buggy near Port Hudson, not far from Bayou Sara.

Sprague's Recollection of P. V.

Sprague relates that P. V. was "evidently a man of some education and ability, a little under the influence of stimulants, and a perfect embodiment of chivalry"—that is, until he was arrested. P. V. had asked the names of regiments and brigades, and where the pickets were.

Soldiers escorted P. V. in his buggy to see their colonel, and the fireworks began.

"Who are you?" said the Colonel.

"What business have you to ask me that question?" [P. V. asked from the buggy.]

"I command this regiment, and I have a right to know who's in my camp. Your conduct has been very suspicious, and I demand to be answered, and answered in a respectful manner."

"It's none of your damned business. I shall go to General Grover, damn you, and report your damned insolence," replied Dr. Whicher.

"You are my prisoner, sir, and you need not try to intimidate me," said the Colonel.

"I try to intimidate you! I swear that's a ___ ___ bright idea! I try to intimidate you in the presence of the whole Yankee Army!... ___ ___ you and your army!"

"You infernal puppy!" said Colonel Warner, "you shut up your mouth. Lt. Norman ... take this man to the General.... He refuses to disclose his name, and I suspect him of being a spy."

"I'm not afraid to disclose my name. My name's Whicher. I'm a surgeon of the Confederate line ... I'm not afraid of any damned Yankee that ever breathed!... I dare you to fight! I'll fight you with pistols, I'll fight you with rifles, I'll fight you with bowie-knives."

Springing upon his feet in the buggy, Dr. Whicher struck his right fist violently into the palm of his left hand, gesticulating fiercely, defying us all and spitting out a torrent of curses.[8]

The troops seized his horse and buggy, his roast chicken and corn bread, and his shirts. Then they turned him over to the provost marshal.

The war ended, and P. V. died two years later, on May 10, 1867 at St. Francisville, Louisiana.

Popular Officer and Doctor

Following his older brother's Southern trajectory, Francis Whicher left Iowa and attended Western Military Institute at seventeen years old.[9] Francis then attended Tulane Medical School in New Orleans.[10] Returning up North with degree in hand, Francis practiced medicine in Muscatine, Iowa.[11] After his father died in early 1856, Francis moved to Louisiana and got established in a community.[12]

In April 1861, Francis Whicher joined the Lake Providence Cadets, which later became part of the 4th Louisiana Infantry.[13] He was popular with the recruits who elected him captain of a company.

Francis Whicher had a very short military career. He died of pneumonia on January 6, 1862 in New Orleans.[14]

From Catholic Student to Confederate Artillery Officer

The college students ran across the yard at double-speed with bayonet-tipped muskets. They stopped and divided into two pin-cushions, thrusting the bayonets outward and upward to repel cavalry attacks.

The Zouave drills had everything Andrew J. Quigley could want: Fencing with the bayonet, agility, and precision. They were modeled after the most elite fighting men in the world, Algerians in the French Army. Best of all, Andrew and company had esprit de corps.[15, 16]

Andrew J. Quigley was born in Iowa in 1837.[17] His father, Patrick Quigley, was a native Irishman who emigrated to St. Louis, then moved to Dubuque. He eventually became mayor and represented Dubuque County in the Wisconsin Territorial Legislature in 1837.[18, 19] Patrick Quigley cast his lot with George Wallace Jones, personally and politically.

Dubuquers knew Andrew's father for his "integrity, honesty and devoted interest to the public welfare." The *Dubuque Herald* commented on Andrew's father: "[He] would stand up in a legislature, in the City Council, in a political convention, and declare his views, even if he stood alone, and would vote alone, if necessary, to leave his name as a protest of the record."[20]

Andrew's father was a devout Catholic who hosted the first Catholic worship services in Dubuque in his house. He sent Andrew to St. Mary's College and Seminary in Emmitsburg, Maryland, in 1855. A good student, Andrew earned excellent marks in Bible, Greek, Philosophy, and Latin.[21]

Andrew was greatly influenced by Professor Daniel Beltzhoover. This West Point-trained math teacher was commandant of the Mountain Cadets who drilled and marched in parades. An *alumnus* of Mt. St. Mary's remembered that Professor Beltzhoover had "drilled us thoroughly on Eardin's and Casey's tactics.... The Zouave Drill formed an important feature of our training."[22]

While Andrew was taking classes, his father, Patrick Quigley, and George Wallace Jones visited Washington, D.C. Senator Jones took Patrick Quigley to meet his friend Senator Jefferson Davis who was convalescing at home with a "diseased eye." Patrick Quigley kept Davis company most of the day. According to Jones, Patrick Quigley became a "great admirer and friend"—that is, a political friend—of Jefferson Davis.[23]

The following year, Andrew received a bachelor of arts degree from Mt. St. Mary's on June 29, 1859. A reporter for the *Catholic Mirror* predicted that Andrew would be noted for his religion, morality, talents, and achievements.

Andrew returned to Dubuque and, in 1860, studied law.[24] His father shared Jefferson Davis's belief that any state could secede from the Union. Patrick Quigley used the penname "Senex" to state this belief in the *Dubuque Herald*. He wrote:

It is not surprising to find so many men, who, we should suppose, ought to know better, denying the right of a sovereign State on any account to separate from the Union. To deny this right is to deny State sovereignty, and to deny State sovereignty is to deny the legality of all Gov't under this Union of States.[25]

About a month before Fort Sumter, Andrew's old professor Beltzhoover headed to Louisiana to enter the Confederate service.[26] At least thirty of his current and former students followed him to Louisiana, including Andrew.

On July 6, 1861, Andrew was appointed second lieutenant with the Louisiana First Heavy Artillery and transferred to Fort St. Philip (across the Mississippi River from Fort Jackson), located to protect New Orleans from attack by ships.

Back in Dubuque, Republicans and pro-war Democrats smeared Patrick Quigley and the Jones allies as "secessionists."[27] When reporters learned that Andrew's older brother had also entered the Confederate service, the *Dubuque Daily Evening Union* suggested that Patrick Quigley was ornery enough to do the same.[28]

The following spring, on Good Friday, April 18, 1862, the Union Navy launched a campaign to capture New Orleans. For six straight days, shipboard mortars lobbed 200-lb. shells at Fort Jackson and Fort St. Philip, with the ships remaining outside the reach of Confederate cannons. Second Lieutenant Andrew J. Quigley and others sheltered inside Fort St. Philip's massive casements.

In the predawn darkness of April 24, Union vessels approached Fort Jackson and Fort St. Philip. Confederate artillery opened fire, and Union vessels fired five-second shells, followed by rapid-fire grapeshot and canister, turning the Mississippi into a "fiery channel." Acrid smoke clouded the river. All batteries at Fort St. Philip fired furiously except for the upper water battery, manned by recruits too green to even handle shotguns.[29] Andrew gathered some veterans and took over the upper water battery. Captain William J. Seymour describes the action:

> The roar of the artillery was deafening; the rushing sound of the descending bombs, the sharp, whizzing noise made by the jagged fragments of exploded shells, the whirring of grape shot and hissing of cannister balls—all this was well calculated to disturb the equanimity of the strongest nerved man.[30]

A chaplain yelled that hell could not be more terrible than the sight of Fort Jackson. Andrew and crew pressed on, with "gallantry, energy, coolness, and bravery worthy of imitation." Union vessels sailed past the forts and captured New Orleans. Inevitably, Fort St. Philip and Fort Jackson surrendered on April 28.[31] Andrew was paroled, went to Brooklyn, Alabama, and was exchanged.

He reentered active service as an ordnance officer at Vicksburg, Mississippi. He reported to Lt. Col. Daniel Beltzhoover, his old drillmaster at Mt. St. Mary's. The *Dubuque Daily Times* mistakenly reported that Andrew led a "cowardly and murderous" attack on a Union commissary wagon train in Hartsville,

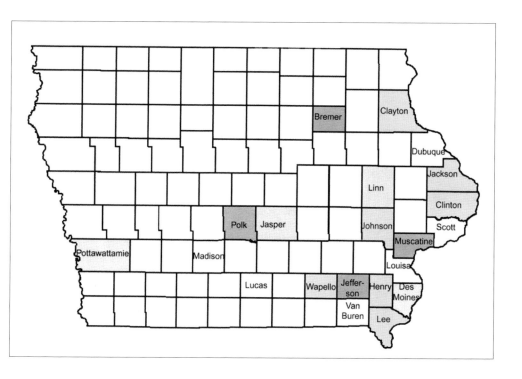

Above: The seventy-six Iowans lived in these counties before serving the Confederacy. (*Census Bureau*)

Right: Secretary of State William H. Seward (pictured) seized Ambassador George Wallace Jones's correspondence and placed him in prison for two months. (*Library of Congress*)

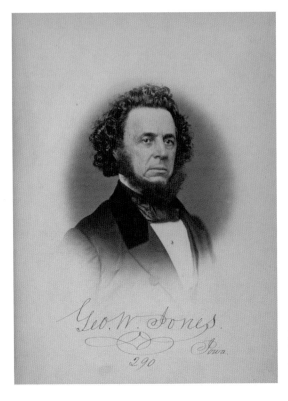

Iowa U.S. Senator George
Wallace Jones, father of
two Iowa Confederates.
(*Library of Congress*)

Jefferson Davis as U.S. Senator
in 1859. (*Library of Congress*)

President James Buchanan (pictured) appointed George Wallace Jones as minister to Grenada, present-day Colombia. (*Library of Congress*)

Secretary of War Edwin M. Stanton authorized law enforcement officials to arrest anyone who discouraged enlistment. (*Library of Congress*)

(DECEASED)
DUBUQUE.

Dennis Mahony's editorials in the *Dubuque Herald* often criticized the Lincoln war effort. He was arrested and imprisoned without trial in 1862. (*History of Dubuque County, Iowa, 1880*)

The partisan U.S. Marshal for Iowa, Herbert M. Hoxie, arrested Iowa Democrats who he suspected were disloyal. (*State Historical Society of Iowa*)

Samuel J. Kirkwood, Iowa's governor for most of the war. (*Library of Congress*)

Artistic Junius L. Hempstead became a warrior who suffered in a POW camp. (*Kathryn Neese*)

DUBUQUE.

Republicans castigated former Gov. Stephen Hempstead because of his son Junius's Confederate service. (*History of Dubuque County, Iowa, 1880*)

Mrs. Lavinia Hempstead and her husband agonized over their son Junius's captivity as a POW. (*State Historical Society of Iowa*)

Annie (Miller) Jones and her husband, Charles S. D. Jones, left for Virginia in early 1862. (*Stephanie O'Neill*)

General Bushrod R. Johnson (pictured) had taught Charles S. D. Jones and George R. G. Jones at Western Military Institute. (*Library of Congress*)

Jefferson Davis received several letters from Charles S. D. Jones during the war and one afterwards. (*Library of Congress*)

Several prominent Iowa Democrats asked Charles Mason to help free their Confederate sons from prison or obtain a pardon. (*State Historical Society of Iowa*)

Several Iowa Confederates or their parents contacted President Andrew Johnson, asking for a pardon. (*Library of Congress*)

Herman H. Heath offered to serve the Confederacy and then became a Union officer. (*Library of Congress*)

Albert H. Newell died at Fort Delaware POW camp. The town fathers of Danville, Iowa, didn't want to bury his body in the local cemetery.
(*Jim Williams, Randel Bailey*)

William V. Burton fled to Missouri to avoid conscription in the Union Army. (*Barbara Wells*)

John F. Henry stayed in Iowa until mid-1863 when he made the perilous journey through Union lines. (*History of the Henry Family, 1900*)

Dr. John F. Henry (father of Iowa Confederate John F. Henry) had been personal physician to David Davis, an architect of Abraham Lincoln's presidential nomination. (*History of the Henry Family, 1900*)

Fort Henry, Tennessee, was named after Confederate Senator Gustavus A. Henry (Iowa Confederate John F. Henry's uncle). (*History of the Henry Family, 1900*)

Congressman Josiah Bushnell Grinnell worried about Copperheads long before the murder of the marshals in October 1864. (*Library of Congress*)

James H. Williams was first an Iowa and then a Virginia state legislator. (*Library of Virginia*)

Right: Former Iowa Congressman Lincoln Clark argued with James H. Williams about the legality of suspending the writ of habeas corpus. (*State Historical Society of Iowa*)

Below: James H. Williams and Cora deMovelle Pritchartt were engaged, broke it off, then married after the war. (*Phil and George Williams*)

Engraved by J.C.Buttre

Lincoln Clark

OF DUBUQUE, IOWA.

Confederate officer Spier Whitaker Jr. was later commissioned as a major during the Spanish-American War. (*State Archives of North Carolina*)

Right: Judge James Grant (pictured) tried to get his captured cousin, Spier Whitaker Jr. paroled and exchanged for one of Spier's boyhood friends from Davenport. (*State Historical Society of Iowa*)

Below: Married life was stressful for Charles S. D. and Annie Jones, John and Nancy Shipley, and Moses S. and Julia Douglass. (*Library of Congress*)

Left: Quartermaster John Shipley gathered food, as did this unidentified Confederate. (*Library of Congress*)

Below: Refugees such as Moses S. Douglass's wife, Julia, fled homes throughout the South. (*Library of Congress*)

1861   The War For the Union.   1865

1861 Photographic War History. 1865

306.   Refugees Leaving the Old Homestead.
[FOR DESCRIPTION OF THIS VIEW SEE THE OTHER SIDE OF THIS CARD.]

Rebel Prisoners, Camp Morton, Indianapolis

Above: Camp Morton POW Camp, Indianapolis, held William A. Musser. (*Library of Congress*)

Right: John T. Lovell left a booming law practice in Dubuque to serve the Confederacy. (*Library of Virginia*)

J. T. Lovell.

Successful attorney Spier Whitaker Sr. served as military aide to North Carolina's governor. He returned to Davenport after the war. (*State Archives of North Carolina*)

Union officials blamed General John Winder (William S. Winder's father) for hellish Andersonville Prison. (*Library of Congress*)

George Washington Swailes had trouble donating cemetery land because of his Confederate service. (*Biographical Review of Henry County, Iowa*)

Lt. William H. Wall dressed something like Lt. John Grimball of the C.S.S. *Shenandoah* (pictured). (*Library of Congress*)

Left: James Ramsey Moore was an Iowa medical student who became a Confederate assistant surgeon. (Kathryn Neese)

Below: This unidentified surgeon represents conditions faced by J. B. Edelen and surgeons on both sides. (*Library of Congress*)

Dr. Philip Van Patten resigned after treating soldiers during the Battle of Shiloh. (*Kathryn Neese*)

James Ramsey Moore, J. B. Edelen, and Philip Van Patten likely had dress uniforms similar to this unidentified member of the Confederate Medical Corps. (*Library of Congress*)

Left: Teamster Napoleon Bonaparte Morgan may have used a bullwhip like this unidentified soldier in a Union uniform. (*Library of Congress*)

Below: William H. Farner refugeed slaves to the Texas interior, to put them out of reach of Union troops. (*Library of Congress*)

657.   A Negro Family coming into the Union Lines.
[FOR DESCRIPTION OF THIS VIEW SEE THE OTHER SIDE OF THIS CARD.]

Warner Lewis Sr. was a close friend of U.S. Senator George Wallace Jones. Two of Lewis's sons entered the Confederate service. (*History of Dubuque County, Iowa, 1880*)

George Conner Hayden's path led from Iowa to Kansas to Texas. (*David Hayden*)

Jacob Taylor Hayden (pictured) and his four brothers, including George Conner Hayden, wore Confederate gray. (*Samuel Ross Penny*)

Robert R. Lawther was a Muscatine grocer and city treasurer before becoming a Confederate colonel. (*Wendell Lawther*)

William Campbell.

Cavalryman William Campbell had many adventures during the Civil War. (*Library of Virginia*)

Abraham Lincoln (pictured) made witty remarks as he debated Stephen A. Douglas. William Campbell witnessed one of these events. (*Library of Congress*)

William Campbell arrived from Colorado in time to fight at Wilson's Creek, Missouri. He then went back to Iowa before heading to Virginia to enlist. (*Census Bureau*)

General Sterling Price (pictured) addressed William Campbell and his fellow hunters at the Battle of Wilson's Creek. (*Library of Congress*)

General Robert E. Lee (pictured) had a horse, Lucy Long, that Iowa Confederate William Campbell bought after the war. (*Library of Congress*)

General John Hunt Morgan (pictured) led a great raid into Kentucky, Indiana, and Ohio. John Haps was one of his troopers. (*Library of Congress*)

John Haps left the Confederate service with a Spencer repeating rifle, not the Colt carried by this unidentified soldier. (*Library of Congress*)

northern Tennessee, in November 1862. In reality, Andrew had remained in Vicksburg.[32]

In early 1863, Andrew participated in the Vicksburg campaign. When General John Pemberton surrendered on July 4, 1863, a Dubuque resident, Captain D. J. O'Neil of the 3rd Iowa, found Andrew and mailed a letter to his father, Patrick Quigley.[33] Paroled four days later, Andrew was not exchanged until December 20. He never was incarcerated in a POW camp. For the remainder of the war, he worked as a quartermaster in Alabama and Mississippi. He signed his final parole papers on May 10, 1865.

Three months after the end of the war, Andrew's father died. Quigley moved to Dubuque by 1867 and practiced law for at least a year.[34] He then practiced law in St. Louis and became a judge in Colorado. He also got married and had children.[35]

When Andrew was nearly fifty, he wrote a fellow Mt. St. Mary's *alumnus*. He mentioned: "Really happy days [at Mt. St. Mary's], when, with hopeful hearts and buoyant frames, we counseled and advised each other as to the different courses lying before us in a country consecrated by our fathers to Civil and Religious Liberty."[36]

Later that year, Andrew and other Confederate veterans marked the death of Jefferson Davis by meeting in Denver and writing a public letter. They stated:

History will accord him [Jefferson Davis] a niche high up in the temple of fame, and rank him first among the bravest and best of our land.... And we salute our comrades in the far South with arms reversed and sorrowing hearts, remembering that "Tis a cause, and not the fate of a cause, which is a glory."[37]

Two years later, on January 15, 1891, Andrew J. Quigley died.

The Iowan on the Confederate Honor Roll

Walking beside a wagon full of surveying instruments, the dusty trail seemed endless. Whenever Warner Lewis Jr. saw prairie grass in the distance, he remembered his older brother's surveying team. Placid prairie grass had turned into a conflagration, roaring, leaping, and killing his brother. Determined to avoid that fate, Warner Jr. remained alert.[38]

Born in Iowa in 1840, Warner Lewis Jr. grew up basking in the sunlight of his father's political friends. His father, Warner Lewis Sr. was a Virginia native who had moved with his wealthy father (and 100 slaves) to Missouri in 1818.[39] Warner Sr. served in the Black Hawk War, met Jefferson Davis, and became a close personal and political friend of Iowa U.S. Senator George Wallace Jones.[40, 41] Because of that friendship, Warner Sr. gained local fame as mayor of Dubuque, Iowa representative and senator, and Surveyor General of Iowa, Wisconsin, and Minnesota.[42, 43]

The Lewis-Jones friendship led to Warner Sr.'s eldest son, Charles, attending Western Military Institute to study civil engineering with the eldest Jones boy.[44] He thanked George Wallace Jones:

> I feel myself under great obligations to you, for the interest you have manifested in my son's welfare, and if he should live and be a respectable man … I shall not fail to remind him of the abiding obligations that rest upon him towards you for your kindness to him.[45]

The life of surveyors was risky. Charles was in a surveying party in northwest Iowa in 1855, where he died in a horrific prairie fire.

The next year, sixteen-year-old Warner Jr. enrolled at Western Military Institute. George R. G. Jones (third son of George Wallace Jones) was also a cadet. Warner Jr. transferred to Union College in Schenectady, New York, in 1858. He joined the Kappa Alpha Society.[46]

While Warner Jr. studied, his father wanted to retain his job as Surveyor General. Senator George Wallace Jones asked his close friend, Senator Jefferson Davis, to write a letter of recommendation for Warner Sr. Davis wrote President Buchanan on May 1, 1858: "I think there is an appropriateness in retaining him as the Surveyor of that portion of our common territory which he exposed his life in defending from the butcheries of the tomahawk and scalping knife."[47]

Warner Sr. thanked Senator Jefferson Davis for his "act of friendship." Warner Sr. stated: "I shall in all probability, never be placed in a condition to reciprocate this mark of kindness practically, [but] you will ever be remembered by me with the most profound respect & esteem."[48]

Two years later, in May 1860, Warner Jr. and William A. B. Jones (George Wallace Jones's middle son) joined a surveying team in Dubuque. They walked half the distance to Dakota Territory, across "naked, bald prairie." When they returned to Dubuque, Warner Jr. dropped out of Union College and started studying law.[49, 50]

Warner Jr. became friends (or acquaintances) with at least six future Confederates from Dubuque, including Iowa state representative James H. Williams.

Five months after the war began, Warner Jr. enlisted in Co. "C," 5th Tennessee Regiment, Provisional Army (later known as the 35th Tennessee Infantry), on September 5, 1861.[51] On a rainy Virginia day not long afterwards, he visited James H. Williams at his parents' house, and they spent the day playing cards.[52]

Warner Jr.'s name popped up in Dubuque in February 1862. The *Times* mistook him for a Confederate recruiting officer in Missouri, Colonel Warner Lewis. They did not realize he was one of Col. Warner Lewis's slaveholding cousins. Notably, the *Times*—a Republican paper—politely stated, "We wish the boy no harm beyond what he may meet in the common events of war. It settles the question of loyalty beyond a peradventure."[53]

Warner Jr. was appointed second lieutenant. He was wounded at the Battle of Shiloh on April 6, 1862, where many Iowa Union troops also became casualties. Less than two months later, Union troops captured Warner Jr. and a younger brother, Thomas (who served in a different unit) in Tishomingo County, Mississippi. They served time in Camp Chase and then Johnson's Island Prison Camp in Ohio. On November 22, 1862, as the winter chill set in, the brothers traveled to Vicksburg for exchange.

The following year, 1863, the Dubuque Provost Marshal complained about Warner Lewis Sr. and other "secession sympathizers."[54]

Mid-way through the war, Warner Jr. was promoted to first lieutenant and served as acting adjutant for Co. "H," 35th Tennessee Infantry.

During the Battle of Chickamauga, which occurred over two days, September 19–20, 1863, Warner Jr. and his fellow officers were on the Confederate right flank. The first day, they saw little action. The second day was a crucible. Advancing, they came within 70 yards of strong Yankee breastworks made of "logs, rocks, and rails." On Warner Jr.'s right side, Union troops poured enfilading fire. For two hours and thirty minutes, the 35th Tennessee held this exposed position as many men fell. Ordered to pull back, they gathered all their wounded and rested a few hours.

Then, back into the breech. The 35th Tennessee pushed back the Union pickets and again faced strong Yankee breastworks. Fierce fighting was followed by a wave of Union artillery and small-arms fire, breaking the Confederate lines and pushing them back 100 yards. "A complete rout seemed inevitable," but Warner Jr. and other officers rallied their men to attack.[55] Union cannons again ripped the Confederate lines until a battery was placed on a ridge and returned fire. Several Confederate regiments ran out of ammunition, but the 35th Tennessee's Col. Benjamin J. Hill saw the Union lines waver. He convinced nearby regiments to attack once more. Fixing bayonets and charging, Warner Jr. and his fellow soldiers pushed back the Union line.

Col. Hill later commented on Warner Jr. and his fellow officers: "[They] all acted well, performing their whole duty, as they had done on many former occasions. In fact, all my officers, with but two exceptions, did themselves great credit.... They are certainly entitled to a high degree of praise."[56]

About a year later, Warner Jr.'s name was placed on the Honor Roll. It was the Confederate government's award for meritorious service. The Confederate government did not have the time or money to issue medals for those on the Honor Roll. Warner Lewis Jr. was the only Iowa Confederate so honored for valor in battle.

In the winter of 1864–1865, he was in the Texas Hospital in Auburn, Alabama, where he may have convalesced through the end of the war. Following the surrender at Appomattox, Warner Jr. passed the bar exam and practiced law in Nashville, Tennessee.[57] He moved back to Dubuque in 1870 and practiced law for at least three years. He then worked for his father in the Dubuque County Recorder's Office.[58] Curiously, three of the nine Dubuque County officers in 1875 were fathers of former Confederates.

After a few years, Warner Jr. returned to Nashville, where he died in 1884.[59] A Union Army veteran from Dubuque, Josiah Conzett, recalled Warner Lewis Sr. and his family. Conzett stated: "They were fine old people ... but intensely Southern in their feelings. Those feelings were also shared by his two sons: Warner and Thomas ... [who] went South and joined the rebel army. Warner lived through it."[60]

Iowa Family Sacrifices All to the Confederacy

The trip back from California seemed slower and sadder than their departure. Failure in the gold mines smashed his dreams. Uncertain of the future, Dr. George D. Crosthwait and his three sons headed back to an Iowa in a huge economic downturn.

George D. Crosthwait was born in Virginia in 1808 and soon moved to Tennessee.[61] His father had good political connections and was friends with Generals Andrew Jackson and Sam Houston.

George Crosthwait graduated with an M.D. from Transylvania University in Lexington, Kentucky. He returned to Murfreesboro, Tennessee, to practice medicine. Dr. Crosthwait married Eliza T. Burton, and they had a large family. He was active in Tennessee politics and served in the state legislature on the Whig ticket.

About a year later, Dr. Crosthwait moved his family to Iowa City. He quickly was elected to the Iowa State Senate in 1852, but he resigned just before his two-year term was finished in 1854 and headed for California. He returned three years later amid the financial Panic of 1857, taking a temporary job as postmaster of Shueyville.[62, 63]

In August 1860, he and five other Iowa City residents called for a state convention of the Constitutional Union Party to be held in Iowa City. A Republican observer stated that Dr. Crosthwait usually sided with the Democrats.[64, 65]

A Confederate comrade wrote the following tribute to Dr. Crosthwait's sons:

> In the early days of 1861, when the South marshaled her sons to defend her firesides, the call reached ... three brothers, Shelton, Frank, and Bromfield Crosthwait. They were sons of Tennessee....
>
> They had in the fifties removed to Iowa. Here ... they still retained their love for the mother land, and, when the call to arms came, they made haste to return to it and offer their services in defense of what they deemed the rights of the South.[66]

The Oldest Brother

Shivering on the wet January night, musket on his shoulder, Shelton Crosthwait slogged toward the Yankee lines. The slippery ground diverted his mind from the impending trial by fire.[67]

Shelton Crosthwait was born in 1837 in Rutherford County, Tennessee. A friend described him as intellectually minded, "punctual, gentle, and brave." Shelton juggled academic studies with working as a printer and a newspaper compositor in Iowa City. He reportedly spoke in favor of "Southern rights."[68]

Shelton "burned with zeal" to defend Tennessee. So he gave up his business prospects in Iowa City and headed for Rutherford County. His younger brother, Frank, also went to Tennessee. They might have traveled separately, but they ended up in the same company. The day Shelton arrived in Rutherford County, he attended a barbecue.[69]

His uncle, a local judge, gave a political speech, and then someone called on Shelton to speak. Shelton gave a moving speech in tune with secession-minded Tennesseans. Shelton enlisted later that day in the "Smyrna Grays," Co. "E," 20th Tennessee Infantry.[70] At age twenty-three, he signed up for a one-year commitment. Seven months later, he was dead.

His comrade, Ralph J. Neal, called him a "model young man." Neal noted that Shelton had no ambition to rise above private.

On January 18, 1862, Shelton and his brother, Frank, and their comrades headed toward Fishing Creek, Kentucky, their first regular battle, and many of them carried flintlock muskets. They spent a wet January night, slogging through muddy roads toward the Yankee lines. The next morning, the forces met in combat. The Tennesseans' wet gunpowder increased the time for reloading weapons and caused many misfires.[71]

Shelton was killed that day at the Battle of Mill Springs, Kentucky (known to Confederates as Fishing Creek). It was the Union's first solid victory of the Civil War. About 40 percent of the Twentieth Tennessee were killed, wounded or captured. Neal recalled:

> No man could possibly have displayed more heroic courage than did he [Shelton] on the battlefield at Fishing Creek. Early in the action, he received a wound, but pressed right on, saying, "Boys, they have shot me, but I can still shoot," nor did he stop until he was pierced through by a ball, and fell dead on the field....
>
> In his death, Company E lost one of its best men, and the South one of its most deserving patriots.[72]

Three months later, news of Shelton's death reached Iowa City. The *State Press*, in Iowa City, mistakenly stated that his brother, Bromfield, had also died—and that their father was a Confederate. According to the *State Press*: "They were serving with their father in the rebel army, and deserved their fate, though not so much as he who by his example lead them into such associations."[73]

The Youngest Brother

Slipping out the back door in the early morning fog, Bromfield R. Crosthwait tried not to awaken any dogs or chickens. His plans were fuzzy. While brothers Shelton and Frank went to Tennessee, hoping to enlist, he would go southwest.

Bromfield R. Crosthwait was born in 1845 in Rutherford County, Tennessee.[74] The last of the brothers to enlist, Bromfield went to St. Clair County in west-central Missouri, along the Sac River. He enlisted in the Missouri State Guard and participated in the Battle of Lexington in September 1861.[75] Three months later, sixteen-year-old Bromfield enlisted in Co. "C," 1st Missouri Infantry, for twelve months. He identified himself as a student. Bromfield's unit later became the 2nd Missouri Infantry.

He participated in the Battles of Elkhorn Tavern (also known as Pea Ridge) and Iuka. He was wounded at the Battle of Corinth on 4 October 1862. He died that evening. He was seventeen years old.

Soon afterwards, his father heard rumors that a "young boy Crosthwait" had died at Corinth. Still grieving Shelton's death, Dr. Crosthwait contacted General Braxton Bragg. The general, in turn, telegrammed Col. Francis M. Cockrell who stated:

> The gallant youth, Private B.R. Crosthwait, was pierced through the body by a musket ball whilst charging the enemy's works at Corinth, Miss., on the 4th of October, last (1862), having almost reached the enemy's battery, and died in our hospital that night. He was buried near the battlefield.[76]

General Cheatham added a note of his own: "I regret the sad tidings this letter contains; but it is the price of liberty, and we must pay it."

Frank B. Crosthwait

Leaning against an elm tree, chin resting on a branch, his eyes followed a cannonball bouncing and bumping toward him. Frank B. Crosthwait stepped away and moved his head just before the ball struck the branch. He laughed, "At least my head wasn't there."[77]

Frank B. Crosthwait spent his early years in Murfreesboro, a place that had a magnetic attraction for him. He worked as a farm laborer in Johnson County, Iowa, in the late 1850s.

Around the time of Fort Sumter, Frank accompanied his older brother, Shelton, to Tennessee. Frank also enlisted in Co. "E," 20th Regiment Tennessee Infantry, on June 20 or July 2, 1861, at Camp Trousdale, enlisting for twelve months.[78]

One of his army friends, Ralph J. Neal, described Frank as brave, honest, "intellectual in his tastes, true to his convictions ... brave as a Spartan."[79] Frank was a color bearer during the Battle of Shiloh. During a lull in the fighting, Ralph saw Frank dodge the bouncing cannonball.

Frank was promoted to ordnance sergeant on May 16, 1862 and third lieutenant the following September. Neal recalled that Frank "was hardly old enough to be called a man, only about twenty."[80]

In late December 1862, time came full circle for Frank; he was back in Murfreesboro, where he had spent his earliest years. On the night of December 28, Frank and other soldiers attended a party at Smyrna Depot with their friends and sweethearts. Hearing that Yankees were headed their way, Frank returned to General John C. Breckinridge's Division.

The next day, Federal cavalry arrived, and Murfreesboro resident B. L. Ridley described his first impressions of battle: "It sounded like the breaking of millions of sticks, and the cannons boomed like a trip hammer sounds over a stubborn piece of heated iron. Then followed the woo-oo-oo-ing of the solid shot, the w-h-i-z-z-i-n-g, w-h-i-n-i-n-g howl of a shell."[81]

Two days later, on December 31, Breckinridge ordered two brigades to attack Union General Rosecrans. Both were repulsed. Then Breckinridge sent Frank's brigade—and another one—to attack by a different route. Frank's comrade, Ralph recalled:

He had a strange premonition that he would fall in that battle. When we were called upon to make that desperate charge from the Cowan House, he said to me: "Ralph, I would willingly give a limb to be safely through this fight. I shall not come out of it. When it is over, do not think I was taken unawares, for I feel the nearness of death as I have never felt it before."

We were very close friends, and I said to him: "Frank, I would not go into this charge feeling as you do. Keep out of this fight. You will never be criticized, for we all know your courage; and you are too useful a soldier to be spared."

But he replied: "I would rather die a soldier than to live a coward."[82]

Frank's regiment became separated from the rest of the brigade and, under withering fire, retreated across a cotton field, past rocky bluffs, to a bend in the river. The Confederates regrouped.

As Union troops advanced across the cotton field, Frank's commanding officer ordered the men to fix bayonets, scale the bluffs, and drive the enemy back. The 20th Tennessee's regimental history states "the bluff ranged from six to ten feet high." The regiment charged, the left flank struggling to climb the bluff amid a hail of bullets, the right flank easily climbing the rocks and bagging seventy-five Union troops. Frank Crosthwait died while scaling the bluff. A comrade called him one of "the bravest officers we had."[83]

After the battle, Confederates went to retrieve the bodies. Ralph recalled:

Frank was found lying with his face upturned and his feet toward the foe. His handkerchief was in his left hand. He had torn it in strips, knotted the pieces, and with it tried to stop the flow of blood from a severed artery; but, faint with loss of blood, he fell back, passing his bloody hand across his brow, and the end came.[84]

Two days after Frank died, local residents returned to Murfreesboro. One woman wrote:

Prisoners entering every street, ambulances bringing in the wounded, every place crowded with the dying, the Federal general, Sill, lying dead in the courthouse.... Frank Crosthwait's lifeless corpse stretched on a counter. He had been visiting my house and was killed on Wednesday. The churches were full of wounded where the doctors were amputating legs and arms.[85]

Frank was posthumously appointed second lieutenant. In spring 1863, about three months after Frank died, Dr. Crosthwait received a message from General Cheatham: "Sad news this to carry to a father already bereft of two gallant sons. They have left a name that will entail eternal honor on all who bear it."[86]

Swapping Land led to Confederate Service

Onlookers hummed with excitement as real-life Yankees stepped before the sequestration judge. Dr. John Hayden ordered his thoughts before speaking, remembering the long and twisty road that led him there.

Born in Pennsylvania, Dr. John had moved to Kentucky as a child, married a Virginia native, and they had children in Kentucky. He bought four slaves, farmed, and practiced medicine. Dr. John moved with his family to Van Buren County in 1847 (shortly before Iowa became a state).[87,88]

Eleven years later, in 1858, Dr. John bought 320 acres of land in Lykins County, Kansas Territory.[89, 90] This was the beginning of the family's move to Kansas and later, Texas. The next year, 1859, part of the family bought land in Kansas and lived there. In summer 1860, a newlywed son brought his bride to Kansas, and Dr. John moved there, too. The rest of the family remained in Van Buren County.

Dr. John "had strong Southern sympathies and was pro-slavery." Some of his sons had similar leanings. In contrast, many of their new Kansas neighbors were still riled by the fraudulent votes that had led to the pro-slavery Lecompton Constitution. Trouble lay just beneath the surface in Kansas Territory.

In summer 1861, after Fort Sumter, Harvey Foster, a pro-Union Texan, arrived in Kansas. He hoped to swap his Fort Worth property (and that of a neighbor named Boden) for land in the loyal North. It was serendipitous that Foster met the Hayden family. Dr. John soon came to Kansas to meet Foster.

Fortune smiled on Dr. John the day the Jayhawkers drove him out of Kansas. Most importantly, he escaped with his life. But he also returned to Van Buren County with Foster. There they settled the paperwork, swapping Dr. John's Iowa land for Foster's Texas holdings. With this trade, the Hayden family history took a new direction with unexpected troubles.

On September 27, 1861, Dr. John and his remaining family members left Iowa for Texas, making a detour to pick up his sons George and Augustus and their families. A son-in-law remained in Kansas, protecting the family's property rights.

The Haydens had a rocky start in Tarrant County, Texas, in fall 1861. The Confederate court system seized their Texas property under the Sequestration Act of the Confederate States, passed on August 31, 1861.[91, 92]

Hayden family historian Samuel Ross Penny explains that this act allowed the government to take over property of alien enemies of the Confederacy. Dr. John appealed the seizure. He claimed that his property had been purchased in good faith before the sequestration laws were enacted and that he had moved to Texas because he supported states' rights and the Southern cause. As a loyal citizen of the Confederacy, Dr. John said the Sequestration Act didn't apply to him.[93]

In 1862, he won his case. That same year, all five brothers enlisted in Co. "C," Griffin's Battalion, Texas Infantry. Four of them enlisted on the same day.

George Conner Hayden

Eldest brother George Conner Hayden was born in Kentucky in 1832. He married Sarah Struble in Keosauqua, Iowa, in 1858. He soon bought land in Kansas Territory, as did his father and brother, Augustus. In 1859, George C. and Sarah expected a child as they moved to Kansas Territory. The next year, late in 1860, they moved back to Van Buren County, Iowa, where their second daughter was born. George C., Sarah, and their daughters packed up again in fall 1861 and moved with his parents to Tarrant County, Texas.[94]

His biographical sketch states that George C. "was a pro-slavery man and a man of decided political convictions, and conscientiously cast his lot with the lost cause."[95] The following summer, on July 20, 1862, George C. enlisted in Co. "C," Griffin's Battalion, with three of his brothers, Augustus C., John R., and Daniel W., for the duration of the war.[96] (This battalion later became the 21st Texas Infantry.) George C. left behind Sarah (expecting a third child) and two daughters.

Private George C. Hayden spent most of the war on detached service, driving a wagon, doing engineering work, and working as a mechanic and a carpenter for a quartermaster.[97] Historian Robert L. Kerby notes:

One way for a soldier to evade field service was to secure a detail, as an agriculturalist, a mechanic, an artisan, a teamster, or a clerk. By the spring of 1864, wives throughout the [Trans-Mississippi] Department were begging their soldier husbands to try "to come home, and recruit your health, & perhaps get a detail also, so that you will not have to return soon."[98]

George's military experience was similar to his brothers. They, too, saw little combat. Instead, they spent most of the war in detailed service, on furlough, or on sick leave.

After the war, George and Sarah returned to Kansas, farmed, and had eleven children. George C. Hayden died on May 23, 1914 in Gardner, Kansas.[99]

Jacob Taylor Hayden

The second-oldest brother was Jacob Taylor Hayden. He was thirteen when the family moved to Iowa, and twenty-seven when they moved to Texas.[100]

Jacob T. enlisted as a second sergeant in Griffin's Battalion on March 10, 1862, the first brother to do so.[101] His unit later became Co. "C," 21st Texas Infantry, the same company and regiment that his four brothers joined. Promoted from second sergeant to junior second lieutenant, he spent much of the rest of the war in Houston, Texas, away from fighting. Jacob T. and two privates were detailed to catch a draft deserter in 1862. He ended the war in Houston.

After Appomattox, Jacob Taylor Hayden taught school and farmed, married, and had children. He died in Haskell, Texas, on August 14, 1909.

Augustus Caesar Hayden

The third brother was Augustus Caesar Hayden, born in 1836. Gus was eleven when his family moved to Van Buren County. Gus married Elizabeth Burchett in Van Buren County on September 26, 1860. By summer 1861, they relocated to Lykins County, Kansas, and farmed. Their first child was born in Kansas.[102]

In the fall of 1861, Gus Hayden brought his wife and newborn baby to Texas. His obituary states: "He had the courage of his convictions. When the Civil War came, he cast his lot with the South ... and believed in the cause of the South." Gus enlisted as a private in Griffin's Battalion.[103] He was slightly wounded at the Battle of Calcasieu Pass on May 6, 1864. Gus spent the rest of the war on furlough and detached service.

After the war, he moved his family back to Kansas. Gus died in Gardner, Kansas, on December 11, 1928.

John Randolph Hayden

The fourth brother was John Randolph Hayden, born in 1843. He was four when his family moved to Iowa and eighteen when they moved to Texas.[104]

John Randolph Hayden enlisted on July 20, 1862.[105] He spent the war on furlough for illness, and on detached service in Texas. After the war, John Randolph Hayden rounded up cattle, got married, had a child, and moved to Kansas. He died in Clovis, New Mexico, on June 11, 1911.

Daniel Webster Hayden

The fifth brother was Daniel Webster Hayden. Born in 1844, Daniel came to Iowa at age three and moved to Texas at age seventeen.[106]

Daniel Webster Hayden enlisted in Griffin's Battalion with three older brothers.[107] Daniel Webster Hayden died of illness on November 29, 1863 in Tarrant County.

Reluctant Confederate With a Southern Wife

George Burgoon had lived in Texas for ten years before enlisting. He also had a wife from Arkansas whose family favored secession. All in all, his "interests were with the South," but twenty years later, George said he had been a "reluctant" Confederate.[108]

Born in 1832 in Ohio, George's mother was born in Maryland and his father in Ohio. They moved to Scott County, Iowa, in 1847. Five years later, in 1852 when George was twenty years old, they moved to Tarrant County, Texas.[109] George married an Arkansas native, Letta J. Fortener, in 1856.

At the firing upon Fort Sumter, Letta and her side of the family favored secession. About a year later, George enlisted in the 19th Texas Cavalry on May 19, 1862.[110] That fall, George's regiment joined William Henry Parsons's Brigade, a unit that saw wide-ranging action in the Trans-Mississippi region.

George's biographical sketch states that he participated in skirmishes in Arkansas, and in General Marmaduke's April 1863 raid on Cape Girardeau, Missouri. A year later, George served in the Red River campaign in Louisiana in April 1864. His regiment disbanded in Texas in May 1865.[111]

After the Trans-Mississippi troops surrendered, George and Letta farmed in Jasper County, southwest Missouri, and raised four children. They later divorced. George Burgoon died in 1915 at age eighty-two in Jasper County, Missouri.

Changes, Changes

A Northern man getting a job in the South and marrying a lovely lady didn't raise any eyebrows back home. Political positions could change, too; James Madison Williams's parents understood this fact. But they were surprised by the speed of change. They never imagined their son would become an ardent Confederate.

James was born in Ohio in 1837. At about age eighteen, he moved with his family to sparsely populated Homer, Hamilton County, Iowa, in 1855 or 1856. His father was a watchmaker and minister in the Swedenborgian Church. James left for a job in Augusta, Georgia, on July 21, 1858, little knowing he would never return.

Historian John Kent Folmar explains that James quickly adapted to Southern life. James took dancing lessons, sang in a choir, joined a baseball club, and entered the Clinch Rifles militia. A loyal son, he sent money to his cash-strapped parents in Iowa.[112]

James's family detected changes in his thinking. His mother, Eleanor, wrote him on May 29, 1859: "Your ideas on slavery sound rather odd. It is doubtless very agreeable to the master to be relieved from all the severe labor, but is it agreeable to the slave to perform it? Is it living by the golden rule?"[113]

The following May 1860, James's mother was amused at his political statements, but she worried that he would "become so much enamored with the South and her institutions that you would not feel like returning to your Western home."[114]

James next fell in love with an Augusta belle, Lizzie Rennison. He wrote his Unionist parents and sister that "the days of the Union are numbered," and the sooner it happens, the better. Shortly after Lincoln's election, James and Lizzie married and moved to Mobile, Alabama, where James took a bookkeeping job.[115]

Outspoken sister Bella, a strong Republican, tried on January 15, 1861 to coax James home for a visit: "I do not think you need to be fearful of coming in contact with "John Brown-ism."[116]

After Fort Sumter, James joined a Mobile militia, the Washington Light Infantry, number two. Local recruits affirmed him by electing him sergeant.[117]

James enlisted in the 21st Alabama Infantry on October 4, 1861. He started a war-long correspondence with Lizzie. James was in a peaceful backwater for most of the war, defending ocean-side forts in the vicinity of Mobile. He assured Lizzie on November 13, 1861: "I love my wife and I love my country."[118]

Lizzie stayed in Mobile during most of the war. James often reminded her of his affection. A ship, possibly coming down the Mississippi River, brought a letter from Iowa. He wrote Lizzie of the "damp chill" caused by the "dark fog of war."[119]

James's ambition marched to Southern drums on January 23. He cheerfully accepted orders and had fun whenever possible. About a month after the Battle of Shiloh, James became deeply homesick. He wrote Lizzie of the Iowa memories that washed over him.[120]

As James gained promotion to officer, he embraced the "peculiar institution" and bought a body servant. A different slave served their mess.

Life in the Confederate Army was quite a contrast to civilian jobs as clerk or bookkeeper. James pondered his life on June 22, 1862: "[Union troops] can never conquer us if the people are true to themselves—and how can they be otherwise? I can't believe that Southern born men will ever submit to the degrading yoke of a hated abolition master."[121]

James never completely forgot his parents and siblings. For example, he sometimes sent letters on blockade runners *en route* to Havana, Cuba, hoping his correspondence would reach Iowa. Later in the war, he sent and received letters under a flag of truce.[122]

Homesickness hammered James on his four-year anniversary of leaving Iowa. He wrote Lizzie about what it was like to say goodbye to his family, perhaps for the last time. The following month, on August 18, 1862, James wrote his father: "My whole soul is in the success of our struggle for independence." It is uncertain when James learned that his little brother John H. Williams had enlisted in the First Iowa Cavalry.[123]

Lizzie gave birth to two children during the war. She lived with James from October 1862 until May 1863, when she returned to Mobile to deliver a son.

During the Battle of Mobile Bay in early August 1864, James commanded Fort Powell. A Union ironclad (Monitor-style) rapidly fired shells and grapeshot into the fort. With two of James's artillery pieces disabled, and exploding Union shells flinging sand in every direction, James feared his magazine would explode. He evacuated his men and blew up Fort Powell on August 7.[124]

Furious Confederates condemned James. Editor John Forsyth of the *Mobile Advertiser and Register* called James's action a "disgraceful surrender." Relieved from duty, a military court tried James for "shamefully abandoning a fort which he had been commanded to defend." The court found that he had "acted with sound discretion," but his commanding officer, Lieutenant General Richard Taylor, suspended James from his command, stating that he "did not make such a defense of the fort as he should have done."[125]

James appealed to Secretary of War James A. Seddon, "in the name of Justice, and as a soldier of the Confederacy whose honor is dear to him," but Seddon declined to intervene. After cooling his heels for four months, James returned to his command in early December 1864.

Still wincing from shame, James decided to challenge editor Forsyth to a duel. Forsyth ended the matter by publicly apologizing.

James wrote his last wartime letter to Lizzie from Spanish Fort (east of Mobile) on March 22, 1865. He wrote, "If the Yankees don't come this time I will be vexed."[126]

James and the 21st Alabama surrendered on May 4, 1865, at Cuba Station, Alabama. They were paroled on May 10 at Meridian, Mississippi. He returned to Mobile a week later. Turning down two job offers in the North, James and Lizzie remained in Mobile and raised a family. He clerked in a probate court, helped reorganize the Alabama state militia in 1872, and helped found a chapter of the United Confederate Veterans.

James Madison Williams died in 1903 and was buried in an unmarked grave. The editor of the *Mobile Daily Register* called James "a patriotic and earnest citizen and an honest man, a gentleman, in the fullest sense of the word."[127]

Operating Behind Enemy Lines

From Muscatine Grocer to Confederate Colonel

Cold, driving rain slammed the troops, bruised and footsore after their Missouri defeats. Trudging south through the Indian Territories, Colonel Robert R. Lawther felt fever take hold. Soon he could barely take deep breaths, much less stay in a saddle. Lawther saw a Confederate surgeon who diagnosed him with "*Phthisis Pulmonalis*, Chronic Hepatitis, and a general prostration."[1,2]

Robert Ralston Lawther was a Pennsylvania native with a Scottish father.[3,4] He had been brought up in a strict Presbyterian sect. Lawther moved to Muscatine, Iowa in 1855 when he was twenty-one.[5,6] He was a tall man, 6 feet, 3 inches, with blue eyes, dark hair, and a fair complexion.[7]

He ran a grocery in Muscatine. Lawther married Ellen E. Hoopes in 1858. Ellen was a Kentucky native and a long-time Muscatine resident. About a year later, their son, Harry, was born.

Civic-minded Lawther donned his grocer's apron and also served as the Muscatine treasurer and the township Clerk and Treasurer. After his term expired in January 1860, he moved to Jefferson City, Missouri, the state capital, to start a grocery store. Ellen and young Harry stayed with her father in Muscatine that summer.[8,9]

The next year, in April 1861, Lawther enlisted in the first company of the Missouri State Guard. His unit became the Third Missouri Cavalry, and he was elected major on December 31, 1861.[10]

A Muscatine resident saw Lawther in Missouri in late 1861. The *Muscatine Journal* stated: "Bob [Lawther] treated him like a gentleman, furnishing him and his friends with tobacco and other conveniences. It seems he has some humanity left in him, although a traitor, striving to ruin his country."[11] Lawther led a charge at Pea Ridge in March 1862 and captured an artillery battery, resulting in a promotion to colonel.

His commanding officer, Major General Sterling Price, recommended that Lawther recruit a regiment of partisan raiders in northern Missouri. Price called Lawther "an officer of distinguished gallantry, daring, and enterprise."[12] The Confederate Secretary of War approved the appointment. The recruits were to receive a $50 bounty, and they had to provide their own horses and weapons. Their pay was $25 a month and all the booty they could seize from the Union army.

Lawther made his recruits swear allegiance to "the Confederate States against all her enemies and oppressors."

Federal troops captured Lawther in August 1862 in Osage County, Missouri. They placed him in Gratiot State Prison in St. Louis. A provost marshal called him "one of the darkest kind of traitors and a Northern man." Federal authorities levied three charges, spanning the previous year:

1. Recruiting and commanding a band of "Guerrilla Insurgents and Robbers who waged illegal warfare," "plundering and stealing" private property.
2. Being a spy, since he was out of uniform.
3. Helping or ordering "insurgents" in summer 1861, to "burn and destroy the Greys Creek and Osage Bridges" to keep Federal Troops from moving by rail to Jefferson City.[13]

Lawther denied these charges, stating that Union troops captured his recruiting commission (and three other commissions), signed by the Confederate Secretary of War. He threatened to contact the Confederate authorities. Lawther said: "In punishing me with close confinement, you are inflicting the same amount of punishment upon Federal officers of like rank.... [The Confederate government is] not slow to retaliate."[14]

Four months into his captivity, Lawther complained that his officers "have been closely confined in a damp, loathsome prison." He objected to waiting 100 days before learning he was charged with bridge-burning. He called the author of the charges "a liar and beneath the notice of a Gentleman."[15]

Lawther was transferred to Alton Penitentiary in Illinois on January 7, 1863, and Camp Chase on January 31. He was exchanged two months later at City Point, Virginia, after seven months of confinement.

Safely back in Arkansas in August 1863, Lawther formed temporarily dismounted cavalry of Marmaduke's Missouri men. By January 1, 1864, Lawther commanded the 10th Missouri Cavalry. Officers in Marmaduke's brigade asked that he be promoted to brigadier general, calling him "an upright and affable gentleman." Major General Fagan called Lawther "a gallant and competent officer."[16,17]

In September and October 1864, Lawther participated in General Sterling "Pap" Price's "Grand Expedition" into Missouri which ended in defeat. After the long retreat through Indian Territory and Texas, Lawther resigned on November 29. When the war ended, he surrendered in Galveston.

Four months after Appomattox, Lawther visited his old home in Pennsylvania. The *Philadelphia Inquirer* reported that a "deputation of citizens" drove Lawther out of town.[18]

The following year, 1866, he gave a toast to General James Longstreet at a picnic near Galveston. Lawther raised his glass and said, "General Longstreet, the hero of forty-nine pitched battles, and the idol of every true lover of Constitutional Liberty."[19]

Lawther stayed in Galveston and then Dallas, running a wholesale grocery and then a feed store. Active in United Confederate Veterans, Robert R. Lawther died of paralytic stroke in 1911.

From Iowa State Representative to Confederate Colonel

Wearing civilian clothes, riding his horse deeper into southern Illinois, Colonel Cyrus Franklin was struck by the fence rails, barns, and livestock all untouched by war. Friendly chats with strangers led to a few intimate discussions with farmers sympathetic to the Confederacy. When Franklin collected enough information, he headed back to Missouri, planning to write Jefferson Davis.

Born in Ohio in 1822 to Virginia natives, Cyrus Franklin served in the Mexican-American War. Afterwards, he moved to Ottumwa and practiced law.[20, 21] One of Franklin's acquaintances from Wapello County, John M. Hedrick, later became a Union general. He wrote an unflattering obituary about Franklin.

Hedrick describes Franklin as "tall, angular, restless, furtive, and peculiar." They met at a Fourth of July celebration, where Hedrick said that Franklin "was dressed in a coarse cotton shirt, tow breeches, coarse shoes, without socks, and a rye-straw, homemade hat. This garb was evidently assumed for effect."[22]

According to Hedrick, Franklin had little success in his law practice, but once he entered politics, he was a captivating stump speaker. Franklin served two terms in the Iowa General Assembly, starting in 1854. He had a short stint as speaker pro tem of the Iowa House.

By mid-1860, Franklin practiced law in Keokuk. He and his wife, Mary, had a five-year-old daughter, Lucy.

According to Hedrick, Franklin was a scheming man with few close Iowa friends. In the days leading up to Fort Sumter, Franklin reportedly rode his horse "in the grey dawn of the morning ... to the southwest ... to stir up the north Missourians to the point of revolt."

Hedrick claims that Franklin ingratiated himself with Missouri Democrats, which led to his appointment as Colonel in the Missouri State Guard. Hedrick asserts:

> No man has ever had less excuse for being a traitor than Cyrus Franklin. He had no personal Southern affiliations, and was Northern born and bred. He had no human chattels in peril.... But he was an intensely pro-slavery Democrat.... He believed in the divine and constitutional right of slavery.[23]

Hedrick states: "[Franklin] had an exaggerated notion of the superiority of the Southern people, and of their courage on the battlefield.... He had the courage of his convictions."

Hedrick states that Franklin persuaded George Laswell, of Ottumwa, as well as a young man from Blakesburg, to head South with him. On August 14, 1861, Cyrus Franklin was a colonel of the Missouri State Guard on active duty in the field. The Missouri State Guard became a Confederate unit.

A month later, Franklin fought in the First Battle of Lexington in Missouri.[24] Col. Franklin and his fellow regimental officers were praised for "their gallantry, zeal and great endurance."[25]

Franklin later assumed command of the 2nd Regiment N.E. Missouri Cavalry. Two of his horses were killed in action. He served in the brigade led by General Martin Green. Hedrick faults Franklin for serving in a brigade guilty of "harassing, robbing, and murdering the people of north Missouri who remained loyal to the American flag."[26]

Union General Samuel R. Curtis wrote from the Department of the Missouri to Secretary of War Edwin Stanton on January 15, 1863. Curtis wrote that Confederate "recruiting guerrilla agents strive to organize their bands" in "southern Iowa and large districts of Missouri."[27]

Granville Leeper was one of Franklin's recruiters who crisscrossed Missouri, Nebraska, and Iowa. At Franklin's request, Leeper went up to Schuyler County, Missouri, in late 1861, and escorted Franklin's family south of the Missouri River.[28, 29]

According to Leeper, Franklin sent him back to Schuyler County—an area thought to be teeming with Missourians eager to serve the Confederacy—to guide them back to Franklin's regiment.

Mid-way through the war, on June 7, 1863, Union troops captured Leeper and sent him to Gratiot Street Prison in St. Louis to be tried by a military tribunal. The authorities took statements from Leeper and compiled witness testimonies.

Leeper testified that when Union troops became active in Schuyler and Putnam County, Missouri, in 1862, he moved to Omaha and Council Bluffs, spending months there. He also said he spent time in Appanoose County, Iowa, but "did nothing" there.

One Putnam County witness contradicted Leeper. The witness testified that when he saw Leeper in Hill Town in Appanoose County, Leeper said "he was going to wait until the leaves got out this spring & then he was going to raise a company" and come down to Putnam County and "give the Union boys hell." This is the first testimony I've seen that indicates a Confederate recruiter was active in Iowa.[30]

Just before the trial, Leeper escaped, ending up in California.

Franklin's Units

Prior to Leeper's arrest, Franklin was in Richmond, Virginia. A couple of months later, the 1st and 2nd Regiments of N.E. Missouri Cavalry were consolidated and formed the 7th (or Franklin's) Regiment Missouri Infantry.

Hedrick states that Franklin narrowly escaped capture at the surrender of Vicksburg.

On November 16, 1863, four months after the fall of Vicksburg, Franklin was in Arkansas. He wrote Jefferson Davis, accusing Confederate Generals Shelby and Marmaduke and their officers of robbing civilians—both pro-Union and pro-Confederate—during their raids into Missouri. Franklin wrote:

> If such work is not soon arrested … not a friend will be left in all that country.…
> The Shelby-Marmaduke raids … have transferred to the Confederate uniform all
> the dread and terror which used to attach to the Lincoln blue.
>
> The last horse is taken from the widow and orphan, whose husband and father
> has fallen in the country's service. No respect is shown to age, sex, or condition.
> Women are insulted and abused.
>
> On the other hand … the Federal commander, is winning golden opinions by his
> forbearance, justice and urbanity.[31]

Col. Franklin says something very interesting: He writes, "I traveled extensively through Illinois recently." Franklin did this in late summer or fall 1863. He continues: "I found everything working there just as we would desire." Franklin talks about his discussion with Southern sympathizers in Illinois. Franklin writes: "Your army and Government have a spotless name, and the respect of all, and the sympathy of many there. Then to return here, and find our own dear and faithful women in dread of our army is too bad." After receiving Franklin's letter, Jefferson Davis called for an investigation.

According to Bruce S. Allardice, author of *Confederate Colonels: A Biographical Register*, it is possible that Franklin had spoken with or written to Jefferson Davis before his trip to Illinois. Franklin wanted to learn what Illinoisans thought about the Confederacy. Perhaps he was thinking of ways to recruit new Illinois men—this at a time when the Confederacy needed friends and soldiers.[32]

After the war ended, Cyrus Franklin moved with his wife and daughter to Tennessee, and then Osceola, St. Clair County, Missouri.

Cyrus Franklin died on January 17, 1885. Writing his obituary reflections, General Hedrick stated that Franklin "had the courage of his convictions, and lost all in fighting for so despicable a cause." Hendrick added that Franklin was "ashamed to visit the people who once honored him" in Iowa.[33]

Hard-Luck Iowa Lawyer Becomes a "War Dog"

Thundering down the urban streets, he led the troopers into the heart of the city. Captain Virgil M. Pendleton had learned the lesson that audacity and speed win the day. But he didn't know that trouble lay just around the corner.

Kentucky native Virgil moved with his wife, Mary, and a two-year-old son to Burlington, Iowa, in the late 1850s. Virgil was approved to argue before the Iowa Supreme Court. He started to gamble on the side.[34, 35, 36]

In the late 1850s, his law practice stalled, a baby girl arrived, and he could not pay his debts. The State of Missouri prosecuted him for "gaming," and Virgil's creditors sued him. Adding insult to injury, Lodge No. 1 in Burlington expelled him for "conduct unbecoming."[37,38]

Shaking off the humiliation, Virgil sold real estate and tried to collect debts for others. In a moment of sunshine, the Burlington lodge reinstated him as master mason, but dark economic clouds eclipsed the day. His last newspaper advertisement ran on May 28, 1861, about a month after Fort Sumter.[39]

Virgil headed to Kentucky. He enlisted as a private on June 1, 1861, in the 1st Regiment Kentucky Infantry.[40] A year later, he enlisted in the 8th Kentucky Cavalry as a captain. Virgil served under Col. R. S. Cluke.

News about Virgil got back to Burlington. A soldier reported seeing him at Shiloh. An Iowa attorney sneered: "At the breaking out of the Rebellion, [Virgil] attempted to recruit a company for the Southern cause, but only succeeded in recruiting himself."[41]

The *Burlington Hawk-eye* editor acknowledged that Virgil enlisted because he "thought the South was right." The editor credited Virgil with "a little manhood" but not much intelligence or patriotism.[42]

Virgil accompanied General John Hunt Morgan on his Christmas 1862 raid into Kentucky.

On December 27, Morgan's troops were crossing the Rolling Fork River. Many Union infantry and cavalry were closing in on them, firing deadly accurate artillery into the Confederates. About 700 men, including several of Cluke's companies, were at risk of being cut off and captured.[43] One of Morgan's men later recalled:

> With an enemy in front and the river behind them it looked especially gloomy for the men under Cluke. This 8th Kentucky Cavalry ... styled themselves "Cluke's War Dogs," and it looked now as if the "war dogs" were to get all the war they could possibly desire....
>
> One of the enemy's batteries was proving especially destructive, and Captain Virgil Pendleton of the 8th Kentucky was ordered to charge this battery. He killed the cannoneers or drove them from their guns, and this silenced these destructive agents for a quarter of an hour.[44]

Virgil's clock was ticking. Ninety days later, the 8th Kentucky Cavalry appeared outside of Mount Sterling, Kentucky, and demanded that the town surrender. The Federals refused.

Col. Cluke led a column of cavalrymen into the "heart of the city." Virgil charged through the streets of Mount Sterling and was mortally wounded. He died six days later, on March 27, 1863. One of Virgil's compatriots said, "No braver soldier or more loyal patriot ever gave his life for the South."[45]

The "Full and Wonderful Life" of a Confederate Cavalryman

Gray-haired William Campbell leaned back in his rocking chair and told a visitor about the third day at Gettysburg. Campbell had arrived in the morning with General J.E.B. Stuart's cavalry. General Lee asked for volunteers for a dangerous errand. The task: Tear down a rail fence that stood between the two opposing armies. Campbell and his friend Curtis volunteered. The problem was that Union troops stood ready to shoot them to pieces.

Campbell was born in King and Queen County, Virginia, in 1837 to a slave-holding family. Late in life, Campbell described life on plantations as "the most distinctive and ideal situation the country had produced."[46]

Campbell came from a long line of "sober, conscientious men of strong religious tendencies." His father advised family members to lead a calm, godly life. Campbell didn't always follow this advice.

He became an orphan at five years old. He inherited two slaves who were hired out. Campbell became aware of "the West"—as present-day Illinois and Iowa were known—when an uncle moved to Galena, Illinois, to make his fortune. The family feared for the uncle's safety, writing letters that sounded "as if they never expected to see him alive, but wished him God speed." Campbell's ears perked up whenever people talked of the West.[47]

He attended Richmond College for a year but ran low on cash, so he left school and worked in a general store. A year later—the spring of 1858—he quit, sold his slaves, and traveled to Galena where two of his uncles lived. He met a local tanner, Ulysses S. Grant, who later became famous. Campbell got a job in McGregor, Clayton County, Iowa, from the brother of one of his aunts.

Two local Irish immigrants taught Campbell the sport of spear fishing. They fished at night. For light, they burned big molasses barrels. Campbell wrote: "They used a long pole with a sharp iron and four beards on the prongs. After many lessons and gay times with these witty Irishmen I learned the art. There were many kinds of large fish in the waters."[48]

One of Campbell's aunts was related to U.S. Senator George Wallace Jones. When in Galena, Campbell frequently saw Senator Jones.

Campbell attended the Lincoln and Douglas debate in Freeport, Illinois. He watched Lincoln rise "in his deliberate way," hand his hat to a bystander, and say, "Please hold my hat while I stone Stephen." Campbell thought that Douglas won the debate.[49]

Campbell was soon entranced by gold fever. In the spring of 1860, he left McGregor for Colorado to dig gold, but it wasn't the thrill he expected.

After a year of digging, he felt wanderlust. Campbell hopped a ride on a stagecoach carrying the U.S. mail, heading to the Great Salt Lake. They drove through a buffalo herd. Campbell observed that "a stage [coach] meeting a herd would have to push its way slowly along. They were always gentle until they stampeded."

A guard, armed to the teeth, sat next to the stagecoach driver. One of the passengers was Horace Greeley, editor and owner of the *New-York Tribune*. Greeley is credited with the statement, "Go west, young man." Hearing that Greeley planned to interview Brigham Young, apostle of the Mormons, Campbell begged to go along. He ended up hearing a "heated discussion on polygamy." He decided that Brigham Young won the argument.

Early in 1861, as Southern states seceded, Campbell experienced a passion of his own: hunting. He was up in the mountains with a companion, Ned Tesson, when they encountered a mountain lion. Campbell stated:

> There was a terrible roar and a mountain lion stood out on a ledge above us. Tesson shot and the animal must have been hit for he rushed down the steep and was almost upon us before I could get aim. Another shot and he was silent and drew back under the edge of the rock. We loaded again and approached very cautiously … he was lying licking his wounds. He started up and this time we killed him. A great tawny, beautiful creature. He had no mane. We carried him back to camp on a pony.[50]

Campbell went on a three-month hunting expedition with Arapaho Indians, led by an "old frontiersman," Nelson Newlin. Campbell loved many of the Arapaho customs, and spending life outdoors and in tents.

In late summer 1861, Campbell and seventy-four other hunters traveled to Fort Laramie on the North Platte River. He learned for the first time that the war had begun, and Virginia had seceded. He stated: "It did not take me long to decide as to my duty. Virginia was invaded by foes, and I must hasten to her defense."[51]

The men talked it over and found that all but three of them sympathized with the South and wanted to serve her as soon as possible, and so, seventy-two hunters broke camp, walking 1,000 miles, by way of Denver and the upper waters of the Arkansas River, until they reached General Sterling Price. It took them four weeks, but they arrived at the Battle of Wilson's Creek on August 10, 1861.

Union General Lyon wanted to drive the Confederates out of Missouri, and General Price "determined to meet him." Campbell stated:

I still remember the sound of the first cannon I heard the morning of Lyon's attack; how the noise echoed and re-echoed along the hills and valleys of the meandering creek.

I realized for the first time that I stood in the actual presence of war, and that two contending armies of equal strength were about to grapple in deadly conflict. General Price ... looked the personification of war.

[Minutes later] Cannon after cannon belched forth and with these came the sharp sound of musketry firing by the sharp shooters as they came in sight of each other along the creek.[52]

Campbell and the hunters were not assigned to any unit, so they watched for two hours, itching to join the fight. General Price rode up and told a staff member to direct the hunters into battle. Price said, "I wish you to know that you have been held back to accomplish a great task. I shall expect to hear from you."

One of the hunters said, "Boys, take aim as though you were shooting deer," and then, "forward, march." Some 150 yards away, the Union troops advanced toward them. A Union officer dashed out on horseback, waving a sword, followed by an escort, to the cheers of his men. Campbell watched as one of his companions took aim and shot the officer who they later deduced was General Lyon. The Union troops fired and the Confederate line seemed to vanish, but a Missouri regiment joined the hunters and they charged, driving the Yankees past the creek. Seventeen of the seventy-two hunters died that day.

The rest of the hunters stayed on with General Price, but Campbell returned to McGregor, settled his affairs, visited Galena, and took a roundabout way to Virginia.

When he was a few miles from Stonewall Jackson's troops, he was walking along a railroad and came upon a Federal sentry. This "tall, raw-looking youth" aimed his gun at Campbell, and he surrendered. Campbell later recalled:

I asked some question. He was proud of his job and soon he showed me his gun. I backed away as I admired it and as soon as I had him at the right distance, I told him he was my prisoner. His chagrin was pitiful. All this time he had been holding his horse. We mounted. I put him in front and rode into Romney. I had hardly dismounted before I was arrested by my own people as a Northern spy.[53]

Ten days later, Campbell talked himself out of prison, citing mutual acquaintances. He went to Richmond and then home, where he learned his sister was dead. As soon as he could get a good horse, he joined the Essex Light Dragoons, which became part of the 9th Virginia Cavalry.[54]

Campbell's unit, Co. "F," was assigned picket duty along the Rappahannock River. Predictably, "camp duties became burdensome" to him.

He didn't stay bored long. General McClellan moved his massive Union army into Virginia in his peninsular campaign. In June 1862, General Robert E. Lee ordered General J. E. B. Stuart to send cavalry "to the rear of McClellan's army" and determine their location.

Moving out, they encountered Yankee pickets and drove past them. Campbell's company charged up a hill, catching Union soldiers trying to form a line. Drawing his saber, Campbell told Lt McLane of the 5th New York Regulars to surrender, but "he turned with sword for a fight." Blade clashed against blade, but Campbell's men closed in, and McLane surrendered.[55]

Later in the ride, J. E. B. Stuart told his men to build a temporary bridge over the Chickahominy River. Tearing down an old barn, they built a bridge in a few hours, crossed over it, and returned to Richmond. The Confederate cavalry had "made a complete circuit of McClellan's Army."

Stuart's wild ride yielded hundreds of Union prisoners and horses, and significant bragging rights. The Confederates lost only one man, Captain John Latane. His death and burial were memorialized in the poem, "The Burial of Latane," and a painting-turned-lithograph that became a fund-raising tool for the Confederacy.

Most soldiers tell stories of both boredom and excitement. Campbell was no different. Late in 1862, he assumed extra duties as clerk to Col. R. L. T. Beale. For a couple of hours each morning, Campbell worked hard, reading reports from orderly sergeants and writing his own regimental reports, listing numbers sick, on detail, and killed and wounded after a battle.

Campbell befriended Isaac Curtis, a scout on General Stuart's staff. Together, they had odd and sundry adventures. Once, they chased and caught a suspected spy.

The following year, in late June 1863, General Lee's army invaded the North. Campbell and Curtis caught wind of a large Union wagon train. They investigated and found that it was guarded by two companies of cavalry. Campbell and Curtis corralled a few of General Stuart's bodyguards and they thundered after the train. They missed it, but they captured a quartermaster with $40,000 on his person. Campbell recalled, decades later, that he never did get a commission on that money.

Campbell's regiment arrived at Gettysburg the morning of the third day of fighting. He and Curtis prepared to tear down a fence that separated Union and Confederate troops. Campbell recalled:

We must not think of anything but getting down the fence. We were both well mounted. Soon the signal came and we dashed forward. As my horse neared the fence he stopped. I could not force him on. The rain of shells was awful. I jumped down and holding the horse with one hand I worked at the fence with the other. I could see Curtis hard at it. Shot and shell were pouring. It did not seem a man could live. A shot went thru my side breast and arm. Now another signal and the army went thru.[56]

Comrades saw his rider-less horse. They said, "Poor Campbell, dead at last." Campbell survived but spent the next five months recuperating. The following year, he and Curtis were back in the saddle.

In August 1864, they needed new horses, so, with permission, the men sneaked across Union lines to steal some. They crossed a river, a swamp, and thick woods. By the time they spotted some Union horses, there was only an hour of sunlight left. Campbell and Curtis trailed behind three soldiers, watching them move from their camp and head toward a dwelling enclosed by a fence. The Confederates "hid and listened" as two men rode into the yard, closed the gate, and went inside the house. Campbell and Curtis jumped the fence to find a man holding the horses. They demanded his surrender, but the man let go of the reins and ran. Campbell recalled:

> Each of us sprang for a horse. Curtis was soon in the saddle, but in my effort to mount I let my bridle slip loose and the horse sprang away, following the loose horse. I ran at once for the gate thinking they would try to get out. Just as I reached it an order came to halt ... I threw up my gun to shoot.
>
> Before I could do it a shot rang out from behind me and the Yankee fell. Curtis had ridden up behind and realizing our danger had shot. Almost at the same instant one of the loose horses ran up beside him and he grabbed the bridle. Hardly had he done so before I was in the saddle and we were off like the wind.[57]

Taking to the swamp, they eventually saw the Union picket line. One of them called out and said to come forward and give the countersign. Campbell and Curtis decided to take their chances. Campbell recalled:

> I always did the talking. I rode a short distance in advance and hailed them and asked to what command they belonged. Some N. Y. Cavalry regiment.... I responded "We are two Confederates inside your lines; we know the penalty is death. We are well armed, each has two six shooters and a double barrel shot gun. If you give way and let us pass, we will not fire a shot, but if not, then look out." Here we started, and the Yankees to our joy gave us the road.[58]

Time passed. Near the end of three years of service, in early March 1865—a month-and-a-half before Lee's surrender—Campbell asked to be reassigned to Col. John Mosby's Partisan Virginia Rangers. Campbell stated two reasons: First, since 1858, he had been a "citizen" of Iowa who voted and owned land. Second, he had nearly fulfilled his original commitment. Campbell's superior officers expressed unanimous but reluctant approval. Colonel Tom Waller wrote, "He is a good, true, and faithful soldier ... I dislike to give him up." Colonel R. L. T. Beale noted Campbell's distinguished service.[59]

Campbell was never transferred. His request probably slipped through the cracks of a crumbling administrative superstructure.

At Appomattox, Campbell reflected: "All the world seemed changed except that Robt. Lee was wise and good, and I trusted that he knew what was best. Laying down arms was the hardest battle I had to fight. Now to go home. I had no home."[60]

Campbell ran into a friend from Colorado in Richmond, wearing a Union officer's uniform. The old friend put Campbell in touch with one of his Galena uncles. Campbell soon arrived in Galena. His Uncle George said, in his presence, "When the young man apologizes for his recent conduct, I will be glad to receive him." Campbell said, "Uncle George, my only apology is that I did not fight harder."

Campbell never saw his uncle again. Campbell travelled to Chicago and stayed several weeks. He later recalled: "I decided that the feeling of antagonism to the Southern cause was more than I could stand. I was hot tempered, and I would not be able to live and work with them in peace."[61]

He returned to Virginia, "bought a stock of goods for a country store," and opened a shop. Reconstruction was hard for Campbell. He stated: "To keep the Negroes in their place when there were three to one in number was a man's job. The Federal agents sent down to annoy us were almost more than the proud sons of the South could stomach."[62]

He married Miss Janet R. R. Latane, and they had a daughter, Mary. Campbell represented Essex County in the Virginia House of Delegates in 1890 and 1891.[63] When Mary grew up, she reflected on her father's storytelling:

Being a child of the Confederacy and always thrilled at the conversation that followed the meeting of my father's friends, I have pictured in my childish mind the great General Lee riding on gray Traveler, serene and clear-eyed, and behind him my father, gay and confident. As far as I knew or cared, this was the whole of the Confederacy, General Lee leading wisely and my father doing a gay bit of fighting to expel this horde of invaders who had come into our lovely land.

So they have come to many a battle and finally to a gallant and glorious surrender at Appomattox. I was very sure that defeat was the finest thing in the world, and a man defeated was a hero, for had not my father and General Lee surrendered, and I had never heard a word of sadness or regret.

One evening after talk of men and battles ... my father said, "Have I never told you how I came into possession of one of General Lee's horses after the surrender? It was in the fall of 1866. I was back in the County of Essex ... when I had an offer to buy a small spirited mare which a returned soldier offered to sell for $125. I found her very satisfactory for riding and drawing a light wagon. One morning, I stopped to talk to a friend, and I suddenly noticed his eyes riveted on the horse."

He said, "Campbell, where did you get that horse?" When I told him, he said, "I have seen General Lee ride her when Traveler was resting. Naturally, I was much surprised and intensely interested. General Lee at that time was in Lexington, Virginia, as President of Washington College. I decided to write and ask him about such a horse.... If she belonged to him, I wanted him to have her."[64]

Robert E. Lee responded to Campbell on October 27, 1866:

I have written to my son, Robert, as you suggested, to ride over and see her, if he has any recollections of her ... I rode her frequently after the return of the Army from Maryland to Virginia in 1862 to the Spring of 1864 and especially while around Fredericksburg and at the Battle of Chancellorsville.[65]

Author C. L. Gray explains: "During Second Manassas, Lee was holding Traveler's bridle reins when the gray became spooked. Lee fell and broke both his hands. Upon the Army's return from Maryland, [General J. E. B.] Stuart sought to buy General Lee a quieter and gentler horse."[66]

Lee recalled that his sorrel mare had been moved to Lynchburg, Virginia, and then to North Carolina around the surrender of Appomattox. A couple of weeks later, Robert E. Lee sent his second son, General William H. F. (Rooney) Lee, who was also Campbell's old commander. Campbell told his daughter, Mary:

We walked down to the stables, and as soon as the mare was brought up, he said, "Yes, that is Lucy Long, presented to my father by General Longstreet [actually, General Stuart] and ridden when Traveler was resting in the spring of '62 and again in '63."...

General Robert Lee had told his son not to accept the horse as a gift on any consideration. So after spending the night, he paid me the $125 and rode away leading Lucy Long.[67]

Late in life, Campbell wrote: "Life has been full and wonderful. Great happiness and great sorrow have come to me.... I hate no man—my heart goes out in love to all humanity. I have tried to live a courageous life. I pray God that no fear may enter my soul when I pass into the great unknown."[68]

William Campbell died two months later, on June 21, 1925.

John Haps—
The Dutch-Iowan Who Became a Confederate

The order to disband spread like wildfire through Jefferson Davis's de facto bodyguard. John Haps and a few Kentucky troopers stole a quartermaster's wagon, loaded it with guns, and lit out for Mississippi. Union troops never stopped them. When Haps dismounted in Holly Springs, he had three six-shooter pistols and an eight-shooter Spencer rifle. He never surrendered.

John Haps started life in Holland as Johannes Haps. At the age of nine, in 1847, his family sailed with other Catholic Dutchmen to the United States, arriving at New Orleans. Most of the group sailed up the Mississippi and settled in Ottumwa and in Keokuk. The new immigrants to Ottumwa attended Mass at the Eddyville Catholic Church.[69, 70, 71]

Johannes became John Haps and lived in Keokuk with his parents. Years later, during the Civil War, he wrote on his Confederate disability papers that he had been born in Eddyville.

Haps worked in Keokuk as a "Penman," probably someone who wrote letters and filled out forms in English for other Dutch immigrants.

Haps moved to Holly Springs, Mississippi, in the late 1850s and ran a newspaper there. Those skills later came in handy during the war.[72]

In mid-October 1860, Jefferson Davis stopped in Holly Springs *en route* to Washington, D.C., to take his seat in the U.S. Senate. A group of citizens met him at the depot, to hear him speak about the possible election of Abraham Lincoln. Jefferson Davis said: "If you procure a uniform befitting your appearance, I will present you with a stand of arms that will cost me as much money as the uniforms cost you."[73]

That marked the beginning of the Jefferson Davis Rifles; 102 men visited a tailor and ordered cadet gray uniforms from Boston for $45 apiece. They informed Senator Davis of their action, and they soon received 102 breech-loading Maynard rifles. Haps later recalled, "From that time on, we drilled constantly."[74]

Mississippi seceded in January 1861. Haps sold the newspaper a month later and formally enlisted in the Jefferson Davis Rifles, which became Co. "D," 9th Mississippi Infantry. Haps's regiment went to Pensacola and helped secure Forts Barrancas and McRee, both abandoned by Federal troops. Haps later recalled that when his one-year enlistment expired, in February 1862, he and thirty-four others "got horses, shotguns, and all necessary things" and offered their services to General Bragg at Pensacola. Haps claims that they were rejected, so they "rode to Chattanooga, and joined the 2nd Kentucky Cavalry."

Col. Basil W. Duke commanded the 2nd Kentucky Cavalry. Duke called his troops "reckless, daredevil youngsters, always eager for adventure and excitement." Four or five of the cavalrymen were typesetters, and they made use of their talents.[75]

On one excursion into Lexington, behind Union lines, Haps and company broke into the *Lexington Observer and Reporter*. They changed the newspaper's sign to read, "Morgan's Headquarters, Adjutant General's Office." Haps printed a twelve-page pamphlet titled *Tactics for Mounted Riflemen* with his own name on the cover.

After they left Lexington, the editor of the paper complained that Haps had left the print shop a mess, ankle-deep with trash and pieces of type. The editor said, "We are not anxious to receive another visit from said Haps."[76]

Haps and crew also printed *The Vidette*, a newspaper for Morgan's troops, in July 1862 in Hartsville, Tennessee. Haps recalled the last copy, printed in Hopkinsville, Kentucky:

> I had taken my detail to Hopkinsville (while the command was feasting at a picnic some fifteen miles back), captured a printing office ... had seven galleys of type ready to make up for the paper, when the advance guard came ... up on a trot, the

bugle sounding for us to fall in. Hastily placing the seven galleys on the hand press and taking a dozen or more proofs, the rear guard admonished us it was time to fall in.

We caught up with the rear guard later, with the Yankees in sight in our rear. The copies of the proofs were distributed and read while the command was on the run to get away from the Yankee soldiers, who were pursuing, but we got away all right.[77]

On another outing, Haps's unit sneaked through Union picket lines by pretending to be Yankees. They probably went undetected because some wore Union Army uniforms—since their own uniforms had worn out—and because they brought along a captured Union soldier. Haps kept the Union soldier quiet by "tightly gripping the prisoner's throat."[78]

The biggest adventure was General John Hunt Morgan's Great Raid into Kentucky, Indiana, and Ohio in summer 1863. Even fifty-seven years after this event, an elderly Haps called it "a pleasure."

Morgan's men covered some 700 miles behind Union lines. They were often dodging Colonel Wolford's 1st Kentucky Cavalry U.S.A., and various Indiana and Ohio home guards and militias.

John Haps and his fellow soldiers were in the saddle, on some days, twenty-one hours a day. Col. Duke later reminisced, "The men in our ranks were worn down and demoralized with the tremendous fatigue."[79]

Near the end of the Raid, Haps was so exhausted that he fell asleep on the banks of the Ohio River near Buffington Island. Fighting broke out a few hundred yards away. Col. Duke and many of his troops were captured—and Haps slept through it all.[80]

When Haps awoke, reins still in hand, he scrambled onto his horse and looked for other Confederates. He found some, riding away from Union troops, so he formed a rearguard to protect Morgan's men. They dodged a Union gunboat on the river. The commanding Union general sent a flag of truce to Morgan, with orders to surrender. Morgan asked for two hours to consult his men, which was granted. Haps and the others unanimously voted to race for the Ohio River. They laid hay across the road to keep the dust from rising and tipping off the Yankees. "Each man gathered an armful of hay for his horse to walk on." Haps led the rearguard, and the race was on.[81]

A day or so later, Haps was shot by accident by another Confederate. The bullet went through his right hip and out his gluteus maximus. A Good Samaritan took Haps into his house and nursed him for four months. When Haps could be moved, they turned him over to Union officers. Haps hobbled off and escaped, but they recaptured him and sent him to Camp Chase and Fort Delaware.[82]

Haps was exchanged in September 1864, and he rejoined Duke's 2nd Kentucky Cavalry in Abingdon, Virginia. Still walking stiffly, with an inflamed hip and discharge from his wounds, Haps endured a bitterly cold, snowy winter. He and the other troopers lacked warm clothing, food, and supplies. On January 22, 1865, three Confederate surgeons declared Private John Haps "unfit for duty at present" and told him to come back in six months to be re-examined.[83]

But Haps remained "on special duty" in southwest Virginia. In early April 1865 as Jefferson Davis fled Richmond and Lee tried to break out of Petersburg, Duke's men tried to unite with Lee, but when they heard about Appomattox, Duke's men caught up with Jefferson Davis and his cabinet in North Carolina. They provided an additional escort for the president as he tried to reach a viable Confederate force. Haps was part of this escort of some 2,000 men, mostly Kentucky cavalrymen.

A few days later, the cavalrymen began deserting, and the generals dismissed most of the remaining troopers on May 8, 1865, near the Savannah River in Georgia.[84, 85]

After the war, Haps moved to East St. Louis, Illinois, and founded a newspaper. He married and had children. Haps named one of his sons after his beloved former commander, John Hunt Morgan.

At age fifty-eight, he broke a leg when a tornado hit East St. Louis. At age sixty-four, Haps encountered a Texas steer. The local press described the scene:

> Maddened by its long ride in a crowded stock car from the southwest plains, the steer, armed with horns six feet across, broke from an unloading chute ... at the National stockyards....
>
> John Haps was leaning against the fence in front of his home at 806 First street when the steer, head down, charged up First street at full speed toward the fence. With a single toss of its broad horns, it hurled Haps over the fence and into the yard.
>
> Bellowing with rage, the steer stood in front of the high fence and pawed the ground several minutes, while Haps took refuge in the house.[86]

Haps moved back to Mississippi in 1908 after his wife and two of their children had died. He entered the Confederate Soldiers' Home at Beauvoir, Jefferson Davis's old residence. Still industrious, Haps planted a beautiful flower garden for residents and visitors to enjoy.[87] Haps flew a Confederate flag over the gate to his garden. He assured his children: "The father and grandfather of us all [referring to himself] is in the far South, having the best time of his life since the death of your Mother."[88]

During World War I, Haps grew vegetables in his garden to help support the war effort against Germany. He realized that since Southern and Northern boys were fighting side by side against a common enemy, this was truly a united country. He took down the Confederate flag and put up the Stars and Stripes. Haps also wrote this poem:

No man can serve two masters,
No man can follow two flags.
Furl the one you love so well,
Cherish its memory to the end of time;
It was born and baptized in blood,
Now let it rest in peace.
Hoist the other toward high heaven,
Let it float over land and sea,
Proud emblem of liberty.[89]

John Haps died on December 2, 1924, not quite eighty-six years old.

Appendix I: Statistics

A few sets of data surprised me, and they may stimulate further questions.

Birthplaces of the Seventy-Six Iowa Confederates
A total 42 percent of Iowa Confederates were born in the South, and 28 percent were born in the North. A further 21 percent were born in the Ohio Valley, which could be classified as either North or South, depending on the neighborhood, and 9 percent of Iowa Confederates were born in a foreign country.

Birthplaces of Parents
A total 39 percent of parents of Iowa Confederates were both born in the South, and 31 percent of the parents were split between South and North; 14 percent of the parents were born in the North; 2 percent were split between the North and a foreign country; and 15 percent of parents were foreign born. (These numbers are rounded up.)

Divided Families
Nineteen men (that is, 25 percent of Iowa Confederates) had one or more immediate family members who served the Union.

Service in the Confederacy
The largest number of Iowa Confederates served in the infantry. Cavalry was a close second, followed by the artillery. Diminishing numbers of Iowans served in the Confederate civil service, and only for part of the war. One Iowan ran an armory, one was an *aide-de-camp* to a Confederate governor (tasked with quelling rebellious Unionists), and one man divided his service between the Confederate Army and Navy.

Desertions

Eleven Iowa Confederates (14.4 percent) deserted. This figure is a little higher than the 12.8 percent of all combined Union troops who deserted, according to historian Ella Lonn (drawing on Thomas L. Livermore's estimates) and much higher than the overall Confederate desertion rate of 9.6 percent (citing Provost Marshal General James B. Fry's estimate). Nine of the eleven Iowa Confederates deserted in 1862 or 1863, but the other two deserted in April or May 1865, when many Confederate troops melted away. Two sets of brothers make up the largest number of Iowans who deserted.

Post-War

Sixty-six Iowa Confederates survived the war. More than one-third of them (twenty-three) visited Iowa after the war. Half of that group remained in Iowa the rest of their lives. As noted previously, Confederate service sometimes became a post-war campaign issue (just as it had been during the war).

Appendix II: Names

Iowans who lived two years in-state before Confederate service (and counties of residence)

Seneca McNeil Bain (Jasper County)
Green Ballinger (Lee County)
William Wirt Bird (Dubuque County)
John C. Booth (Polk County)
Joseph Collins Brownfield (Clayton County)
Samuel Bulger (Clinton County)
George Burgoon (Scott County)
Joseph Amos Burgoon (Scott County)
William Valentine Burton (Van Buren County)
William Campbell (Clayton County)
Watkins Joseph Cantillon (Dubuque County)
James Nathaniel Cobb (Lucas County)
James Madison Collier (Madison County)
William P. Cresap (Des Moines County)
Bromfield R. Crosthwait (Johnson County)
Frank Crosthwait (Johnson County)
Shelton Crosthwait (Johnson County)
James Marion Dicken (Bremer County)
Moses Scruggs Douglass (Madison County)
Benjamin William Dudley (Lee County)
J. B. Edelen (Des Moines County)
Frederick von Ende (Des Moines County)
William Henri Farner (Lee, Polk, Pottawattamie Counties)
Edward S. Flint (Delaware County)
Samuel K. Fowler (Lee County)
Cyrus Franklin (Wapello County)
John Haps (Lee County)
Charles Bernidot Harris (Jackson County)
George Webster Harris (Jackson County)
Augustus C. Hayden (Van Buren County)
Daniel W. Hayden (Van Buren County)
George C. Hayden (Van Buren County)
Jacob T. Hayden (Van Buren County)

John R. Hayden (Van Buren County)
Junius Lackland Hempstead (Dubuque County)
John Flournoy Henry (Des Moines County)
Joseph S. Howard (Lee, Lucas Counties)
Charles Scott Dodge Jones (Dubuque County)
Gabriel Scott Jones (Dubuque County)
George Rice Gratiot Jones (Dubuque County)
Ambrose Key (Louisa County)
Andrew V. Knight (Wapello County)
George S. Laswell (Wapello County)
Robert R. Lawther (Muscatine County)
Thomas W. Lewis (Dubuque County)
Warner Lewis Jr. (Dubuque County)
John Terrill Lovell (Dubuque County)
Winchester Miller (Jefferson County)
James Ramsey Moore (Lee County)
Napoleon Bonaparte Morgan (Madison County)
William A. Musser (Pottawattamie County)
Albert H. Newell (Des Moines County)
Virgil M. Pendleton (Des Moines County)
Cornelius V. Putman (Lee, Linn Counties)
John A. B. Putman (Lee, Linn Counties)
Andrew Jackson Quigley (Dubuque County)
Daniel O'Connell Quigley (Dubuque County)
Miles Ramay (Louisa County)
John C. Shipley (Muscatine County)
William Smith (Madison County)
George Washington Swailes (Henry County)
George Talty (Scott County)
John Talty (Scott County)
Patrick Talty (Scott County)
Simon Talty (Scott County)
Philip Van Patten (Clinton, Lee Counties)
Benton Boone Wainscott (Decatur County)
Jefferson Straton Wainscott (Decatur County)
Wilson Hunt Wainscott (Decatur County)
William Henry Wall (Henry County)
Francis Whicher (Muscatine County)
Patterson Venable Whicher (Muscatine County)
Spier Whitaker Jr. (Scott County)
Spier Whitaker Sr. (Scott County)
James H. Williams (Dubuque County)
William Sidney Winder (Lee County)

Endnotes

Abbreviations: CSR (Confederate Service Record); WD (James H. Williams Diaries)

Introduction

1. Cooper, W. J., *Jefferson Davis, American* (2000), xiv.
2. Mulley, C., *The Women who Flew for Hitler* (2017), ix.

Chapter 1

1. Potter, D. M., *Impending Crisis: America Before the Civil War, 1848–1861* (2011), p. 43.
2. Wubben, H. H., *Civil War Iowa and the Copperhead Movement* (1980) p. 233.
3. 1840 Federal Census, Dubuque County.
4. Mayors of Dubuque, Iowa, 1837–Present.
5. Davidson, J. N., "Negro Slavery in Wisconsin and the Underground Railroad" (1897), p. 36
6. Dykstra, R., *Bright Radical Star* (1993), 12.
7. Parish, J. C., *George Wallace Jones* (1912), pp. 5-7.
8. Mahoney, T. R., "Rise and Fall of the Booster Ethos in Dubuque, 1850–1861" (2002), p. 382.
9. Parish, *op. cit.*, p. 176.
10. *Ibid.*, pp. 40-41.
11. Macy, J., *Anti-Slavery Crusade* (1919), p. 109.
12. Milton, G. F., *Eve of Conflict* (1934), pp. 107-109.
13. Parker, L. F., "A Pioneer Lyceum," Leonard F. Parker papers.
14. Douglass, T. O., Pilgrims of Iowa (1911), pp. 128-129.
15. Potter, D. M., *Lincoln and His Party in the Secession Crisis* (1995), p. 47.
16. Wubben, *op. cit.*, p. 20.
17. Milton, *op. cit.*, pp. 272-273.
18. Parish, *op. cit.*, pp. 52-54.

19. G. W. Jones to Laurel Summers, March 6, 1858, Laurel Summers Papers.
20. Sage, L. L. *William Boyd Allison* (1956), p. 39.
21. Milton, *op. cit.*, p. 312.
22. Parish, *op. cit.*, pp. 56-57.
23. Cooke, G. W., *Ralph Waldo Emerson* (1882), p. 140.
24. Wyatt-Brown, B., *Shaping of Southern Culture* (2001), p. 182.
25. Bartlett, D. W., *Life and Public Services of Hon. Abraham Lincoln* (1860), p. 104.
26. Dubuque Times, August 6, 1859, in Wulkow,H., *Dubuque in the Civil War Period* (1949), pp. 40-43.
27. *Iowa State Journal*, August 27, September 3, 1860.
28. Fulton, C. J., "Jefferson County Politics Before the Civil War," *Annals of Iowa* (1914), pp. 450-451.
29. Potter, 1995, *op. cit.*, pp. 6, 9.
30. *Ibid.*, p. 13.
31. Lathrop, H.W., *Life and Times of Samuel J. Kirkwood* (1893), 112.
32. Wubben, *op. cit.*, pp. 26, 233.
33. Potter, 1995, *op. cit.*, p. 52.
34. *Ibid.*, p. 52.
35. *Ibid.*, p. 157.
36. *Ibid.*, pp. 16-17.
37. Holzer, H., *Lincoln, President-Elect* (2008), p. 168.
38. Wyatt-Brown, *op. cit.*, pp. 177-178.
39. *Ibid.*, 199-200.
40. Potter, 1995, *op. cit.*, pp. 41-42.
41. *Ibid.*, 200.
42. Wyatt-Brown, *op. cit.*, p. 183.
43. Rosenberg, M. M., *Iowa on the Eve of the Civil War* (1972), pp. 31-33.
44. *Ibid.*, pp. 31-33.
45. McPherson, J. M., *Battle Cry of Freedom* (1988), pp. 195-196.
46. Curran, R. E., ed., *John Dooley's Civil War* (2012), p. 289.

Chapter 2

1. State Democratic Press editor, spring 1861, Wubben, *op. cit.*, p.39.
2. Abraham Lincoln, First Inaugural Address, March 4, 1861, Jones, A.T., ed., *Political Speeches and Debates of Abraham Lincoln and Stephen A. Douglas* (1895), p. 533.
3. Charles Mason, August 8, 1861, *Burlington Weekly Hawk-eye and Telegraph*, August 17, 1861.
4. Wubben, *op. cit.*, p. 49.
5. Neely, M. E., *Fate of Liberty* (1991), pp. 19-21.
6. Miles, T. J., *Conspiracy of Leading Men of the Republican Party to Destroy the American Union* (1864), p. 5.
7. Wubben, *op. cit.*, p. 54.
8. G. W. Jones to Jefferson Davis, November 30, 1858, DIY History.
9. Parish, *op. cit.*, G. W. Jones on visiting Lincoln, pp. 236-242.
10. G. W. Jones to Jefferson Davis, May 17, 1861, Parish, *op. cit.*, p. 62

11. G. W. Jones to Laurel Summers, May 17, 1861, Laurel Summers Papers.
12. "Traitor Jones," *Muscatine Journal*, December 27, 1861.
13. *Burlington Hawk-eye*, February 8, 1862.
14. "The Traitor Jones," *Chicago Post*, February 14, 1862.
15. "Operations in Tennessee," *New York Times*, February 7, 1862.
16. "A Rich Document," *Burlington Weekly Hawk-eye and Telegraph*, July 12, 1862.
17. *Ibid.*
18. Warner Lewis to Laurel Summers, January 10, 1862, Laurel Summers Papers.
19. Parish, *op. cit.*, pp. 245-246.
20. Neely, *op. cit.*, p. 52.
21. Neely, *op. cit.*, pp. 53-54.
22. Rehnquist, W. H., *All the Laws by One: Civil Liberties in Wartime* (1998), pp. 59-60.
23. Wubben, *op. cit.*, pp. 64-67.
24. Abraham Lincoln to Erastus Corning, June 12, 1863, Moore, F., *Rebellion Record*, Vol. VII (1864), pp. 299-303.
25. *Ibid.*
26. Wubben, *op. cit.*, 65-67.
27. Sage, *op. cit.*, pp. 56-58.
28. Wubben, *op. cit.*, pp. 65-67.
29. Abraham Lincoln to Erastus Corning, June 12, 1863, Moore, *op. cit.*, p. 305.
30. Albany Democratic Committee to Abraham Lincoln, June 30, 1863, Moore, *op. cit.*, p. 306.
31. Wubben, *op. cit.*, pp. 64-65.
32. Wubben., *op. cit.*, p. 65.
33. "Secret Movements of Northern Traitors," *Dubuque Daily Times*, July 20, 1862.
34. Klement, F. L., *Lincoln's Critics: The Copperheads of the North* (1999), pp. 14-17.
35 Sage, *op. cit.*, pp. 53-56.
36. *Burlington Weekly Hawk-eye and Telegraph*, May 26, 1863.
37. *Muscatine Journal*, July 23, 1863.
38. *Journal of Tenth General Assembly of the State of Iowa* (1864), 47.
39. *Burlington Weekly Hawk-eye and Telegraph*, June 4, 1864.
40. Wubben, *op. cit.*, pp. 111-112.
41. *Ibid.*
42. *Ibid.*
43. S. J. Kirkwood to Thomas Clagett, *Burlington Hawk-eye*, 8/17/1863, Wubben, *op. cit.*, 112.
44. Wubben, *op. cit.*, pp. 111-112, 168.
45. *Magazine of Poetry: Quarterly Review Illustrated*, Vol. IV (1892), p. 177.
46. Stephen Hempstead to Charles Mason, January 27, 1865, Charles Mason Papers.
47. J. L. Hempstead to D.C. Cram, September 2, 1865, VMI Archives.
48. J. L. Hempstead CSR.
49. "Candidate for County Judge," *Dubuque Daily Evening Union*, September 25, 1861.
50. "Judge Hempstead and His Rebel Son," *Dubuque Daily Evening Union*, October 4, 1861.
51. "Spirit of Ex-Governor Hempstead is Borne Over the Dark River," *Dubuque Herald*, February 17, 1883.

52. Confederate officers to Jefferson Davis, August 12, 1861, J.L. Hempstead CSR.
53. "Hon. Stephen Hempstead," *History of Dubuque County, Iowa* (1880), 803.
54. WD, September 14, 1861.
55. Murray, J. O., *Immortal Six Hundred* (1905), pp. 87-88, 93-95.
56. Murray, *op. cit.*, pp. 29-32.
57. J. L. Hempstead Diary, "'How Long will this Misery Continue?'" Beatty, B. and Caprio, J., eds., *Civil War Times Illustrated* (1981).
58. *Ibid.*, September 24, 1864.
59. *Ibid.*, September 28, 1864.
60. *Ibid.*, October 5, 1864.
61. *Ibid.*, September 18, 1864.
62. *Ibid.*, September 29, 1864.
63. *Diary of Capt. Henry C. Dickinson, C.S.A.*, December 29, 1864 (1910).
64. Stephen Hempstead to Charles Mason, January 27, 1865, Mason Papers.
65. Stephen Hempstead to Charles Mason, February 23, 1865, Mason Papers.
66. J. L. Hempstead to Abraham Lincoln, February 16, 1865, Mason Papers.
67. *Ibid.*
68. Stephen Hempstead to Charles Mason, February 23, 1865, Mason Papers.
69. J. L. Hempstead to Stephen Hempstead, March 12, 1865, Mason Papers.
70. J. L. Hempstead to Lavinia Hempstead, March 31, 1865, Mason Papers.
71. Stephen Hempstead to Andrew Johnson, April 17, 1865, Mason Papers.
72. Stephen Hempstead to Charles Mason, May 25, 1865, Mason Papers.
73. J. L. Hempstead to Paul Cantwell, August 20, 1865, J.L.P. Cantwell Papers.
74. *Ibid.*, September 21, 1865.
75. *Ibid.*, November 22, 1865.
76. Hempstead, J., "How the Six Hundred Officers Fared," *Confederate Veteran* (1908).
77. "Decease of Mrs. Hempstead and Mr. McNamara," January 4, 1871, *Dubuque Herald*.
78. Parish, *op. cit.*, pp. 9-11.
79. *Ibid.*, p. 10.
80. Kellie-Smith, G., "Difficult with Learning or Learning to be Difficult?" (2003), p. 251.
81. Parish, *op. cit.*, p. 10.
82. Davis, V., *Jefferson Davis, Ex-President of the Confederate States of America*, Vol. I (1890), pp. 82-89.
83. Parish, *op. cit.*, p.14.
84. *Ibid.*, pp. 27, 31.
85. 1840 Federal Census, Dubuque County.
86. Parish, *op. cit.*, pp. 65-66 and 24-25.
87. Mahoney, 2002, *op. cit.*, pp. 382-383.
88. Rosenberg, *op. cit.*, pp. 67-68.
89. Green, J. R., *Military Education and the Emerging Middle Class in the Old South* (2008), pp. 10 and 136-137.
90. WMI Register, 1850–1861.
91. Warren, C., *History of Harvard Law School*, III (1908), p. 66.
92. G. W. Jones to Jefferson Davis, November 30, 1858, DIY History.
93. Parish, *op. cit.*, pp. 41-51.
94. Rosenberg, *op. cit.*, pp. 31-33.
95. Mahoney, 2002, *op. cit.*, pp. 406, 417.

96. G. W. Jones to Augustus Jones, May 27, 1861, G.W. Jones Correspondence, Seward Papers.
97. Parish, *op. cit.*, pp. 216-223.
98. Parish, *op. cit.*, pp. 225-227.
99. Lehman, M. J., "Observations on Chagres Fever," *Annual Report of the Supervising Surgeon-General of the Marine Hospital Service* (1889), p. 100.
100. Cooper, R., "A Case of Ague (Chagres Fever)" *British Journal of Homeopathy* (1875), pp. 698-700.
101. Varney, N. S., "Statement of Nils S. Varney," Iowa City, Iowa Medical Center (2012).
102. Parish, *op. cit.*, pp. 226-227.
103. Wulkow, *op. cit.*, pp. 40-43.
104. G. W. Jones to Augustus Jones, May 27, 1861, Seward Papers.
105. G. W. Jones to Jefferson Davis, May 17, 1861, Seward Papers.
106. G. W. Jones to Jefferson Davis, January 20, 1861 Crist, L.L., ed., *Papers of Jefferson Davis, Vol. VII*, 1861, p. 17.
107. Josephine Jones to G. W. Jones, July 10, 1861, Seward Papers.
108. C. S. D. Jones to G. W. Jones, September 8, 1861, Seward Papers.
109. *Ibid.*
110. C. S. D. Jones to G. W. Jones, April 9, 1861, Seward Papers.
111. *Ibid.*
112. G. W. Jones to Charles Mason, September 11, 1865, Mason Papers.
113. Josephine Jones to G. W. Jones, August 25, 1861, Seward Papers.
114. G. W. Jones to Augustus Jones, May 27, 1861, Seward Papers.
115. Josephine Jones to G. W. Jones, August 25, 1861, Seward Papers.
116. *Ibid.*
117. C. S. D. Jones to G. W. Jones, July 6, 1861, Seward Papers.
118. C. S. D. Jones to S. E. Hunter, July 1, 1861, Wilkie, F., *Pen and Powder* (1888), pp. 157-159.
119. C. S. D. Jones to G. W. Jones, July 31, 1861, Seward Papers.
120. C. S. D. Jones to G. W. Jones, September 25, 1861, Seward Papers.
121. *Ibid.*
122. Josephine Jones to G. W. Jones, August 25, 1861, Seward Papers.
123. Wubben, *op. cit.*, p. 54
124. G. W. Jones to R. E. Lee, January 15, 1869, Mary Custis Lee Collection, 1835–1918.
125. Cooper, W. J., *op. cit.*, 288.
126. Davis, V., *op. cit.*, pp. 579-581.
127. G. W. Jones to Jefferson Davis, November 30, 1858, DIY History.
128. Parish, *op. cit.*, pp. 235-241.
129. *Muscatine Journal*, December 21, 1861, p. 2.
130. G. W. Jones to Jefferson Davis, May 17, 1861, Seward Papers.
131. B. M. Samuels to W. H. Seward, December 24, 1861, Mason Papers.
132. Parish, *op. cit.*, pp. 245-246.
133. Jones., J. W., *The Davis Memorial Volume* (1897), p. 50.
134. C. S. D. Jones to Jefferson Davis, August 10, 1863, C.S.D. Jones CSR.
135. C. S. D. Jones to Jefferson Davis, May 2, 1863, C.S.D. Jones CSR.
136. C. S. D. Jones to Jefferson Davis, December 23, 1886, Jefferson Davis Collection.
137. Receipt to C. S. D. Jones, May 31, 1862, C. S. D. Jones CSR.
138. C. S. D. Jones to C. D. Memminger, November 11, 1862, C. S. D. Jones CSR.

139. C. S. D. Jones to Jefferson Davis, May 2, 1863, C. S. D. Jones CSR.

140. C. S. D. Jones to Jefferson Davis, August 10, 1863, C. S. D. Jones CSR.

141. "From Richmond," *Dubuque Daily Times*, November 29, 1863.

142. Cook, "Story of the Six Hundred," *Confederate Veteran*, Vol. V (1897), 116-117.

143. T. F. Bayard to G. W. Jones, October 9, 1864, G. W. Jones Correspondence, Des Moines.

144. C. S. D. Jones to T. F. Bayard, October 20, 1864, T. F. Bayard Papers.

145. "Capture of Dubuque Rebels," *Dubuque Daily Times*, May 26, 1864.

146. G. W. Jones to J. A. Bayard, October 9, 1864, G. W. Jones Correspondence, Des Moines.

147. G. W. Jones to T. F. Bayard, November 28, 1864, T. F. Bayard Papers.

148. C. S. D. Jones to Jefferson Davis, March 25, 1865, C. S. D. Jones CSR.

149. *Ibid.*

150. J. J. Miller to James Speed, September 20, 1865, C. S. D. Jones CSR.

151. "JONES," *Daily Iowa State Register*, May 4, 1866.

152. *Dubuque Directory* (1870).

153. R. E. Lee to G. W. Jones, March 22, 1869, Lee Family Papers, 1824–1914.

154. C. S. D. Jones to William Corly, November 3, 1878, Notre Dame University Archives.

155. Waples, "Return of Physician," March 7, 1877, Iowa Hospital for the Insane.

156. C. S. D. Jones to Jefferson Davis, December 23, 1886, Jefferson Davis Collection.

157. *Ibid.*

158. *Ibid.*

159. Luke 12:3, *King James Bible*.

160. Mahoney, 2002 *op. cit.*, pp. 383-384.

161. H. H. Heath to H. St. George Offutt, April 9, 1861, H. H. Heath Confederate Civilian Record.

162. C. S. D. Jones to G. W. Jones, July 6, 1861, Seward Papers.

163. Josephine Jones to G. W. Jones, August 25, 1861, Seward Papers.

164. H. H. Heath to U.S. Senators, February 21, 1870, Houghton Library.

165. P. J. Kelly to George Williamson, May 16, 1862, P. J. Kelly CSR.

166. Aurner, C. R., "Johnson County in the Civil War," *Leading Events in Johnson County, Iowa*, Vol. I (1912), p. 505.

167. "An Iowa Renegade," *Memphis Daily Argus*, in *Dubuque Daily Times*, May 7, 1861.

168. *Ibid.*

169. P. J. Kelly to Leonidas Polk, September 6, 1861, P. J. Kelly, *op. cit.*

170. *Ibid.*

171. P. J. Kelly to Leonidas Polk, April 11, 1862, P. J. Kelly, CSR.

172. P. J. Kelly to George Williamson, May 16, 1862, P. J. Kelly, CSR.

173. "Recruiting for the National Service," *New York Times*, July 13, 1862.

174. *Ibid.*

175. *Ibid.*

176. Palmer, N., Summaries of A.H. Newell and Rev. Albert Newell.

177. Palmer, *op. cit.*

178. A. H. Newell CSR.

179. Williams, J., "Private Albert H. Newell".

180. Williams, J., *op. cit.*

181. Susan Carpenter to C. C. Carpenter, April 20, 1865, Wubben, *op. cit.*, p. 216.

182. E. W. Eastman to Andrew Johnson, July 8, 1865, Bergeron, P. H., ed., *Papers of Andrew Johnson: May-August 1865* (1990), p. 369.

183. Williams, J., *op. cit.*

184. C. S. Manning Testimony, G. S. Bailey Union Citizens File.

185. Murray, C., "Madison County During the War" (1908).

186. Wubben, *op. cit.*, pp. 67-68 and 122-123.

187. Marshall, J. A., *American Bastille* (1871), pp. 421-425.

188. Wubben, *op. cit.*, p. 69.

189. *History of Madison County, Iowa* (1879), p. 72.

190. *Muscatine Courier*, December 27, 1862, Wubben, *op. cit.*, pp. 68-69.

191. H. M. Hoxie to John Kasson, February 24, 1863, Adjutant-General's Correspondence.

192. Winterset Citizens to S. J. Kirkwood, Adjutant-General's Correspondence.

193. Wubben, *op. cit.*, p. 68.

194. H. M. Hoxie to E. M. Stanton, February 25, 1863, enclosure no. 4 to S. J. Kirkwood to Stanton, March 13, 1863, *War of Rebellion*, Ser. III, Vol. III (1899), pp. 66-72.

195. *Ibid.*

196. Murray, C., *op. cit.*

197. Klement, F., "Rumors of Golden Circle Activity in Iowa during the Civil War Years," *Annals of Iowa* (1965), 535-536.

198. Stevens, W. B., *Centennial History of Missouri* (1921), pp. 214-217.

199. Federal Census, 1860, Van Buren County, Iowa.

200. Stevens, W. B., *St. Louis: History of the Fourth City*, Vol. II (1909), pp. 37-40.

201. Marvel, W., *Lincoln's Autocrat* (2015), p. 220.

202. Neely, *op. cit.*, pp. 51-54.

203. Barbara Wells to author, e-mail, October 10, 2014.

204. J. D. Sandford to Provost Marshal, St. Louis, September 1, 1862, Missouri Union Provost Marshal Records.

205. Stevens, 1909, *op. cit.*, pp. 37-40.

206. W. V. Burton CSR.

207. Barbara Wells to author, e-mail, October 10, 2014.

208. "William V. Burton's $250,000 Estate in Trust," undated clipping.

209. *Confederate Veteran* (1922), p. 473.

210. Henry, J. F., *A History of the Henry Family* (1900), pp. 99-101.

211. *Transactions of the McLean County Historical Society* (1899), pp. 359-363.

212. *Burlington Daily Hawk-eye and Telegraph*, February 17, 1862.

213. Wubben, *op. cit.*, p. 40.

214. August 23, 1861, *Burlington Daily Hawk-eye*, Lendt, D., *Demise of the Democracy: The Copperhead Press in Iowa* (1973), p. 75.

215. Marvel, *op. cit.*, p. 220.

216. Henry, *op. cit.*, pp. 99-101.

217. Shambaugh, B. F., *Messages and Proclamations of the Governors of Iowa*, Vol. III (1903), pp. 13-14.

218. Draft Registrations, First Congressional District, Iowa.

219. J. F. Henry Sr. to Charles Mason, July 12, 1865, Mason Papers.

220. "Jubilee in Burlington," *Burlington Weekly Hawk-eye and Telegraph*, July 11, 1863.

221. *Muscatine Weekly Courier*, July 23, 1863.

222. Henry, *op. cit.*, pp. 99-101.

223. J. F. Henry Sr. to Charles Mason, July 12, 1865, Mason Papers.

224. Neely, *op. cit.*, pp. 75-77.

225. J. F. Henry CSR.

226. Matthews, G. R., *Basil Wilson Duke CSA* (2005), pp. 193-194.

227. Quisenberry, A. C., *Register of Kentucky State Historical Society* (1917), pp. 44-46.

228. J. F. Henry Sr. to Charles Mason, July 12, 1865, Mason Papers.

229. J. F. Henry Sr. to Charles Mason, July 26, 1865, Mason Papers.

230. Wubben, *op. cit.*, pp. 43-44;

231. J. B. Grinnell to S. J. Kirkwood, August 18, 1862, Upham, "Arms and Equipment for Iowa Troops in the Civil War," *Iowa Journal of History and Politics* (1918), p. 15.

232. *Muscatine Weekly Courier*, July 23, 1863, Lendt, *op. cit.*, p. 90.

233. *Iowa State Register*, September 16, 1863, Wubben, *op. cit.*, p. 127.

234. Wubben, *op. cit.*, p. 114.

235. *Journal*, Tenth General Assembly of the State of Iowa, p. 24.

236. Payne, C. E., *Josiah Bushnell Grinnell*, (1938), p. 160.

237. Payne, *op. cit.*, pp. 180-181.

238. Parker, L. F., notes, *History of Poweshiek County, Iowa*.

239. E. D. Williams obituary.

240. Baker, N. B., General Orders 37, October 5, 1864, "Murder of the U.S. Marshals in Poweshiek County," Appendix N, Report, Adjutant-General's Office (1865).

241. M. Gleason deposition, "Trial of Gleason," *Davenport Daily Gazette*, November 5, 1867.

242. J. Mathews to Major Duncan and W.M. Stone, October 1, 1864, Appendix N., *op. cit.*

243. J. J. Alyea testimony, Trial of Gleason, *op. cit.*, November 2, 1867

244. *Ibid.*

245. J. Mathews, *op. cit.*, October 1, 1864.

246. T. Reed testimony, Trial of Gleason, *op. cit.*, November 5, 1867.

247. J. Mathews, *op. cit.*, October 1, 1864.

248. Burlington Weekly Hawk-eye, October 8, 1864.

249. *Montezuma Republican*, in *Muscatine Journal*, in *Burlington Hawk-eye*, October 15, 1864.

250. J. Bowers, S. A. Allen grand jury statements, December 14, 1864.

251. Parker, *op. cit.*, pp. 218-219.

Chapter 3

1. 1860 Federal Slave Schedule, Shenandoah Valley, Virginia

2. Johnston, F., *Memorials of Old Virginia Clerks* (1888), pp. 367-368.

3. August 23, September 9, 1861, WD.

4. Goodspeed, *op. cit.*, p. 455.

5. September 22, 1859, Lovell Diary.

6. January 9, 1860, January 8, 16, 1861, WD.

7. January 22, 1859, WD.

8. Goodspeed, *op. cit.*, p. 346.

9. May 12, 1861, WD.

10. Johnston, *op. cit.*, pp. 367-368.
11. D. C. Cram to J. H. Williams, May 3, 1861, *Dubuque Daily Times*.
12. D. C. Cram to J. H. Williams, May 10, 1861, *Dubuque Daily Times*.
13. May 12, 1861, WD.
14. *Journal of the Iowa House of Representatives, Spring 1861*, p. 49.
15. *Dubuque Herald*, May 23, 1861.
16. "Inkerman," *Dubuque Herald*, June 2, 1861.
17. *Dubuque Herald*, December 14, 1860, Wubben, *op. cit.*, p. 29.
18. *Dubuque Daily Times*, May 16, 1862.
19. *Journal* of the Iowa House, *op. cit.*, p. 118.
20. "Inkerman," *Dubuque Herald*, June 2, 1861.
21. Johnston, *op. cit.*, pp. 367-368.
22. J. H. Williams, *Dubuque Herald*, June 29, 1861.
23. L. Clark to J. H. Williams, *Dubuque Herald*, July 10, 1861.
24. J. H. Williams to L. Clark, *Dubuque Herald*, July 11, 1861.
25. J. H. Williams to J. E. B. Stuart, December 28, 1863, J. H. Williams CSR.
26. "Ominous," *Dubuque Times*, July 17, 1861.
27. "A Dubuque Representative in the Secesh Army," *Dubuque Daily Times*, May 16, 1862.
28. July 22, 1861, WD.
29. July 24 to 31, 1861, WD.
30. August 2 and 12, 1861, WD.
31. August 5, 7, 12, 1861, WD.
32. August 8,9, 1861, WD.
33. August 14, 1861, WD.
34. August 13,1861, WD.
35. August 24, 26, 1861, WD.
36. September 2, 1861, WD.
37. October 12, 1861, WD.
38. September 14, 1861, WD.
39. November 2, 1861, WD.
40. Avirett, J. B., *Memoirs of General Turner Ashby* (1867), p. 131.
41. November 4, 1861, WD.
42. Cora D. Pritchartt to J. H. Williams, November 4, 1861. Their correspondence is in the Williams Family Papers.
43. November 16, 1861, WD.
44. November 19, 1861, WD.
45. J. H. Williams to Cora, November 25, 1861.
46. Cora to J. H. Williams, November 27, 1861.
47. J. H. Williams to Cora, December 10, 1861.
48. J. H. Williams to Cora, November 25, 1861.
49. *Ibid.*
50. J. H. Williams to Cora, November 30, 1861.
51. J. H. Williams to Cora, December14 1861.
52. Cora to J. H. Williams, December 26, 1861.
53. J. H. Williams to Cora, December 18, 1861.
54. Cora to J. H. Williams, January 24, 1862.
55. Cora to J. H. Williams, March 26, 1862.
56. Cora to J. H. Williams, June 21, 1862.

57. Cora to J. H. Williams, June 1, 1862.
58. Cora to J. H. Williams, March 17, 1862.
59. Cora to J. H. Williams, July 10, 1862.
60. Cora to J. H. Williams, February 18, 1863.
61. J. H. Williams to Cora, December 26. 1862.
62. J. H. Williams to Cora, February 2, 1863.
63. J. H. Williams to Cora, February 3, 1863.
64. Cora to J. H. Williams, February 9, 1863.
65. J. H. Williams to Cora, March 27 1863.
66. J. H. Williams to Cora, March 31. 1863.
67. Cora to J. H. Williams, April 13, 1863.
68. Cora to J. H. Williams, April 13, 1863.
69. J. H. Williams to Cora, June 10, 1863.
70. J. H. Williams to Cora, June 16, 1863.
71. J. H. Williams to Cora, July 8, 1863.
72. J. H. Williams to Cora, July 25,1863.
73. Cora to J. H. Williams, August 8, 1863.
74. Cora to J. H. Williams, July 30, 1865.
75. J. H. Williams to Cora, February 13, 1863.
76. Robinson, W. M., *Justice in Grey* (1941), pp. 364-365.
77. J. H. Williams to Cora, March 30, 1863.
78. J. H. Williams to Cora, September 25, 1863.
79. J. H. Williams to Cora, September 24, 1863.
80. J. B. Minor, October 15, 1863, J. H. Williams CSR.
81. T. G. Green to Jefferson Davis, October 10, 1862, J. H. Williams CSR.
82. J. H. Williams to J. E. B. Stuart, December 28, 1863, J. H. Williams CSR.
83. J. H. Williams to Cora, February 3, 1864.
84. J. H. Williams to Cora, October 24, 1864.
85. *Ibid.*
86. J. W. Thomson to J. C. Breckinridge, March 17, 1865, J. H. Williams CSR.
87. Fitz Lee to J. C. Breckinridge, February 25, 1865, with R. E. Lee note, J. H. Williams CSR.
88. Cora to J. H. Williams, July 30, 1865.
89. J. H. Williams to Cora, January 28, 1866.
90. J. H. Williams to Cora, August 9, 1866.
91. J. H. Williams to Cora, April 26, 1869.
92. J. H. Williams to Cora, November 8, 1866.
93. J. H. Williams to Cora, April 16, 1869.
94. Rachleff, P., "The Readjusters," *Organizing Black America* (2001), p. 521.
95. Rachleff, P., *Black Labor in Richmond, 1865–1890* (1984), p. 108.
96. Armstrong, W. H., *William McKinley and the Civil War* (2000), p. 134.
97. J. H. Williams obituary, *Evening Star*, December 7, 1903.
98. John Jackson ("Black Hawk"), *Confederate Veteran* (1912), p. 410.
99. "Gen. J. H. Williams," December 11, 1903, *Shenandoah Herald*, p. 3.
100. "Mrs. Cora Pritchartt Williams," *Confederate Veteran* (1927), 429.
101. J. O'Hea Cantillon obituary, *Dubuque Daily Herald*, April 1, 1879.
102. "W. J. Cantillon," *Dubuque Evening Globe Journal*, October 25, 1900.
103. Goodspeed, *op. cit.*, pp. 343-344.

104. W. J. Cantillon CSR.
105. *Dubuque Herald*, July 13, 1861.
106. *Dubuque Herald*, August 3, 1861.
107. Hearn, C. G., *Mobile Bay and the Mobile Campaign* (1993), pp. 187-191.
108. "W. J. Cantillon," *Dubuque Evening Globe Journal*, October 25, 1900.
109. 1870 Federal Census, Dubuque, Iowa.
110. *Waterloo Daily Courier*, September 20, 1892.
111. "W. J. Cantillon," *Dubuque Evening Globe Journal*, October 25, 1900.
112. *Dubuque Herald*, September 3, 1865.
113. Mayors of Dubuque, Iowa, 1837–Present
114. G. W. Jones to Jefferson Davis, August 25, 1882, Jefferson Davis Collection.
115. "Senex" (Patrick Quigley), *Dubuque Herald*, January 13, 1861, in Clark, O. B., *Politics of Iowa During Civil War and Reconstruction* (1911), p. 60.
116. Childs, C. C., *Dubuque: Frontier River City* (1984), pp. 85-86.
117. Mahoney, 2002, *op. cit.*, p. 404;
118. *History of Dubuque County*, *op. cit.*, p. 540.
119. D. O'C. Quigley CSR.
120. C. S. D. Jones to S. E. Hunter, July 1, 1861, in Wilkie, F., *op. cit*, pp. 157-159.
121. "Daniel O'Connell Quigley," Encyclopedia Dubuque.
122. 1850 Federal Census, Dubuque, Iowa.
123. Warner Lewis Sr. obituary, *Dubuque Herald*, May 4, 1888.
124. *Alexandria Gazette*, January 11, 1854.
125. *Annual Catalogue ... of ... Cornell College* (1856);
126. Beloit Academy Inventory.
127. T. W. Lewis CSR.
128. *Burlington Weekly Hawk-eye and Telegraph*, June 21, 1862.
129. T. W. Lewis CSR.
130. June 9, 1852, Lovell Diary.
131. Jones, M. C., *Descendants of Gabriel Jones of Essex and Culpeper Counties, Virginia* (1949), 52.
132. March 3, April 1, 27, 1858, WD.
133. "Public Meeting in the County of Culpeper," April 15, 1861, Virginia Secession Convention documents.
134. G. S. Jones to Secretary of Treasury, February 8, 1862, G. S. Jones CSR.
135. Robert Toombs to C. G. Memminger, July 7, 1862, G. S. Jones CSR.
136. Jones, M. E., *op. cit*, p. 52.
137. B. B. Richards to R. B. Griffin, June 28, 1870, Griffin Collection.
138. J. T. Lovell to R. B. Griffin, July 15, 1861, Griffin Collection.
139. W. W. Bird CSR.

Chapter 4

1. Salter, W., *Sixty Years and Other Discourses* (1907), p. 307.
2. Green Ballinger CSR.
3. Salter, *op. cit.*, p. 309.
4. 1850 Slave Census, Barbourville, Knox County, Kentucky.
5. Moretta, J. A., *William Pitt Ballinger* (2000), pp. 15, 59.

6. Ross, *Justice of Shattered Dreams* (2003), 19, 25-28.
7. *Ibid.*, pp. 41-44.
8. E-mails, John Moretta and author, March 11, 2012.
9. Koonce, D. B., *Doctor to the Front* (2000), p. 7.
10. "Terry's Texas Rangers," *Confederate Veteran* (1907), p. 498/
11. Moretta, *op. cit.*, p. 144.
12. Moretta, *op. cit.*, p. 181.
13. Salter, *op. cit.*, p. 309.
14. Moretta, *op. cit.*, p. 181.
15. J. M. B. Dicken CSR.
16. Lucas, W. V., *Pioneer Days of Bremer County, Iowa* (1918), p. 10.
17. Wright, M., "General Douglas H. Cooper, C.S.A." (1954), pp. 178-180.
18. Lucas, *op. cit.*, p. 10.
19. *Centennial History of Mount Vernon, Iowa, 1847–1947* (1948), p. 52.
20. *History of Mt. Vernon, op. cit.*, p. 52
21. Matthews, J. M., *Statutes at Large of the Confederate States of America* (1862), p. iii.
22. J. A. B. Putman CSR.
23. C. V. Putman CSR.
24. *History of Mt. Vernon, op. cit.*, p. 52.
25. *Ibid.*
26. *History of Mt. Vernon, op. cit.*, p. 52.
27. Matthews, J. M., *op. cit.*, p. iii;.
28. C. V. Putman CSR.
29. J. A. B. Putman CSR.
30. "Confederate Texas Troops," Civil War Soldiers and Sailors System.
31. J. M. Wester affidavit, Nancy A. Putman Texas Confederate widow's pension application.
32. E-mail, Wesleyan College Archivist Lynn Ellsworth to author, March 7, 2011.
33. G. W. Leavell CSR.
34. J. M. Ray affidavit, Elizabeth Leavell Florida Confederate widow's pension application.
35. Bird, H. T., *Memories of the Civil War* (1925).
36. Elizabeth Leavell Florida Confederate widow's pension application.
37. Leavell, J. A., "Leavells Generation 8, Part 1."
38. Ashe, S. A., *Biographical History of North Carolina* (1908), pp. 479-484.
39. Battle, *Sketches of the History of the University of North Carolina, 1789–1889* (1889), p. 228.
40. Ashe, *op. cit.*, pp. 479-484.
41. James Grant to J. Thorington, May 10, 1862, Spier Whitaker Jr. CSR.
42. Ashe, *op. cit.*, pp. 479-484.
43. *Ibid.*
44. Allen, W. C., *History of Halifax County* (1918), pp. 202-203.
45. *Ibid.*
46. Powell, W. S., ed., *Dictionary of North Carolina Biography* (1996), p. 172.
47. "Married," *Muscatine Journal*, April 2, 1859.
48. Downer, H. E., *History of Davenport and Scott County, Iowa*, Vol. II (1910), p. 605.
49. Nancy Shipley deposition, Shipley v. Shipley (1863).

50. Sigafoos, R. A., *Cotton Row to Beale Street* (1979), pp. 38-39.

51. Nancy Shipley deposition, *op. cit.*

52. *Ibid.*

53. J. C. Shipley CSR.

54. William Chambers deposition, Shipley v. Shipley (1863).

55. Nancy Shipley deposition, *op. cit.*

56. *Muscatine Journal*, April 18, 1862.

57. Brossart, M., Muscatine County, Iowa, Marriage Index.

58. Conversation, A. F. Shipley and author, May 6, 2012.

59. "Major Shipley Answers Summons," *Muscatine Journal*, July 18, 1911.

60. *History of Cass County, Iowa* (1884), pp. 663-664.

61. E-mail, Christine Brugman to author.

62. *History of Cass County, Iowa, op. cit.*, pp. 663-664

63. 1860 slave distribution map.

64. *History of Andrew and DeKalb Counties, Missouri* (1888), pp. 218-223.

65. E-mail,Christine Brugman to author.

66. W. Smith to B. S. Ewell, November 30, 1863, W. Smith CSR.

67. *History of Cass County, Iowa, op. cit.*, pp. 663-664.

68. 1856 Iowa Census, Des Moines County.

69. 1860 Federal Census, Des Moines County, Iowa.

70. W. P. Cresap CSR.

71. W. P. Cresap Missouri Confederate Pension Application.

72. Antrobus, A. M., "Charles Ende," *History of Des Moines County, Iowa* (1915), pp. 402-409.

73. 1856 Iowa Census, Des Moines County.

74. "Fred V. Ende," *Greenville Morning Herald*, March 25, 1925.

75. 1860 Federal Census, Hunt County, Texas.

76. Antrobus, *op. cit.*, 402-409.

77. F. V. Ende CSR.

78. Barr, A., *Polignac's Texas Brigade* (1998),p. 4.

79. "Polignac's Brigade," Handbook of Texas Online.

80. 1856 Iowa Census, Madison County.

81. 1860 Federal Census, Madison County, Iowa.

82. Family trees of Julia Ann Reagan, James Scruggs Douglass.

83. J. M. Collier CSR.

84. M. S. Douglas CSR.

85. Collins, *General James G. Blunt: Tarnished Glory* (2005), p. 149.

86. Julia A. and Franklin P. Douglass tombstones;.

87. Baker, family trees of Julia Ann Reagan and James Scruggs Douglass.

88. Kerby, R. L., *Kirby Smith's Confederacy* (1972), p. 312.

89. "Gordon's Regiment, Arkansas Cavalry," Civil War Soldiers and Sailors System.

90. Kerby, *op. cit.*, pp. 337 and 352.

91. Family tree of Moses Scruggs Douglas.

92. Mary Douglass Arkansas Confederate widow's pension application.

93. E-mail, Susan Cobb Beck to author.

94. 1860 Federal Census, Lucas County, Iowa.

95. E-mail, Susan Cobb Beck to author.

96. J. N. Cobb CSR.

97. Daniel, L. J., Shiloh (1997), p. 208.

98. Isbell, T. T., "Patrick Cleburne and the 2nd Tennessee Infantry," *Shiloh and Corinth* (2007), p. 30.

99. E-mail, Susan Cobb Beck to author.

100. *Ibid.*

101. 1856 Iowa Census, Pottawattamie County.

102. 1860 Federal Census, Pottawattamie County, Iowa.

103. Popchock, B., ed., *Soldier Boy: The Civil War Letters of Charles of Musser, 29th Iowa* (1995), p. 2.

104. W. A. Musser CSR.

105. Winslow, H. L., *Camp Morton 1861–1865 Indianapolis Prison Camp* (1940), pp. 325, 330.

106. Winslow, *op. cit.*, p. 337.

107. C. O. Musser to father, November 27, 1863, Popchock, *op. cit.*, p. 97.

108. Winslow, *op. cit.*, pp. 339-343.

109. C. O. Musser to father, January 17, 1864, Popchock, *op. cit.*, p. 103.

110. C. O. Musser to father, May 20, 1864, Popchock, *op. cit.*, p. 131.

111. Winslow, *op. cit.*, pp. 350 and 353-360.

112. C. O. Musser to father, August 17, 1864, Popchock, *op. cit.*, p. 143.

113. C. O. Musser to father, October 8, 1864, Popchock, *op. cit.*, pp. 157-158.

114. W. A. Musser CSR.

115. Popchock, *op. cit.*, p. 7.

116. C. O. Musser to father, April 1, 1865, Popchock, *op. cit.*, p. 200.

117. Popchock, *op. cit.*, pp. 7-8.

Chapter 5

1. Ellis, J. W., "Virginia Colony," *History of Jackson County, Iowa*, Vol. I (1910), pp. 563-564.

2. Mahoney, T. R., *Provincial Lives* (1999), p. 171.

3. Mahoney, 2002, *op. cit.*, pp. 382-383.

4. "Judge John T. Lovell," French Bassett's Notes on Prominent Virginians.

5. J. T. Lovell to G. B. Waples, March 6, 1852, Waples Papers.

6. J. T. Lovell to G. B. Waples, September 24, 1851, Waples Papers.

7. J. T. Lovell to G. B. Waples, July 20, September 27, 1852, Waples Papers.

8. J. T. Lovell to G. B. Waples, September 27, March 6, 1852, Waples Papers.

9. J. T. Lovell to G. B. Waples, April 13, 1853, Waples Papers.

10. J. T. Lovell to G. B. Waples, November 9, 1856, Waples Papers.

11. Goodspeed, *op. cit.*, p. 455.

12. September 7, 1859, Lovell Diary.

13. J. T. Lovell to R. B. Griffin, September 1, 1861, Griffin Collection.

14. J. T. Lovell to G. B. Waples, September 19, 1860, Waples Papers.

15. *Ibid.*

16. "Inkerman," *Dubuque Herald*, May 29, 1861.

17. "The Fourth at Zwingle," *Dubuque Weekly Times*, July 11, 1861, in Petersen, W.J., "Legal Holidays in Iowa," *Iowa Journal of History and Politics* (1945), p. 123.

18. *Delaware College Review*, Vol. VII, No. 4 (1891), p. 62.

19. September 14, 1861, WD.

20. J. T. Lovell to R. H. G. Kean, August 27, 1862, J. T. Lovell Confederate Civilian Record.

21. J. T. Lovell to R. H. G. Kean, March 30, 1864, J. T. Lovell Confederate Civilian Record.

22. Invoices, August 28, November 27, 1863, J. T. Lovell Confederate Civilian Record.

23. James H. Williams to Cora, February 14, 1866, Williams Family Papers.

24. J. T. Lovell to R. B. Griffin, July 2, 1866, Griffin Collection.

25. J. T. Lovell to R. B. Griffin, August 25, 1866, Griffin Collection.

26. J. T. Lovell to R. B. Griffin, April 1, 1867, Griffin Collection.

27. Hale, "John Terrill Lovell, Owner. Editor, and Publisher," *Warren Sentinel*, March 25, 1954.

28. "Death by Lightning," *St. Joseph Missouri Gazette*, in *Daily Wabash Express*, July 18, 1871.

29. "Judge John T. Lovell," French Bassett's Notes on Prominent Virginians.

30. Hale, "John Terrill Lovell, Owner. Editor, and Publisher," *Warren Sentinel*, March 25, 1954.

31. Powell, W. S., *op. cit.*, p. 172.

32. 1860 Federal Census, Scott County, Iowa.

33. Whitaker, F. D. H., "Spier Whitaker, 1798–1869" (1907), p. 6.

34. Scott County Bar resolution, December 1869, in Whitaker, F.D.H., *op. cit.*, p. 6.

35. Whitaker, F. D. H., *op. cit.*, p. 6.

36. *Ibid.*

37. Spier Whitaker CSR.

38. *Richmond Daily Dispatch*, October 25, 1861.

39. Auman, W. T., *Civil War in the North Carolina Quaker Belt* (2014), pp. 38-39.

40. H. T. Clark to Spier Whitaker, March 6, 1862, Governor's Correspondence (N.C.).

41. Auman, W. T. *op. cit.*, p. 40.

42. *Ibid.*

43. Whitaker, F. D. H., *op. cit.*, pp. 6-8.

44. "Col. Spier Whitaker," *Davenport Daily Gazette*, December 3, 1869.

45. Hasian, M., *In the Name of Necessity* (2005), p. 116.

46. Blakey, A. F., *General John H. Winder* (1990), p. xv.

47. Blakey, *op. cit.*, pp. 36-37, 40, 42-43, 48.

48. Blakey, *op. cit.*, pp. 6-9.

49. Blakey, *op. cit.*, pp. 6-9, 45;

50. W. S. Winder CSR.

51. Blakey, *op. cit.*, pp. 147-148.

52. Blakey, *op. cit.*, pp. 1-3, 151, 157-158, 175-177.

53. Blakey, *op. cit.*, pp. 1-3, 182-183.

54. Blakey, *op. cit.*, pp. 1-3.

55. Blakey, *op. cit.*, pp. 203-204.

56. Hasian, *op. cit.*, pp. 115, 121.

Chapter 6

1. Sigafoos, *op. cit.*, p. 31.

2. Lonn, E., *Foreigners in the Confederacy* (1965), p. 28.

3. Lonn, *op. cit.*, pp. 54-55.

4. George Talty CSR.

5. John Talty CSR.

6. Patrick Talty CSR.

7. Simon Talty, CSR.

8. Draft Registration Records, Second Congressional District, Iowa.

9. *Root's Moline Directory 1867.*

10. 1885 Iowa Census, Atlantic.

11. *Council Bluffs Directory 1897.*

12. Kindig, B. R., *Courage and Devotion* (2014), pp. 76-77.

13. W. O'Day, November 6, 1862, W. O'Day CSR.

14. WPA 1930s Graves Registration Survey.

15. *History of Appanoose County, Iowa* (1878), pp. 504-505.

16. S. B. Bulger CSR.

17. Ainsworth, F. C., and Kirkley, J. W., *War of the Rebellion*, Series II, Vol. 1, p. 92.

18. *History of Appanoose County, Iowa* (1878), pp. 504-505.

19. Philip Bulger CSR.

20. National Park Service, "Battle of Arkansas Post, Stepping Stone to Vicksburg."

21. McCaffrey, J. M., *Only a Private* (2004), p. 81.

22. Draft Registration Records, Second Congressional District, Iowa.

23. Philip Bulger Union Service Record.

24. *Roster and Record of Iowa Troops in the Rebellion*, Vol. II (1908), p. 604.

25. *History of Appanoose County, Iowa, op. cit.*, pp. 504-505.

26. 1856 Iowa Census, Decatur County.

27. *Biographical and Historical Record of Ringgold and Decatur Counties, Iowa* (1887), p. 713.

28. 1860 Federal Census, Decatur County, Iowa.

29. B. B. Wainscott CSR.

30. J. S. Wainscott CSR.

31. "Thirty-Fourth Texas Cavalry," Handbook of Texas Online.

32. "Brush Battalion," Handbook of Texas Online.

33. W. H. Wainscott CSR.

34. C. E. Wainscott CSR.

35. "George Washington Swailes," *Biographical Review of Henry County, Iowa* (1906), pp. 415-418.

36. Amber, "George Washington Swailes" transcription note.

37. G. W. Swailes CSR.

38. *Burlington Hawk-eye*, February 27, 1864.

39. "George Washington Swailes" transcription.

40. Burt Emerson to C. W. Killborn, June 29, 1863, J. C. Brownfield CSR.

41. *History of Texas, Together with a Biographical History of Tarrant and Parker Counties* (1895), pp. 553-557.

Chapter 7

1. 1860 Federal Census, Conway County, Arkansas.

2. Register of Cadet Applicants, United States Military Academy, 1853 to 1854.

3. *Iowa Journal of History and Politics*, Vol. XVII (1919), p. 372.

4. G. S. Laswell to Jefferson Davis, January 12, 1864, G. S. Laswell CSR.

5. Cyrus Franklin obituary, *Ottumwa Weekly Courier*, February 18, 1885.

6. G. S. Laswell CSR.

7. *Little Rock Arkansas True Democrat*, 26 September 1861.

8. G. S. Laswell to Surgeon General, June 12, 1862, G. S. Laswell, *op. cit.*

9. G. S. Laswell to J. P. McCowan, June 26, 1862, G. S. Laswell, *op. cit.*

10. G. S. Laswell, October 24, 1862, G. S. Laswell, *op. cit.*

11. G. S. Laswell to Jefferson Davis, January 12, 1864, G. S. Laswell, *op. cit.*

12. Davis, J., *Rise and Fall of the Confederate Government*, Vol. I (1912), p. 316.

13. 1840 Federal Census, Dubuque County.

14. Parish, *op. cit.*, p. 179.

15. B. R. Johnson to Jefferson Davis, January 1, 1862, G. R. G. Jones CSR.

16. J. G. Soulard to G. W. Jones, February 26, 1862, G. W. Jones Correspondence, State Historical Society of Iowa.

17. C. S. D. Jones to G. W. Jones, July 31, 1861, Seward Papers.

18. Josephine Jones to G. W. Jones, August 25, 1861, Seward Papers.

19. G. R. G. Jones CSR.

20. Parish, *op. cit.*, pp. 60-63.

21. B. R. Johnson to Jefferson Davis, January 1, 1862, G. R. G. Jones CSR.

22. Lloyd Tilghman to G. W. Randolph, November 18, 1862, G. R. G. Jones CSR.

23. Lindsley, J. B., ed., *Military Annals of Tennessee, Confederate*, Vol. II (1886), pp. 860-863.

24. L. Tilghman to W. W. Mackall, February 12, 1862, "Bombardment of Fort Henry," Everett, *Rebellion Record*, Supplement, Vol. I (1864), p. 407.

25. "Operations in Tennessee: Additional Details of the Victory at Fort Henry," *New York Times*, February 7, 1862.

26. *Davenport Daily Gazette*, February 13, 1862.

27. *Dubuque Daily Times*, February 14, 1862.

28. *Dubuque Daily Times*, February 25, 1862.

29. Barbiere, J., *Scraps from the Prison Table* (1868), pp. 103-104.

30. Lloyd Tilghman to G. W. Randolph, November 18, 1862, G. R. G. Jones CSR.

31. "Evidence Against Dubuque Rebel Sympathizers," *Dubuque Daily Times*, July 18, 1863.

32. *Annual Report of the Commissioner of Patents*, Vol. I (1872), p. 270

33. Leggett, M. D., *Patents for Inventions*, Vol. II (1874), 780.

34. *Henry County, Iowa, Directory 1859–60*.

35. James Buchanan to W. H. Wall, September 1, 1859, W. H. Wall CSR.

36. *Biographical and Historical Memoirs of Mississippi* (1891), pp. 972-973.

37. J. F. Simmons to Jefferson Davis, March 30, 1861, W. H. Wall CSR.

38. Logan, *Roster and Record of Iowa Troops in the Rebellion*, Vol. I (1908), 906.

39. W. H. Wall to A. G. Brown, August 9, 1862, W. H. Wall CSR.

40. W. H. Wall, Confederate Navy Subject File.

41. Melton, M., *The Best Station of Them all* (2012), p. 166.

42. W. H. Wall, Confederate Navy Subject File.

43. *Biographical and Historical Memoirs of Mississippi* (1891), 972-973.

44. Metcalf, V. H., *Official Records of the Union and Confederate Navies in the War of the Rebellion*, Series One, Vol. 22 (1904), pp. 152-170.

45. Kerby, *op. cit.*, pp. 410-412.

46. Kerby, *op. cit.*, pp. 410-412.

47. Metcalf, *op. cit.*, p. 158.

48. Kerby, *op. cit.*, pp. 410-412.

49. Kerby, *op. cit.*, pp. 410-412.

50. "James Ramsey Moore, M.D.," *Annual of Washington and Jefferson College for 1883*, pp. 119-122.

51. *Ibid.*

52. Flannery, M. A., *Civil War Pharmacy* (2004), pp. 41-42.

53. Gue, B., *History of Iowa from the earliest times*, Vol. IV (1893), pp. 138-139.

54. "James Ramsey Moore, M.D.," *Annual of Washington and Jefferson College, op. cit.*, pp. 119-122.

55. J. R. Moore CSR.

56. "James Ramsey Moore, M.D.," *Annual of Washington and Jefferson College*, 119-122.

57. "Boils and Carbuncles," Mayo Clinic.

58. "Typhoid Fever," Mayo Clinic.

59. "James Ramsey Moore, M.D.," *Annual of Washington and Jefferson College, op. cit.*, pp. 119-122.

60. Pratt, M. B., *Our Relations* (2002), p. 20.

61. 1856 Iowa Census, Keokuk, Iowa.

62. *General Catalogue of Kenyon College, Gambier, Ohio* (1899), p. 45.

63. B. W. Dudley to J. C. Breckinridge, February 1, 1863, in B. W. Dudley CSR

64. Executive Documents, 33rd Congress. (1854), p. 116.

65. *Burlington Weekly Hawk-eye*, June 6, 1856.

66. "Glorious Fourth," July 7, 1857, *Burlington Weekly Hawk-eye and Telegraph*.

67. "Marine Hospital, April 20, 1858, *Burlington Weekly Hawk-eye and Telegraph*.

68. *Ibid.*

69. "Des Moines County Medical Association," May 12, 1860, *Burlington Weekly Hawk-eye and Telegraph*.

70. Executive Documents, 35th Congress, 1857–58, p. 472.

71. *"Hospital at Burlington, Iowa" First Annual Report* (1872), p. 19.

72. J. B. Edelen CSR.

73. Flannery, *op. cit.*, pp. 22-23.

74. Thompson, E. P., *History of the Orphan Brigade* (1898), p. 582.

75. *Burlington Daily Hawk-eye and Telegraph*, May 23, 1862.

76. "Where They Should Go," August 23, 1862, *Burlington Weekly Hawk-eye and Telegraph*.

77. Norton, Rebel Religion (1961), p. 73.

78. Woodforde, J., *Treatise on Dyspepsia, or, Indigestion* (1820), pp. 3-6.

79. "Phillip Van Patten, M.D.," *Biographical and Historical Memoirs of Eastern Arkansas* (1890), pp. 497-499.

80. *Annals of Iowa*, Vol. 1 (1863), pp. 169-171.

81. "Phillip Van Patten, M.D.," *Biographical and Historical Memoirs of Eastern Arkansas, op. cit.*, pp. 497-499.

82. Philip Van Patten CSR.

83. J. C. Tappen to Captain Green, April 12, 1862, *War of the Rebellion*, Ser. 1, Vol. 10, Part 1, pp. 429-430.

84. Flannery, *op. cit.*, p. 214.

85. "Phillip Van Patten, M.D.," *Biographical and Historical Memoirs of Eastern Arkansas, op. cit.,* pp. 497-499.

86. Hunerdosse, "Joseph Howard: Early Iowa Pioneer".

87. McDonnold, B. W., *History of the Cumberland Presbyterian Church* (1893), pp. 336-337, 569-571.

88. Killinger-Jacobson, "Joseph Steward Howard b. Sept. 26, 1834".

89. S. Howard CSR.

90. Norton, *op. cit.,* p. 85.

91. Curran, R. E., *John Dooley's Civil War* (2012), p. 255.

92. Lane, *History of Education in Texas* (1903).

93. Andrews, L. F., *Pioneers of Polk County, Iowa,* Vol. I (1908), pp. 133-134.

94. Crist, L. L., *Papers of Jefferson Davis,* Vol. VII, 1861 (1992), pp. 115, 159.

95. Cullum, *Officers and Graduates of the U.S. Military Academy,* Vol. II (1868), p. 219.

96. J. C. Booth to S. P. Walker, March 11, 1861, J. C. Booth CSR.

97. Davis, *op. cit.,* pp. 317-318.

98. "Fayetteville Arsenal," *Encyclopedia of the American Civil War* (2000), pp. 685-686.

99. Josiah Gorgas to J. C. Booth, March 25, 1862, J. C. Booth CSR.

100. Taylor, "Sixth Battalion", *Histories of the Several Regiments and Battalions from North Carolina,* Vol. IV (1901), pp. 295-296.

101. M. Considine to Richard Lambert, February 2, 1863, M. Considine CSR.

102. "Fiery Trial" in "Under the Rebel Flag," Texas State Library and Archive Commission.

103. McCaslin, R. B., *This Corner of Canaan* (2013), p. 165.

104. Cutler, W. G., "Wyandotte County," *History of the State of Kansas* (1883).

105. Kremer, Co. I, 6th Iowa Infantry, *War of the Rebellion.*

106. "Fiery Trial" in "Under the Rebel Flag," Texas State Library and Archive Commission.

107. Ambrose Key CSR.

108. Kerby, *op. cit.,* p. 261.

109. "20th Regiment, Texas Infantry (Elmore's), National Park Service, Civil War Soldiers and Sailors Database.

110. Clark, "Re. George Key, b. 1795," Ancestry.com;

111. 1856 Iowa Census, Louisa County.

112. 1860 Federal Census, Cooper County, Missouri.

113. Miles Ramay CSR.

114. Ellis, J. T., 1863 Civil War Diary.

115. 1900 Federal Census, Panola County, Mississippi.

116. John Ramay Last Will and Testament.

117. B. Ramay correspondence with author, April 30, 2012.

118. 1850 Federal Census, Jackson County, Iowa.

119. 1860 Census, Grayson County, Texas.

120. Texas Voter Registration Lists, 1867.

121. G. W. Harris CSR.

122. Harris Genealogy Forum.

123. Charles Harris CSR.

124. C. B. Harris Texas Confederate Pension Application.

125. 1860 Federal Census, Wapello County, Iowa.

126. A. V. Knight Texas Confederate Pension Application.

127. A. V. Knight CSR.

128. 1880 Federal Census, Bell County, Texas.

129. Farish, T. E., "Winchester Miller," *History of Arizona*, Vol. VI (1918), pp. 104-108.

130. 1856 Iowa Census, Jefferson County.

131. Winchester Miller CSR.

132. Miller, H. W., and Harter, H., "Miller Family Came Here from Gold Rush," *Tempe Daily News*, April 28, 1976.

133. Farish, *op. cit.*

134. Libby, W., *Confederate Civil War Soldiers and Veterans of Madison County, Iowa* (2010), pp. 4, 7.

135. N. B. Morgan CSR.

136. 1870 Federal Census, Warren County, Iowa.

137. *History of Madison County, Iowa* (1879), pp. 457-458.

138. Texas Muster Roll Index Cards, 1838–1900.

139. 1850 Federal Census, Scott County, Iowa.

140. George Burgoon Iowa land patent.

141. J. A. Burgoon CSR.

142. Knox, Yoder, Civil War Veterans of Northeast Tarrant County.

143. Warren, S. L., "Battles of Cabin Creek," Oklahoma Historical Society Encyclopedia (online).

144. *Memorial and Biographical History of McLennan, Falls, Bell, and Coryell Counties, Texas*, vol. II (1893), pp. 726-727.

145. E. S. Flint CSR.

146. Greer, C. D., "Thirtieth Texas Cavalry," Handbook of Texas Online.

147. *Memorial and Biographical History of McLennan, Falls, Bell, and Coryell Counties, Texas, op. cit.*, pp. 726-727.

148. *Memorial and Biographical History of McLennan, Falls, Bell, and Coryell Counties, Texas, op. cit.*, pp. 885-886.

149. 1856 Iowa Census, Jasper County.

150. 1860 Federal Census, Pike County, Mississippi.

151. *Portrait and Biographical Album of Polk County, Iowa* (1890), pp. 726-727.

152. *Historical Sketch of the Quitman Guards* (1866);

153. S. M. Bain, CSR.

154. Conerly, L. W., *Pike County, Mississippi, 1798–1876: Pioneer Families and Confederate Soldiers* (1909), pp. 178-179.

155. Bunch, J. A., *Military Justice in the Confederate States Armies* (2000), p. 66.

156. Memorial and Biographical History of McLennan, Falls, Bell, and Coryell Counties, Texas, *op. cit.*, pp. 885-886.

157. Mrs. Annie Bain, Texas Confederate Widow's Pension Application.

158. "Dr. Farner's Letter," *Galveston Medical Journal, 1865–1866: A Monthly Record of Medical Science* (1865), pp. 171-173.

159. *History of Waukesha County, Wisconsin* (1880), p. 619.

160. *History of Lee County, Iowa* (1914), pp. 645-646.

161. Hussey, T., *Beginnings: Reminiscences of Early Des Moines* (1919), p. 84.

162. Pelzer, L., "History and Principles of the Democratic Party of the Territory of Iowa," *Iowa Journal of History and Politics*, Vol. VI (1908), pp. 222-224.

163. Johnson, B., *Des Moines: Pioneer of Municipal Progress and Reform of the Middle West*, Vol. I (1911), p. 81.

164. W. H. Farner to Friend Randall, August 14, 1867, Texas State Library and Archives

Commission.

165. Dixon, J. M., *Valley and the Shadow* (1868), pp. 59-61.
166. Nolan, L., "Great Civil War: Opposite Sides," Landmark 26 (1983).
167. Postell, L., "Father and Son, Confederate and Federal Soldiers," *Landmark 13* (1970), 4.
168. Bassett, S. C., *Buffalo County, Nebraska, and Its People*, Vol. I (1916), p. 23.
169. Smiley, J. C., *History of Denver* (1901), p. 634.
170. "Dr. Farner," *Denver Daily Evening News*, December 4, 1861.
171. "Resolutions of the Colorado First," *Weekly Rocky Mountain News*, June 7, 1862.
172. W. H. Farner CSR.
173. Baum, D., and Greer, C. D., "Slaves Taken to Texas for Safekeeping During the Civil War," *Fate of Texas* (2008), p. 96.
174. *Ibid.*
175. W. H. Farner to Friend Randall, August 14, 1867, Texas State Library and Archives Commission.
176. Dixon, *op. cit.*, pp. 59-61.
177. Diary of S. K. Fowler, 2nd Missouri Infantry (Confederate), 1862–1865.
178. 1854 Iowa Census, Lee County.
179. *Annals of the Grand Lodge of Iowa* (1858), pp. 55, 146, 383.
180. *History of Lewis, Clark, Knox, and Scotland Counties, Missouri* (1887), p. 1038.
181. S. K. Fowler CSR.
182. G. T. Fowler CSR.
183. J. J. Fowler, Secretary of State of Missouri, Military Archives.
184. Diary of S. K. Fowler.
185. *Ibid.*
186. *Ibid.*
187. *Ibid.*

Chapter 8

1. *Portrait and Biographical Album, Muscatine County, Iowa* (1889), pp. 371-373.
2. E-mail, B. Shields to author, January 8, 2012.
3. *Catalogue from 1834 to 1872, Tulane* (1871), p. 1851.
4. 1860 Federal Census, Parish of West Feliciana, Louisiana.
5. 1860 Slave Schedule, Bayou Sara, Parish of West Feliciana, Louisiana.
6. "Lytle v. Whicher, *et al.*", January 19, 1858, Louisiana Supreme Court Archives.
7. P. V. Whicher CSR
8. Sprague, H. B., *History of the 13th Infantry Regiment of Connecticut Volunteers* (1867), pp. 134-136.
9. Klausner, A., WMI Register, June 6, 1851.
10. *New Orleans Medical News and Hospital Gazette,*, Vol. III (1857), pp. 117-119.
11. 1856 Iowa Census, Muscatine County.
12. 1860 Federal Census, Carroll Parish, Louisiana.
13. Francis Whicher CSR.
14. "Obituary," *Muscatine Journal*, September 9, 1862.
15. McSweeney and Meline, *Story of the Mountain*, Vol. II (1911), pp. 3-4, 8, 15-16, 25.
16. *Frank Leslie's Illustrated Newspaper*, July 28, 1860.

17. 1850 Federal Census, Dubuque County, Iowa.

18. "Pertinent Statements and Facts," September 3, 1865, *Dubuque Herald*.

19. Mayors of Dubuque, Iowa, 1837–Present.

20. "Pertinent Statements and Facts," September 3, 1865, *Dubuque Herald*.

21. Mt. St. Mary's University Archives, A.J. Quigley file.

22. McSweeney and Meline, *op. cit.* p. 25.

23. G. W. Jones to Jefferson Davis, August 25, 1882, J. Davis Collection, Museum of the Confederacy.

24. 1860 Federal Census, Dubuque, Iowa.

25. "Senex," *Dubuque Herald*, January 13, 1861.

26. A. J. Quigley, CSR.

27. "Bogus Character of the Mahony Convention Shown Up," August 26, 1861, *Dubuque Daily Evening Union*.

28. "Bogus Baby Speakers," September 30, 1861, *Dubuque Daily Evening Union*.

29. Hyslop, S. G., *Eyewitness to the Civil War* (2006), 125.

30. *War of the Rebellion*, Series One, Vol. 18, pp. 282-283.

31. Sledge, *Union's Naval War in Louisiana, 1861–1863* (2015).

32. *Dubuque Daily Times*, December 9, 1862.

33. *Dubuque Daily Times*, July 15, 1863.

34. *Root's 1867 Dubuque Directory*.

35. 1870 Federal Census, St. Louis County, Missouri.

36. A. J. Quigley to A. V. D. Watterson, January 4, 1889, Mt. St. Mary's Archives.

37. "Mourning in Colorado," *Kansas City Times*, December 11, 1889.

38. Ingalsbe J. L., "Northwestern Iowa in 1855," *Iowa Journal of History and Politics*, Vol. XVIII, (1920), pp. 271-272.

39. Sorley, M. E., *Lewis of Warner Hall: The History of a Family* (1979), p. 515;

40. Obituary, *Dubuque Herald*, May 4, 1888;

41. Warner Lewis Sr. to Jefferson Davis, May 9, 1858.

42. Mayors of Dubuque, Iowa, 1837–Present.

43. Warner Lewis Jr., Iowa Territorial and State Legislators (General Assembly) Biographies.

44. Klausner, Western Military Institute Register

45. Warner Lewis to G. W. Jones, September 8, 1850, G. W. Jones Correspondence.

46. *Catalogue Committee, Record of the Members of Kappa Alpha* (1892), p. 66.

47. Jefferson Davis to James Buchanan, May 1, 1858, Surveyor General papers.

48. Warner Lewis to Jefferson Davis, May 9. 1858, Jefferson Davis Papers.

49. Kingsbury, G. W., *History of Dakota Territory*, Vol. I (1915), pp. 74-75.

50. 1860 Federal Census, Dubuque, Iowa.

51. Warner C. Lewis CSR.

52. October 22, 1861, WD.

53. *Dubuque Daily Times*, February 23, 1862.

54. Captain C. Washington to Henry Halleck, February 16, 1862, Union Citizens File.

55. *War of the Rebellion*, Series I, Vol. 30, Part II Reports, p. 5.

56. B. J. Hill to W. A. King, September 20, 1863, *War of the Rebellion*, Series I, Vol. 30, Part II Reports, pp. 181-184.

57. *1867 Nashville Directory*.

58. Wolfe, *Dubuque Directory*, Vol. 2 (1870).

59. *1941 Kappa Alpha Catalogue*, Union College Alumni Records.

60. Conzett, J., *Recollections of People and Events of Dubuque, Iowa* (1971), p. 38.
61. G. R. Crosthwait, Iowa Legislature, online profiles.
62. *Third Annual Exhibition of the Iowa State Agricultural Society* (1857), pp. 6, 11, 442.
63. 1860 Federal Census, Johnson County, Iowa.
64. *History of Johnson County, Iowa* (1883), p. 199.
65. Clark, O. B., *op. cit.*, pp. 26-27;
66. Neal, R. J., "Shelton, Frank, and Brom. R. Crosthwait," *Confederate Veteran*, Vol. VII (1899), pp. 70-71.
67. Neal, R. J., in McMurray, *History of the Twentieth Tennessee Regiment* (1904), p. 434.
68. *State Press*, Iowa City, in *Davenport Daily Gazette*, April 18, 1862.
69. Neal, R. J., 1899, *op. cit.*, pp. 70-71.
70. Shelton Crosthwait CSR.
71. "The Battle of Mills Springs, Kentucky," TAC News, November-December 2006, http://www.ghqmodels.com/newsletters/novdec2006.pdf 1/30/2001 .
72. Neal, R. J., in McMurray, *op. cit.*, p. 434.
73. *State Press*, Iowa City, *Davenport Daily Gazette*, April 18, 1862.
74. Neal, R. J., 1899, *op. cit.*, pp. 70-71.
75. B. R. Crosthwait CSR.
76. Neal, R. J., 1899, *op. cit.*, pp. 70-71.
77. Neal, R. J., in McMurray, *op. cit.*, pp. 125-128.
78. F. B. Crosthwaite CSR.
79. Neal, R. J., 1899, *op. cit.*, pp. 70-71.
80. Neal, R. J., in McMurray, *op. cit.*, pp. 433-434.
81. Ridley, B. L., "Echoes from the Battle of Murfreesboro," *Confederate Veteran*, Vol. XI, No. 2 (1903), pp. 65-67.
82. Neal, R. J., 1899, *op. cit.*, pp. 70-71.
83. McMurray, *op. cit.*, pp. 234-235.
84. Neal, R. J., 1899, *op. cit.*, pp. 70-71.
85. Ridley, B. L., *op. cit.*, p. 154.
86. Neal, R. J., 1899, *op. cit.*, pp. 70-71.
87. 1856 Iowa Census, Van Buren County.
88. 1860 Federal Census, Van Buren County, Iowa.
89. Penny, S. R., "Dr. John W. Hayden Family in Confederate Service".
90. E-mails, S. R. Penny and author, January 17, 28, 2013.
91. *Sequestration Act Passed by the Congress of the Confederate States* (1861).
92. Hamilton, D. W., "Confederate Sequestration Act," in Blair, ed., *Civil War History* (2006).
93. Penny, S. R., *op. cit.*
94. *Ibid.*
95. Blair, E., *History of Johnson County, Kansas* (1915), pp. 322-323.
96. G. C. Hayden CSR.
97. G. C. Hayden Confederate Civilian File.
98. Kerby, *op. cit.*, pp. 398-399.
99. Penny, S. R., *op. cit.*
100. *Ibid.*
101. J. T. Hayden CSR.

102. S. R. Penny, *op. cit.*
103. A. C. Hayden CSR.
104. S. R. Penny, *op. cit.*
105. J. R. Hayden CSR.
106. S. R. Penny, *op. cit.*
107. D. W. Hayden CSR.
108. *History of Jasper County, Missouri* (1883), p. 726.
109. Knox, Yoder, "Civil War Veterans of Northeast Tarrant County," (2008);
110. George Burgoon CSR.
111. *History of Jasper County, Missouri* (1883), p. 726.
112. Folmar, K., *From that Terrible Field* (1981), pp. xi-xiii, xv-xvi.
113. Folmar, K., *This State of Wonders* (1986), pp. 41-42.
114. Folmar, 1986, *op. cit.*, p. 83.
115. Folmar, 1986, *op. cit.*, pp.108-109.
116. Folmar,1986, *op. cit.*, p. 120.
117. Folmar, 1981, *op. cit.*, pp. xi-xiii.
118. Folmar, 1981, *op. cit.*, pp. 7-8.
119. Folmar, 1981, *op. cit.*, pp. 30-31.
120. Folmar, 1981, *op. cit.*, pp. 30-31, 70.
121. Folmar, 1981, *op. cit.*, p. 116.
122. Folmar, 1981, *op. cit.*, pp. 130, 158.
123. Folmar, 1981, *op. cit.*, pp. 100, 130.
124. J. M. Williams CSR.
125. Folmar, 1981, *op. cit.*, p. 175.
126. Folmar, 1981, *op. cit.*, p. 158.
127. Folmar, 1981, *op. cit.*, pp. xv-xvi

Chapter 9

1. DeHaven, C., Gurley, B., *I Acted from Principle* (2002), p. 245.
2. R. R. Lawther CSR.
3. 1870 Federal Census, Galveston, Texas;
4. Pilgrim, M. E., " Civil War Diary of Richard M. Venable," *Prologue: Quarterly of National Archives & Records Administration*, Winter 1996, p. 266.
5. *Memorial and History of Dallas County, Texas*, Vol. II (1892), p. 754.
6. 1856 Iowa Census, Muscatine County.
7. R. R. Lawther CSR.
8. *Muscatine Directory*, Vol. I (1860).
9. 1860 Federal census, Muscatine County, Iowa.
10. R. R. Lawther CSR.
11. *Muscatine Journal*, October 25, 1861.
12. Sterling Price, May 12, 1862, R. R. Lawther CSR.
13. R. R. Lawther CSR.
14. R. R. Lawther to General, Gratiot Street Prison, October 13, 1862, R. R. Lawther CSR.
15. December 13, 1862, R. R. Lawther CSR.
16. Camp of Fagan's Command, May 28, 1864, R.R. Lawther CSR.
17. J. F. Fagan, May 20, 1864, R.R. Lawther CSR.

18. "Summary of News," *Philadelphia Enquirer*, August 10, 1865.
19. "General Longstreet at a Texas Pic-Nic," *Richmond Whig*, May 18, 1866.
20. 1860 Federal Census, Lee County, Iowa.
21. "Cyrus Franklin," Iowa Territorial and State Legislators (General Assembly) Biographical Forms.
22. Hedrick, J. M., "Cyrus Franklin," *Ottumwa Weekly Courier*, February 18, 1885.
23. *Ibid.*
24. Cyrus Franklin CSR.
25. T. A. Harris, September 23, 1861, *War of the Rebellion*, Series I, Vol. 3, p. 192.
26. Hedrick, *op. cit.*
27. S. R. Curtis to Edwin Stanton, January 15, 1863, *War of the Rebellion*, Series I, Vol. 22, Part 2, pg. 44.
28. Granville Leeper CSR.
29. "Granville Leeper," Union Citizens File.
30. Witness testimony, Granville Leeper CSR.
31. Cyrus Franklin to Jefferson Davis, November 6, 1863, *War of the Rebellion*, Series I, Vol. 22, Part 2, pp. 1058–1060.
32. E-mails, Bruce S. Allardice and author.
33. Hedrick, *op. cit.*
34. 1860 Federal Census, Des Moines County, Iowa.
35. Withrow, *Reports of Cases in Law and Equity*, Vol. XI (1866), pp. 7-16.
36. Audrain County, Missouri, Circuit Court Abstracts, 1 (1857).
37. *Proceedings of the Right Worthy Grand Lodge of the United States*, Vol. III (1863), p. 2,362.
38. *Proceedings of the Grand Lodge of Iowa*, Vol. III (1863), p. 321.
39. *Burlington Daily Hawk-eye and Telegraph*, May 28, 1861.
40. V. M. Pendleton CSR.
41. Stiles, E. H., *Recollections and Sketches* (1916), p. 276.
42. "Where They Should Go," *Burlington Weekly Hawk-eye and Telegraph*, August 23, 1862.
43. Belcher, *10th Kentucky Volunteer Infantry in the Civil War* (2009).
44. Young, *Confederate Wizards of the Saddle* (1914), pp. 436-438
45. Young., *op. cit.*, pp. 185-187.
46. Campbell, W., "Autobiographical Sketch," *William and Mary Quarterly*, Second Series, Vol. IX, No. 2 (1929).
47. *Ibid.*
48. *Ibid.*
49. *Ibid.*
50. *Ibid.*
51. *Ibid.*
52. *Ibid.*
53. *Ibid.*
54. William Campbell CSR.
55. Campbell, W., "Stuart's Ride and Death of Latane," *Southern Historical Society Papers, New Series*, Vol. I (1914), pp. 86-90.
56. Campbell, W., 1929, *op. cit.*
57. *Ibid.*
58. *Ibid.*

59. William Campbell CSR.

60. Campbell, W., 1929, *op. cit.*

61. *Ibid.*

62. *Ibid.*

63. *Journal* of House of Delegates of the State of Virginia (1891), p. 4.

64. Campbell, M., "Lucy Long," *William and Mary Quarterly*, Vol. 19, No. 4 (1939), pp. 471-473.

65. R. E. Lee, October 27, 1866, in Campbell, M., *op. cit.*, pp. 471-473.

66. C. L. Gray, "Lucy Long," blog, Headquarters: Army of Northern Virginia.

67. Campbell, M., *op. cit.*, pp. 471-473.

68. Campbell, W., 1929, *op. cit.*

69. 1850 Federal Census, Lee County, Iowa.

70. Ligtenberg, "Christiaan Verwayen and the Lost Disabdera Settlement," AADAS Conference Papers (2001).

71. 1860 Federal Census, Lee County, Iowa.

72. "Capt. John Happs Dies at 85," Associated Press, December 3 or 5, 1924, in *St. Louis Post-Dispatch*.

73. Haps, J., "Haps and Mishaps," *The National Tribune* (1907).

74. *Ibid.*

75. Duke, B. W., *Reminiscences of Basil W. Duke* (1911), p. 87.

76. "Rebels in Lexington, Kentucky," *Sacramento Daily Union*, November 21, 1862.

77. Haps, J., "Haps and Mishaps," *op. cit.*

78. Duke, B. W., *History of Morgan's Cavalry* (1867), pp. 304-305.

79. Coggins, J., *Arms and Equipment of the Civil War* (1962), p. 51.

80. Haps, J., "Hard Riding With Morgan," *Confederate Veteran*, Vol. XXVIII, No. 11 (1920), pp. 437-438.

81. *Ibid.*

82. Simmons, F. E., *Complete Account of the John Morgan Raid* (1863), pp. 74-75.

83. J. Haps CSR.

84. Davis, W. C., *An Honorable Defeat* (2001), pp. 172-174.

85. Matthews, G. R., *Basil Wilson Duke, CSA* (2005), pp. 200-201.

86. "Steer on Rampage: Texas Animal on Tear in St. Louis, Mo.," *Muskegon Daily Chronicle*, August 10, 1904.

87. Rosenburg, B. B., *Living Monuments* (1993), p. 104.

88. John Haps to John Morgan Haps.

89. "Garden of Memory," *Confederate Veteran*, Vol. XXVII, No. 11 (1919), p. 438.

Bibliography

Manuscripts

Arkansas Confederate Pension Applications, Arkansas History Commission, Little Rock

French Bassett's Notes on Prominent Virginians, Library of Virginia, Richmond

Thomas F. Bayard Papers, Library of Congress

Beloit Academy Inventory, Beloit College Special Collections, Beloit, Wis.

John Lucas Paul Cantwell Papers, University of North Carolina

Civil War Draft Registration Records, National Archives, D.C.

Confederate Civilian Records, National Archives, D. C.

Confederate Navy Subject File, National Archives, D. C.

Confederate Service Records, National Archives, D. C.

Confederate Civil War Soldiers and Veterans of Madison County, Iowa, Walt Libby, Winterset

Jefferson Davis Collection, Museum of the Confederacy, Richmond, Va.

Jefferson Davis Papers, W. S. Hoole Special Collections Library, University of Alabama, Tuscaloosa

"Democratic Rangers Case 1864," Grinnell College Archives, Iowa

Josephus Eastman Diary transcript, Grinnell Historical Museum

Josephus Eastman Diary, State Historical Society of Iowa, Des Moines

James Thornton Ellis Diary, 1863, Missouri State Archives, Jefferson City

Florida Confederate Pension Claim Applications, State Board of Pensions, Tallahassee

Diary of Samuel K. Fowler, 2nd Missouri Infantry (Confederate), 1862–1865, Stanford University Libraries Special Collections, Stanford, Calif.

Michael Gleason Case File, State Historical Museum of Iowa, Des Moines

Graduates of the College of Physicians and Surgeons, Keokuk, University of Iowa Special Collections, Iowa City

Governor's Correspondence, North Carolina Office of Archives & History, Raleigh

Ray B. Griffin Collection, University of Iowa Libraries, Iowa City

"The Dr. John W. Hayden Family in the Confederate Service," S. R. Penny, Mesa, Ariz.

H. H. Heath, Houghton Library, Harvard University, Cambridge, Mass.

"Joseph Howard: Early Iowa Pioneer," Evalee Hunerdosse, Newton, Iowa

Morton Boyte Howell Family Papers, Tennessee State Library and Archives

Iowa Legislators Past and Present, www.legis.iowa.gov , The Iowa Legislature, Des Moines

Iowa Wesleyan University Student Records, Archives, Mt. Pleasant

George Wallace Jones Letters, DIY History, University of Iowa, Iowa City

Hempstead, J. L., Virginia Military Institute Archives, Lexington

Iowa land patents, U.S. Department of the Interior, Bureau of Land Management, D. C.

Jefferson County, Kentucky, Mortuary Records

Lee Family Papers, 1824–1914, Virginia Historical Society, Richmond

John T. Lovell 1859 Diary and Autograph Book, Virginia Historical Society, Richmond

Jesse Macy Papers, Box 1, State Historical Society of Iowa, Iowa City

"Murder of U.S. Marshals in Poweshiek County," Appendix N, January 1, 1865, Iowa Adjutant-General's Office, State Historical Society of Iowa, Des Moines

Caroline Murray, "Madison County during the War," Madison County Historical Society, Winterset, Iowa

Mary Custis Lee Collection, 1835–1918, Virginia Historical Society, Richmond

Charles Mason Papers, State Historical Society of Iowa, Des Moines

Mayors of the City of Dubuque, Iowa, 1837–Present, City of Dubuque

Missouri Circuit Court Abstracts, Missouri State Archives, Jefferson City

Missouri Confederate Pension Applications, Missouri State Archives, Jefferson City

Missouri Soldiers' Records, War of 1812–World War I, Missouri Secretary of State, St. Louis

Missouri Union Provost Marshal Records, Missouri Secretary of State, St. Louis

Missouri United Methodist Archives, Fayette

Mt. St. Mary's University Archives, Emmitsburg, Md.

"Summaries for Albert H. Newell and Rev. Albert Newell," Nelda Palmer

"Private Albert H. Newell," Jim Williams

Notre Dame University Archives, South Bend, Ind.

Leonard F. Parker papers, Grinnell College Archives, Grinnell, Iowa

Physicians records, Iowa Hospital for the Insane, Mental Health Institute, Independence, Iowa

Records of the Secretary of the Interior, Appointment Division, Misc. Appointment Papers, Surveyor General, Iowa & Wisconsin, National Archives, D. C.

Register of Cadet Applicants, U. S. Military Academy at West Point, National Archives, D. C.

"Resolutions of the Colorado First," *Weekly Rocky Mountain News*, June 7, 1862, Denver, Co.

George Wallace Jones Correspondence, Wm. H. Seward Papers, University of Rochester, N.Y.

George Wallace Jones Correspondence, State Historical Society of Iowa, Des Moines

Nancy W. Shipley vs. John C. Shipley, June Term 1863, Muscatine County Genealogical Society, Muscatine, Iowa

Laurel Summers Papers, State Historical Society of Iowa, Des Moines

Historical Archives of the Supreme Court of Louisiana, University of New Orleans Earl K. Long Library, New Orleans

Surveyor General, Iowa and Wisconsin, Misc. Papers, National Archives, D.C.

Texas Confederate Pension Applications, and Texas Voter Registration Lists (1867–1869), Texas State Library and Archives Commission, Austin

Union Citizens File, National Archives, D. C.

Union Service Records, National Archives, D.C.

United States Pardons under Amnesty Proclamations 1865 to 1869, National Archives, D. C.

Virginia Secession Convention documents, University of Richmond, Va.

Waples Family Papers, University of Delaware Library Special Collections, Newark

Western Military Institute ephemera, Filson Historical Society, Louisville, Ky.

Western Military Institute Register, Montgomery Bell Academy Archives, Nashville, Tenn.

Williams Family Papers, Virginia Historical Society, Richmond

James Harrison Williams Diaries, University of Virginia Library, Charlottesville

Works Progress Administration, 1930s Graves Registration Survey, National Archives, D. C.

Published Sources

A Centennial History of Mount Vernon, Iowa, 1847–1947 (Mt. Vernon: 1948)

Adjutant-General's Correspondence, Disloyal Sentiment, State Historical Society of Iowa, Des Moines

Allardice, B. S., *Confederate Colonels: A Biographical Register* (Columbia: University of Missouri Press, 2008)

Allen, W. C., *History of Halifax County* (Boston: The Cornhill Co., 1918)

Andrews, L. F., *Pioneers of Polk County, Iowa*, Vol. I (Des Moines: Baker-Trisler Co., 1908)

Annals of Iowa, Vol. I (Iowa City: State Historical Society of Iowa, 1863)

Annual Report of the Commissioner of Patents, Vol. I (D. C.: United States Patent Office, 1872)

Andreas, A. T., *A.T. Andreas Historical Atlas of the State of Iowa* (Chicago: 1875)

The Annual of Washington and Jefferson College for 1883 (Philadelphia: 1884)

Annual Catalogue of the Officers and Students of Iowa Conference Seminary or Cornell College, (Davenport: Luse, Lane, & Co., 1856)

Antrobus, A. M., *History of Des Moines County, Iowa*, Vol. I (Chicago: S. J. Clarke, 1915)

Armstrong, W. H., *William McKinley and the Civil War* (Kent: Kent State University Press, 2000)

Ashe, S. A., ed., *Biographical History of North Carolina from Colonial Times to the Present*, Vol. VII (Greensboro: Charles L. Van Noppen, 1908)

Auman, W. T., *Civil War in the North Carolina Quaker Belt* (Jefferson: McFarland & Co., 2014)

Aurner, C. R., *Leading Events in Johnson County, Iowa*, Vol. I (1912)

Avirett, J. B., *Memoirs of General Turner Ashby and his Compeers* (Baltimore: Selby & Dulany, 1867)

Banasik, M. E., ed., *Missouri Brothers in Gray: The Reminiscences and Letters of William J. Bull and John P. Bull* (Iowa City: Camp Pope Bookshop, 1998)

Barbiere, J., *Scraps from the Prison Table: At Camp Chase and Johnson's Island* (Doylestown: W. W. H. Davis, 1868)

Barr, A., *Polignac's Texas Brigade* (College Station: Texas A & M University Press, 1998)

Bartlett, D. W., *Life and Public Services of Hon. Abraham Lincoln* (New York: H. Dayton, 1860)

Bartlett, E. S., "Letter from Grinnell: E.S. Bartlett to his Children and Grandchildren," *The Annals of Iowa* (Iowa City: State Historical Society of Iowa, Fall 1978)

Bassett, S. C., *Buffalo County, Nebraska, and Its People*, Vol. I (Chicago: S. J. Clarke, 1916)

Battle, K. P., *Sketches of the History of the University of North Carolina, 1789–1889* (Chapel Hill: University of North Carolina, 1889)

Baum, D., *Counterfeit Justice: the judicial odyssey of Texas freedwoman Azeline Hearne* (Baton Rouge: Louisiana State University Press, 2009)

Beatty, B., and Caprio, J., eds., "'How Long will this Misery Continue?' A Confederate Forced to face Starvation and Rebel fire," *Civil War Times Illustrated* XIX (1981)

Bergeron, P. H., ed., *The Papers of Andrew Johnson: May–August 1865* (Knoxville: University of Tennessee Press, 1990)

Biographical and Historical Memoirs of Eastern Arkansas (Chicago: Goodspeed Publ. Co., 1890)

Biographical and Historical Memoirs of Mississippi (Chicago: Goodspeed Publ. Co., 1891)

Biographical Review of Henry County, Iowa (Chicago: Hobart Publ. Co., 1906)

Biographical and Historical Record of Ringgold and Decatur Counties, Iowa (Chicago: Lewis Publ. Co., 1887)

Bird, H. T., *Memories of the Civil War* (1925)

Blair, E., *History of Johnson County, Kansas* (Lawrence: Standard Publ. Co., 1915)

Blair, W. A., *With Malice Toward Some: Treason and Loyalty in the Civil War Era* (Chapel Hill: University of North Carolina Press, 2014)

Blake, H. N., *Reports of Cases Argued and Determined in the Supreme Court of Montana Territory*, Vol. II (San Francisco: Bancroft-Whitney Co., 1877)

Blakey, A. F., *General John H. Winder* (Gainesville: University of Florida Press, 1990)

Bunch, J. A., *Military Justice in the Confederate States Armies* (Shippensburg: White Mane Books, 2000)

Campbell, M., "Lucy Long," *William and Mary Quarterly*, Vol. XVIX (Williamsburg: 1939)

Campbell, W., "Autobiographical Sketch," *William and Mary Quarterly*, 2nd Series, Vol. IX (Williamsburg: 1929)

Campbell, W., "Stuart's Ride and Death of Latane," *Southern Historical Society Papers, New Series*, Vol. I (Richmond: 1914)

Catalogue from 1834 to 1872 (New Orleans: Tulane University School of Medicine, 1871)

Census Bureau, Federal Census, 1850, 1860, 1870, 1880, 1890, 1900, 1910

Census Bureau, Federal Slave Schedules, 1850, 1860

Childs, C. C., Klein, R.F. ed., *Dubuque: Frontier River City, 35 Sketches* (Dubuque: Research Center for Dubuque Area History, 1984)

Choppin, S., ed., *New Orleans Medical News and Hospital Gazette*, Vol. III (1857)

Clark, O. B., *Politics of Iowa During Civil War and Reconstruction* (Iowa City: Clio Press, 1911)

Clark, W., ed., *Histories of the Several Regiments and Battalions from North Carolina in the Great War, 1861–65*, Vol. IV (Raleigh: State of North Carolina, 1901)

Collins, R., *General James G. Blunt: Tarnished Glory* (Gretna, La.: Pelican, 2005)

Confederate Veteran (Nashville: S. A. Cunningham, 1899, 1903, 1904, 1907, 1912, 1919, 1920, 1927)

Conzett, J., *Recollections of People and Events of Dubuque, Iowa, 1846–1890* (Dubuque: 1971)

Cook, R., *Baptism of Fire: The Republican Party in Iowa, 1838–1878* (Ames: Iowa State University Press, 1994)

Cooke, G. W., *Ralph Waldo Emerson: His Life, Writings, and Philosophy* (Boston: James R. Osgood and Co., 1882)

Cooper, W. J., *Jefferson Davis, American* (New York: Alfred A. Knopf, 2000)

Cooper, R., "A Case of Ague (Chagres Fever) and What We Learn from it" in Drysdale, ed., *The British Journal of Homeopathy*, vol. 33 (London: Henry Turner and Co., 1875)

Council Bluffs City Directory 1897

Crist, L. L., ed., *Papers of Jefferson Davis*, Vols. V, VI, VII, VIII, X, XI (Baton Rouge: Louisiana State University Press, 1985, 1989, 1992, 1995, 1999, 2003)

Cullum, G. W., *Biographical Register of the Officers and Graduates of the U.S. Military Academy at West Point, N.Y.*, Vol. II, 1841–1867 (New York: D. Van Nostrand, 1868)

Curran, R. E., ed., *John Dooley's Civil War: An Irish American's Journey in the First Virginia Infantry Regiment* (Knoxville: University of Tennessee, 2012)

Cutler, W. G., *History of the State of Kansas* (Chicago: A. T. Andreas, 1883)

Daniel, L. J., *Shiloh: The Battle That Changed the Civil War* (New York: Simon and Schuster, 1997)

Davidson, J. N., "Negro Slavery in Wisconsin and the Underground Railroad" (Milwaukee: Parkman Club Publications, 1897)

Davis, J., *The Rise and Fall of the Confederate Government*, Vol. I (New York: D. Appleton and Co., 1912)

Davis, V., *Jefferson Davis, Ex-President of the Confederate States of America: A Memoir by His Wife*, Vol. I (New York: Belford Co. Publishers, 1890)

Davis, W. C., *An Honorable Defeat: The Last Days of the Confederate Government* (New York: Harcourt, Inc., 2001)

Delaware College Review (Newark: Delaware College, 1891)

Delbanco, A., ed., *The Portable Abraham Lincoln* (New York: Viking, 1992)

Dickinson, H. C., *Diary of Capt. Henry C. Dickinson, C.S.A.* (Denver: 1910)

Dixon, J. M., *The Valley and the Shadow* (New York: Russell Bros., 1868)

Douglass, T. O., *The Pilgrims of Iowa* (Boston: Congregational Home Missionary Society, 1911)

Downer, H. E., *History of Davenport and Scott County, Iowa*, Vols. I, II (Chicago: S. J. Clarke, 1910)

Dubuque City Directory (Dubuque: 1859, 1867, 1868, 1870, 1875)

Duke, B. W., *History of Morgan's Cavalry* (Cincinnati: Miami Printing and Publ. Co., 1867)

Duke, B. W., *Reminiscences of Basil W. Duke* (Garden City: Doubleday, Page & Co., 1911)

Durham, R. S., ed., *A Confederate Yankee: The Journal of Edward William Drummond, A Confederate Soldier from Maine* (Knoxville: University of Tennessee Press, 2004)

Dykstra, R. R., *Bright Radical Star: Black Freedom and White Supremacy on the Hawkeye Frontier* (Cambridge: Harvard University Press, 1993)

Ellis, J. W., *History of Jackson County, Iowa*, Vol. I (Chicago: S. J. Clarke, 1910)

Ericson, C., "Kissin Kuzzins," *The Cherokeean* (Rusk: Portal to Texas History,1983)

Everett, E., *The Rebellion Record, Supplement*, Vol. I (New York: G. P. Putnam, 1864)

Farber, D., *Lincoln's Constitution* (Chicago: University of Chicago Press, 2003)

Farish, T. E., *History of Arizona*, Vol. VI (Phoenix: Filmer Bros. Electrotype Co., 1918)

Farner, W. H., "Dr. Farner's Letter," *Galveston Medical Journal, 1865–1866: A Monthly Record of Medical Science* (Galveston: Greenville Dowell, 1865)

First Annual Report of the Supervising Surgeon of the Marine Hospital Service of the United States for Year 1872 (D.C.: Government Printing Office, 1872)

Flannery, M. A., *Civil War Pharmacy: A History of Drugs, Drug Supply and Provision, and Therapeutics for the Union and Confederacy* (Binghamton: Haworth Press, 2004)

Folmar, J. K., *From that Terrible Field: Civil War Letters of James M. Williams, Twenty-First Alabama Infantry Volunteers* (Tuscaloosa: University of Alabama Press, 1981)

Folmar, J. K., *This State of Wonders: The Letters of an Iowa Frontier Family, 1858–1861* (Iowa City: University of Iowa Press, 1986)

Gallagher, G. W., *Becoming Confederates: Paths to a New National Loyalty* (Athens: University of Georgia Press, 2013)

Gallaway, B. P., *The Ragged Rebel: A Common Soldier in W. H. Parsons' Texas Cavalry, 1861–1865* (Austin: University of Texas Press, 1988)

Genovese, E. D., *A Consuming Fire: The Fall of the Confederacy in the Mind of the White Christian South* (Athens: University of Georgia Press, 1998)

Gleeson, E., *Illinois Rebels: A Civil War Unit History of G Company, 15th Tennessee Regiment Volunteer Infantry* (Carmel: Guild Press of Indiana, 1996)

Goldfield, D., *America Aflame: How the Civil War Created a Nation* (New York: Bloomsbury Press, 2011)

Goodspeed, W. A., *History of Dubuque County, Iowa* (Chicago: Goodspeed Historical Assn., 1911)

Grear, C. D., ed., *The Fate of Texas: The Civil War and the Lone Star State* (Fayetteville: University of Arkansas Press, 2008)

Green, J. R., *Military Education and the Emerging Middle Class in the Old South* (Cambridge: Cambridge University Press, 2008)

Gue, B., *History of Iowa from the earliest times to the beginning of the 20th Century*, Vol. IV, 1866 to 1903 (New York: Century History Co., 1893)

Haps, J., "Haps and Mishaps: Four Years' Experience in the Confederate Army by a Wandering Printer—Published the Southern Vidette," *National Tribune* (D.C.: 1907)

Harper, R. S., *Lincoln and the Press* (New York: McGraw-Hill, 1951)

Hasian, M., *In the Name of Necessity: Military Tribunals and the Loss of American Civil Liberties* (Tuscaloosa: University of Alabama Press, 2005)

Hearn, C. G., *Mobile Bay and the Mobile Campaign: The Last Great Battles of the Civil War* (Jefferson: McFarland and Co., 1993)

Heath, C. L., "Fayetteville Arsenal," in Heidler, D. S., ed., *Encyclopedia of the American Civil War: A Political, Social, and Military History* (New York: W. W. Norton, 2000)

Henry, J. F., *A History of the Henry Family* (Louisville: John P. Morton & Co., 1900)

Henry County, Iowa, Directory 1859–60 (Mt. Pleasant: Watson Brown, 1859)

Historical Sketch of the Quitman Guards, Company E, 16th Mississippi Regiment, Harris' Brigade (New Orleans, 1866)

History of Andrew and DeKalb Counties, Missouri (St. Louis: Goodspeed Publ. Co., 1888)

History of Appanoose County, Iowa (Chicago: Western Historical Co., 1878)

History of Cass County, Iowa (Springfield: Continental Historical Co., 1884)

History of Des Moines County, Iowa, and its People, Vol. I (Chicago: S. J. Clarke, 1915)

History of Dubuque County, Iowa (Chicago: Western Historical Co., 1883)

History of Jasper County, Missouri (Des Moines: Mills & Co., 1883)

History of Lee County, Iowa (Chicago: S. J. Clarke, 1914)

History of Lewis, Clark, Knox, and Scotland Counties, Missouri (Marceline: Walsworth Publ. Co., 1887)

History of Madison County, Iowa (Des Moines: Union Historical Co., 1879)

History of Muscatine County, Iowa, Vol. I (Chicago: S. J. Clarke, 1911)

History of Poweshiek County, Iowa (Des Moines: Union Historical Co., 1880)

History of Texas, Together with a Biographical History of Tarrant and Parker Counties (Chicago: Lewis Publ. Co., 1895)

History of Waukesha County, Wisconsin (Chicago: Western Historical Society, 1880)

Holzer, H., *Lincoln President-Elect: Abraham Lincoln and the Great Secession Winter, 1860–1861* (New York: Simon and Schuster, 2008)

Hyslop, S. G., *Eyewitness to the Civil War: The Complete History from Secession to Reconstruction* (D. C.: National Geographic Books, 2006)

Ingalsbe, J. L., "Northwestern Iowa in 1855," Shambaugh, B. F., ed., *Iowa Journal of History and Politics*, Vol. XVIII (Iowa City: State Historical Society of Iowa, 1920)

Iowa Secretary of State, 1856 Iowa Census

Isbell, T. T., *Shiloh and Corinth: Sentinels of Stone* (Jackson: University Press of Mississippi, 2007)

Johnson, B., *Iowa: Its History and its Foremost Citizens* (Des Moines: S.J. Clarke, 1918)

Johnson, R. L., *Warriors into Workers: The Civil War and the Formation of Urban-Industrial Society in a Northern City* (New York: Fordham University Press, 2003)

Johnston, F., *Memorials of Old Virginia Clerks* (Lynchburg: Bell Co., 1888)

Jones, A. T., ed., *Political Speeches and Debates of Abraham Lincoln and Stephen A. Douglas, 1854–1861* (Battle Creek: International Tract Society, 1895)

Jones, J. P., *Black Jack: John A. Logan and Southern Illinois in the Civil War Era* (Carbondale: Southern Illinois University Press, 1967)

Jones, J. W., *The Davis Memorial Volume* (Chicago: Dominion Co., 1897)

Jones, M. C., *Descendants of Gabriel Jones of Essex and Culpeper Counties, Virginia* (1949)

Jordan, B. M., *Marching Home: Union Veterans and Their Unending Civil War* (New York: Liveright Publishing Co., 2014)

Journal of Proceedings of the Right Worthy Grand Lodge of the United States, Vol. III (Baltimore: James L. Ridgely, 1863)

Journal of the House of Delegates of the State of Virginia (Richmond: 1891)

Journal of the Iowa House of Representatives, Spring 1861 (Des Moines: 1861)

Journal of the House of Representatives of the Tenth General Assembly (Des Moines: 1864)

Kellie-Smith, G., "Difficulty with Learning or Learning to be Difficult?" in Archer, C. ed., *Trauma, Attachment, and Family Permanence* (London: Jessica Kingsley Publishers, 2003)

Keokuk Directory and Business Mirror (Keokuk: Orion Clemens, 1857, 1859)

Kerby, R L., *Kirby Smith's Confederacy: The Trans-Mississippi South, 1863–1865* (New York: Columbia University Press, 1972)

Kindig, B. R., *Courage and Devotion* (AuthorHouse, 2014)

Kingsbury, G. W., *History of Dakota Territory: South Dakota*, Vol. I (Chicago: S. J. Clarke, 1915)

Klement, F. L., *The Copperheads in the Middle West* (Chicago: University of Chicago Press, 1960)

Klement, F. L., *The Limits of Dissent: Clement L. Vallandigham and the Civil War* (New York: Fordham University Press, 1998)

Klement, F. L., *Lincoln' Critics: The Copperheads of the North* (Shippensburg: White Mane Books, 1999)

Klement, F.L., "Rumors of Golden Circle Activity in Iowa during the Civil War Years," *The Annals of Iowa*, Vol. 37 (Iowa City: State Historical Society of Iowa, 1965)

Koonce, D. B., *Doctor to the Front: The Recollections of Confederate Surgeon Thomas Fanning Wood, 1861–1865* (Knoxville: University of Tennessee Press, 2000)

Kremer, W. P., *Roster of Co. I, 6th Iowa Infantry, War of the Rebellion* (Rutherford, N. J., 1913)

Krick, R., *Lee's Colonels* (Dayton: Morningside Bookshop, 1979)

Krick, R. E. L., *Staff Officers in Gray* (Chapel Hill: University of North Carolina Press, 2003)

Lathrop, C., *History of the First Regiment Iowa Cavalry Veteran Volunteers* (Lyons, Iowa: 1890)

Lathrop, H. W., *Life and Times of Samuel J. Kirkwood, Iowa's War Governor* (Iowa City, 1893)

Leggett, M. D., *Patents for Inventions Issued by the U.S. Patent Office, 1790 to 1873, Inclusive*, Vol. II (D. C.: United States Patent Office, 1874)

Lehman, M. J., "Observations on Chagres Fever," *Annual Report of the Supervising Surgeon-General of the Marine Hospital Service of the U.S.* (D. C.: Government Printing Office, 1889)

Lendt, D. L., *Demise of the Democracy: The Copperhead Press in Iowa, 1856–1870* (Ames: Iowa State University Press, 1973)

Ligtenberg, L., "Christiaan Verwayen and the Lost Disabdera Settlement," Assn. for the Advancement of Dutch American Studies (Holland, Mich.: 2001)

Lindsley, J. B., ed., *Military Annals of Tennessee, Confederate*, Vol. II (Nashville: J. M. Lindsley & Co., 1886)

Lonn, D., *Desertion During the Civil War* (New York: The Century Co., 1928)

Lonn, E., *Foreigners in the Confederacy* (Gloucester, Mass.: Peter Smith, 1965)

Lucas, W. V., *Pioneer Days of Bremer County, Iowa* (Waverly: Waverly Democrat, 1918)

Macy, J., *Anti-Slavery Crusade* (New Haven: Yale University Press, 1919)

Magazine of Poetry: A Quarterly Review, Vol. IV (Buffalo: Charles Wells Moulton, 1892)

Mahoney, T. R., *From Hometown to Battlefield in the Civil War Era: Middle Class Life in Midwest America* (Cambridge: Cambridge University Press, 2016)

Mahoney, T. R., *Provincial Lives: Middle-Class Experience in the Antebellum Middle West* (Cambridge: Cambridge University Press, 1999)

Mahoney, T. R., "The Rise and Fall of the Booster Ethos in Dubuque, 1850–1861," in Bergman, M., ed., *The Annals of Iowa* (Iowa City: State Historical Society of Iowa, 2002)

Marshall, J. A., *American Bastille* (Philadelphia: Stoddardt and Co., 1871)

Marvel, W., *Lincoln's Autocrat: The Life of Edwin Stanton* (Chapel Hill: University of North Carolina Press, 2015)

Matthews, G. R., *Basil Wilson Duke CSA* (Lexington: University Press of Kentucky, 2005)

Matthews, J. M., *The Statutes at Large of the Confederate States of America, Passed at the Second Session of the First Congress* (Confederate States of America, 1862)

McCaffrey, J. M., ed., *Only a Private: A Texan Remembers the Civil War—the Memoirs of William J. Oliphant* (Houston: Halcyon Press, 2004)

McCaslin, R. B., *Portraits of Conflict: A Photographic History of Tennessee in the Civil War* (Fayetteville: University of Arkansas Press, 2007)

McCaslin, R. B., ed., *This Corner of Canaan: Essays on Texas in Honor of Randolph B. Campbell* (Denton: University of North Texas Press, 2013)

McDonnold, B. W., *History of the Cumberland Presbyterian Church* (Nashville: 1893)

McIlhany H. M., *Some Virginia Families* (Staunton: Stoneburner and Prufer, 1903)

McMurray, W. J., *History of the Twentieth Tennessee Regiment* (Nashville: Publications Committee, 1904)

McPherson, E., *The Political History of the United States of America During the Great Rebellion* (D. C.: Philp & Solomons, 1864)

McPherson, J. M., *Abraham Lincoln and the Second American Revolution* (New York: Oxford University Press, 1990)

McPherson, J. M., *Battle Cry of Freedom* (Oxford: Oxford University Press, 1988)

McPherson, J. M., *Embattled Rebel: Jefferson Davis as Commander in Chief* (New York: The Penguin Press, 2014)

McPherson, J. M., *For Cause and Comrades: Why Men Fought in the Civil War* (Oxford: Oxford University Press, 1997)

McSweeney, E. F. X., *The Story of the Mountain*, Vol. II (Emmitsburg: Weekly Chronicle, 1911)

Medical Coloradoana, a Jubilee Volume, 1871–1921 (Denver: Colorado State Medical Society, 1922)

Melton, M., *The Best Station of Them All: The Savannah Squadron, 1861–1865* (Tuscaloosa: University of Alabama Press, 2012)

Memorial and History of Dallas County, Texas, Vol. II (Chicago: Lewis Publ. Co., 1892)

A Memorial and Biographical History of McLennan, Falls, Bell, and Coryell Counties, Texas, Vol. II (Chicago: Lewis Publ. Co., 1893)

Miles, T. J., *The Conspiracy of Leading Men of the Republican Party to Destroy the American Union* (New York: J. Walter & Co., 1864)

Milton, G. F., *The Eve of Conflict: Stephen A. Douglas and the Needless War* (Boston: Houghton Mifflin, 1934)

Mitgang, H., *Lincoln as They Saw Him* (New York: Rinehart & Co., Inc., 1956)

Moore, F., *The Rebellion Record: A Diary of American Events*, Vol. VII (New York: D. Van Nostrand, 1864)

Moretta, J. A., *William Pitt Ballinger, Texas Lawyer, Southern Statesman: 1825–1888* (Austin: Texas State Historical Association, 2000)

Mulley, C., *The Women who Flew for Hitler: A True Story of Soaring Ambition and Searing Rivalry* (New York: St. Martin's Press, 2017)

Murray, J. O., *The Immortal Six Hundred* (Winchester: Eddy Press Corp., 1905)

Muscatine City Directory for 1893–94 (Muscatine: Charles I. Barker, 1893)

Neely, M. E., *The Fate of Liberty: Abraham Lincoln and Civil Liberties* (New York: Oxford University Press, 1991)

Newell, A., *Biography of Rev. A. Newell* (St. Louis: Nixon-Jones Printing, 1894)

Noe, K. W., *Reluctant Rebels: The Confederates Who Joined the Army After 1861* (Chapel Hill: University of North Carolina Press, 2010)

Noll, M. A., *The Civil War as a Theological Crisis* (Chapel Hill: University of North Carolina Press, 2006)

Norton, H., *Rebel Religion: Story of the Confederate Chaplains* (St. Louis: Bethany Press, 1961)

Official Records of the Union and Confederate Navies in the War of the Rebellion (D. C.: United States Naval War Records Office, 1908)

Parish, J.C., *George Wallace Jones* (Iowa City: State Historical Society of Iowa, 1912)

Parker, L. F., *History of Poweshiek County, Iowa*, Vol. I (Chicago: S. J. Clarke, 1911)

Payne, C. E., *Josiah Bushnell Grinnell* (Iowa City: State Historical Society of Iowa, 1938)

Peltzer, L., "History and Principles of the Democratic Party of the Territory of Iowa," *Iowa Journal of History and Politics*, Vol. VI (Iowa City: State Historical Society of Iowa, 1908)

Petersen, W. J., 'Legal Holidays in Iowa,' *Iowa Journal of History and Politics*, Vol. 43 (Iowa City, 1945)

Pilgrim, M. E., 'The Civil War Diary of Richard M. Venable,' *Prologue: Quarterly of the National Archives & Records Administration* (College Park, Md.: 1996)

Pitcock, C. D., and Gurley, B. J., eds., *I Acted From Principle: The Civil War Diary of Dr. William J. McPheeters, Confederate Surgeon in the Trans-Mississippi* (Fayetteville: University of Arkansas Press, 2002)

Popchock, B., ed., *Soldier Boy: The Civil War Letters of Charles O. Musser, 29th Iowa* (Iowa City: University of Iowa Press, 1995)

Porter, D. D., *Naval History of the Civil War* (New York: Sherman Publ. Co., 1886)

Portrait and Biographical Album, Muscatine County, Iowa (Chicago: Acme Publ., 1889)

Portrait and Biographical Album of Polk County, Iowa (Chicago: Lake City Publ. Co., 1890)

Postell, L., "Father and Son, Confederate and Federal Soldiers," *Landmark 13* (Waukesha: 1970)

Potter, D. M., *The Impending Crisis: America Before the Civil War, 1848–1861* (New York: Harper Perennial, 2011)

Potter, D. M., *Lincoln and His Party in the Secession Crisis* (Baton Rouge: LSU Press, 1995)

Powell, W. S., ed., *Dictionary of North Carolina Biography*, Vol. 6 (Chapel Hill: University of North Carolina Press, 1996)

Power, J., *The "Iron Man" and the "Mississippi Company" of Morgan's Raiders* (Bloomington, Ind.: Author House, 2009)

Pratt, M. B., *Our Relations: Dudley-Pratt Families* (Indianapolis: Pratt Poster Co., 2002)

Proceedings of the Grand Lodge of Iowa, Vols. II, III (Iowa City: Order of the Grand Lodge, 1863)

Quisenberry, A. C., *Register of the Kentucky State Historical Society*, 15, No. 45 (Frankfort: Kentucky Historical Society, 1917)

Rachleff, P., *Black Labor in Richmond, 1865–1890* (Philadelphia: Temple University Press, 1984)

Rachleff, P., "The Readjusters," *Organizing Black America: An Encyclopedia of African American Associations* (New York: Garland Publ., 2001)

Randall, J. G., *Constitutional Problems Under Lincoln* (New York: D. Appleton and Co., 1926)

Record of the Members of Kappa Alpha Fraternity (New York, 1892)

Rehnquist, W. E., *All the Laws by One: Civil Liberties in Wartime* (New York: Knopf, 1998)

Reynolds, D. E., *Editors Make War: Southern Newspapers in the Secession Crisis* (Carbondale: Southern Illinois University Press, 1970, 2006)

Ridley, B. L., *Battles and Sketches of the Army of Tennessee* (Mexico: Missouri Printing and Publ., 1906)

Root's Moline City Directory 1867

Rosenberg, M. M., *Iowa on the Eve of the Civil War: A Decade of Frontier Politics* (Norman: University of Oklahoma Press, 1972)

Ross, M. A., *Justice of Shattered Dreams* (Baton Rouge: Louisiana State University Press, 2003)

Ross, R. R., *Early Bench and Bar of Detroit* (Detroit: Richard P. Joy, 1907)

Roster and Record of Iowa Troops in the Rebellion, Vols. I, II (Des Moines: E. H. English, 1908)

Sage, L. L., *William Boyd Allison* (Iowa City: State Historical Society of Iowa, 1956)

Salter, W., *Sixty Years and Other Discourses with Reminiscences* (Boston: Pilgrim Press, 1907)

Sauers, R. A., and Tomasak, P., *The Fishing Creek Confederacy: A Story of Civil War Draft Resistance* (Columbia: University of Missouri Press, 2012)

Scharf, J. T., *History of St. Louis City and County*, Vol. I (Philadelphia: Louis H. Everts, 1883)

Schwieder, D., *Iowa: The Middle Land* (Ames: Iowa State Press, 1996)

Shambaugh, B. F., *Messages and Proclamations of the Governors of Iowa*, Vols. II, III (Iowa City: State Historical Society of Iowa, 1903)

Sigafoos, R. A., *Cotton Row to Beale Street: A Business History of Memphis* (Memphis: Memphis State University Press, 1979)

Sledge, C. L., *The Union's Naval War in Louisiana, 1861–1863* (Pickle Partners Publ., 2015)

Smiley, J. C., *History of Denver* (Denver: Denver Times, 1901)

Soike, L. J., *Necessary Courage: Iowa's Underground Railroad in the Struggle Against Slavery* (Iowa City: University of Iowa Press, 2013)

Sorley, M. E., *Lewis of Warner Hall* (Baltimore: Genealogical Co., 1979)

Sprague, H. B., *History of the 13th Infantry Regiment of Connecticut Volunteers* (Hartford: Case, Lockwood, & Co., 1867)

Springer, A., *History of Louisa County, Iowa, from its Earliest Settlement to 1912*, Vol. I (Chicago: S. J. Clarke, 1912)

Stevens, W. B., *Centennial History of Missouri*, Vol. IV (St. Louis: S. J. Clarke, 1921)

Stevens, W. B., *St. Louis: History of the Fourth City, 1763–1909*, Vol. II (St. Louis: S. J. Clarke, 1909)

Stiles, E. H., *Recollections and Sketches of Notable Lawyers and Public Men of Early Iowa* (Des Moines: Homestead Publ. Co., 1916)

Stranathan, M., ed., *History of Early Cumberland* (Women's Civic Club, Cumberland, Ohio, 1943)

Strausbaugh, J., *City of Sedition: The History of New York City During the Civil War* (New York: Twelve Press, 2016)

Thompson, E.P., *History of the Orphan Brigade* (Louisville: Lewis Thompson, 1898)

Transactions of the McLean County Historical Society, Vol. I (Bloomington: McLean County Historical Society, 1899)

Upham, C. B., "Arms and Equipment for Iowa Troops in the Civil War," *Iowa Journal of History and Politics*, Vol. 16 (Iowa City: State Historical Society of Iowa, 1918)

Varney, N. R., "Statement of Nils S. Varney, Director of Training, Iowa City, IA Medical Center before the Subcommittee on Benefits, House Committee on Veterans Affairs," (D. C.: Department of Veterans Affairs, 2012)

The War of the Rebellion: A Compilation of the Official Records of the Union and Confederate Armies (D. C.: Government Printing Bureau)

Warren, A. G., *Catalogue of the Delta Kappa Epsilon* (New York: Delta Kappa Epsilon Council, 1910)

Warren, C., *History of the Harvard Law School and of Early Legal Conditions in America*, III (New York: Lewis Publ. Co., 1908)

Watkins, S. R., *Co. Aytch: A Confederate Memoir of the Civil War* (New York: Touchstone, 1962)

Weber, J. L., *Copperheads: The Rise and Fall of Lincoln's Opponents in the North* (New York: Oxford University Press, 2006)

White, J. W., *Abraham Lincoln and Treason in the Civil War: The Trials of John Merryman* (Baton Rouge: Louisiana State University Press, 2011)

Williams' Muscatine Directory, City Guide, and Business Mirror, Vol. I, 1859–1860 (R. M. Burnett, 1859)

Winslow, H. L., *Camp Morton 1861–1865 Indianapolis Prison Camp* (Indiana Historical Society, 1940)

Winter, W. C., ed., *Captain Joseph Boyce and the 1st Missouri Infantry, C.S.A.* (St. Louis: Missouri History Museum, 2011)

Wilkie, F. B., *Pen and Powder* (Boston: Ticknor and Co., 1888)

Withrow, T. F., *Reports of Cases in Law and Equity Determined in the Supreme Court of the State of Iowa*, Vol. XI (Chicago: Thomas F. Withrow, 1866)

Woodforde, J., *Treatise on Dyspepsia, or, Indigestion* (Somerset, England: E. Penny, 1820)

Wright, M., "General Douglas H. Cooper, C.S.A.," *Chronicles of Oklahoma* (Oklahoma City: Oklahoma Historical Society, 1954)

Wubben, H. H., *Civil War Iowa and the Copperhead Movement* (Ames: Iowa State University Press, 1980)

Wyatt-Brown, B., *Shaping of Southern Culture: Honor, Grace, and War, 1760s–1880s* (Chapel Hill: University of North Carolina Press, 2001)

Yahn, Rachel, "Fayetteville Arsenal: A Place of Pride and Community Effort," *Tar Heel Junior Historian* 40:1 (Raleigh: North Carolina Museum of History, 2000)

Young, B. H., *Confederate Wizards of the Saddle* (Boston: Chappie Publ. Co., 1914)

Zimring, D. R., *To Live and Die in Dixie: Native Northerners Who Fought for the Confederacy* (Knoxville: University of Tennessee Press, 2014)

Newspapers

Alexandria Gazette (Va.)
Baltimore Sun (Md.)
Bryan News Letter (Texas)
Burlington Hawk-eye and Telegraph (Iowa)
Daily News (Denver, Colo.)
Daily Iowa State Register
Daily State Journal (Austin, Texas)
Daily State Register (Iowa)
Daily Wabash Express (Terre Haute, Ind.)
Dallas Morning News (Texas)
Davenport Daily Gazette (Iowa)
Denver Daily Evening News (Denver, Colo.)
Dubuque Daily Evening Union (Iowa)
Dubuque Evening Globe-Journal (Iowa)
Dubuque Herald (Iowa)
Dubuque Times (Iowa)
Galveston Daily News (Texas)

Greenville Morning Herald (Texas)
Kansas City Times (Mo.)
Mobile Advertiser and Register (Ala.)
Muscatine Courier (Iowa)
Muscatine Journal (Iowa)
Muskegon Daily Chronicle (Mich.)
National Tribune (D. C.)
New York Times (N. Y.)
Ohio State Journal (Columbus, Ohio)
Ottumwa Weekly Courier (Iowa)
Philadelphia Inquirer (Pa.)
Richmond Daily Dispatch (Va.)
Richmond Times-Dispatch (Va.)
Richmond Whig (Va.)
Rocky Mountain News (Denver, Colo.)
Sacramento Daily Union (Calif.)
Shenandoah Herald (Woodstock, Va.)
Sioux City Journal (Iowa)
St. Louis Post Dispatch (Mo.)
State Press (Iowa)
Tempe Daily News (Ariz.)
Warren Sentinel (Front Royal, Va.)
Waterloo Daily Courier (Iowa)
Winchester Evening Star (Va.)

Miscellaneous

Baker, Leigh, family trees of Moses Scruggs Douglass, Julia Ann Reagan, and James Scruggs Douglass, ancestry.com
"Battle of Arkansas Post, Stepping Stone to Vicksburg," National Park Service, www.nps.gov/
Warren, S. L., "Battles of Cabin Creek," Encyclopedia of Oklahoma History and Culture, www.okhistory.org
"Confederate Texas Troops" and "Gordon's Regiment, Arkansas Cavalry," National Park Service, Civil War Soldiers and Sailors System, www.nps.gov/
Encyclopedia Dubuque, www.encyclopediadubuque.org
"Brush Battalion," "Polignac's Brigade," "Tenth Texas Field Artillery (Pratt's)," "Thirtieth Texas Cavalry" (by Greer, C. D.), "Thirty-third Texas Cavalry," "Thirty-fourth Texas Cavalry," Handbook of Texas Online, Texas State Historical Assn., Austin, tshaonline.org/handbook
Knox, B., and Yoder, Y., Civil War Veterans of Northeast Tarrant County, www.txgenweb.org
Leavell, J. A., "Leavells, Generation 8," littlecalamity.tripod.com/Genealogy/LeavellFam8.html
Gray, C. L., "Lucy Long," headquartersanv.blogspot.com
Lane, J. J., "History of Education in Texas," U.S. Bureau of Education circular (1903)
Mayo Clinic, "Boils and Carbuncles," and "Typhoid Fever," mayoclinic.org
1860 slave distribution map, Library of Congress, D. C.
"George Washington Swailes," genealogytrails.com/iowa/henry/bios02.htm
"Under the Rebel Flag: Life in Texas During the Civil War," Texas State Library and Archives Commission, Austin, Tex., www.tsl.texas.gov/

Whitaker, F. D. H., "Spier Whitaker, 1798–1869," University of North Carolina, Chapel Hill

Wulkow, H., Dubuque in the Civil War Period (master's thesis, Evanston: Northwestern University, 1949)

Index